CAV
STRIKE OPERATIONS

Miniature Gaming Rules

TABLE OF CONTENTS

CREDITS

CAV: Strike Operations by:
  Jon Walker

CAV created by:
  Ed Pugh

Contributing Authors:
  Ron Hawkins
  Al Pare
  Matt Ragan

Editing:
  Jennifer Schoonover

Illustrations:
  Chris Lewis
  Daniel Tyka
  Jon Walker

Graphic Design & Layout:
  Jon Walker

Special Thanks to:
  Justin Fritz
  Brandon Baker
  Roger Rexroad

Visit: www.cavhq.com

Talon Games
2235 W Towanda Ave.
El Dorado KS 67042

Reaper Miniatures
9062 Teasley Ln.
Denton TX 76210

CAV: Strike Operations
Copyright Talon Games 2015
First Printing June 2015

ISBN 978-1-930048-01-0

TLN 24950

Welcome to CAV: Strike Operations!

CAV: Strike Operations (CAV: SO) is a tabletop sci-fi miniatures game set in an ever-expanding universe nearly 300 years (2274 AD) in our future. Taking its name from the 10+ meter tall war machines that dominate the battlefield, CAV: SO is a game for two or more players that is easy to learn and fast to play.

As a player in CAV: SO, you will be able to choose from a wide variety of models and factions that will allow you to showcase your own style of play and tactics. Model figures are available to represent the men and machines fighting in CAV: SO that a player may choose to collect, assemble, and paint to bring their battlefield to life. Every game of CAV: SO features a multitude of options to ensure every battle is as challenging as it is fun and a construction system has also been included allowing for an even greater level of customization.

Make sure to also visit the official CAV: Strike Operations website at **www.cavhq.com** for official news and the latest game information. Besides finding downloadable versions of any charts or record sheets mentioned in this rulebook, you can find new game scenarios, fiction, and painting and terrain tips, as well as a FAQ and errata section that is regularly updated with any new information regarding the game rules.

Thank you for purchasing the CAV: Strike Operations rulebook and it is our sincerest hope you have as much fun playing CAV: SO as we do. Now on to the "Big Dance"!

IMPORTANT

Besides teaching you how to play the game, the CAV: SO rule book is designed to provide a player with an understanding of the game universe they will be fighting in and the weapons that will be used.

Every attempt has been made to answer any questions that may arise but, should one come up, feel free to contact us with any questions, comments, or concerns.

For email, address your inquiry to:

questions@talon-games.com

CAV: Strike Operations forum:

http://forum.reapermini.com

We will try to answer every question as soon as possible. It will greatly aid our response time if your questions are phrased to be answered with a simple "yes" or "no". ■

Syde's Guide to the Galaxy (Volume 24, updated 2274)
Dr. Eleanor Syde, DSocSci
New World Publishing, Terra

Foreword

While many of my esteemed colleagues have written vast tomes on the history of the galaxy, I have always tried to organize the majority of my guide to reflect the era that most of you are familiar with and most assuredly influences everything around us in the here and now. The last three centuries are but a blip in the passage of time, but nowhere in our previous history has so short a period had more of an affect on so many. *ES*

A Galaxy Divided

"All will see the light and you, my children, shall guide the faithless on their final path of salvation!"
— The Grand Inquisitor, The Empire of Malvernis

As of 2274, the known galaxy encompasses hundreds of worlds, the majority of which fall under the auspices of seven major galactic states and the five known races that control them. Many other independent worlds and small trading/defense collectives exist as well, scattered throughout the heavens.

The Adon Economic Confederation

The largest and oldest of the galactic states, the Adon Economic Confederation is made up of ten member nations, each of which provides troops to their collective self-defense force, NADO. The Adonese have long been the stabilizing force throughout the galaxy since setting forth to the stars from their home world of Adon.

The Almirithil Principality

The Principality is a small group of worlds settled by the defeated remnants of the losing nations from the Adonese world war. After their exile from Adon, the surviving leaders fled to the Mirith system, setting up their "government in exile" far rimward from their former home.

The Ritterlich Republic

Since the "unification" of the Ritterlich under a central government many centuries ago and ruled by their military elite, the Ritter have made expansion from their homeworld a priority. The Ritterlich have built the largest space navy of any of the galactic nations, requiring constant vigilance as to their future ambitions from their galactic neighbors.

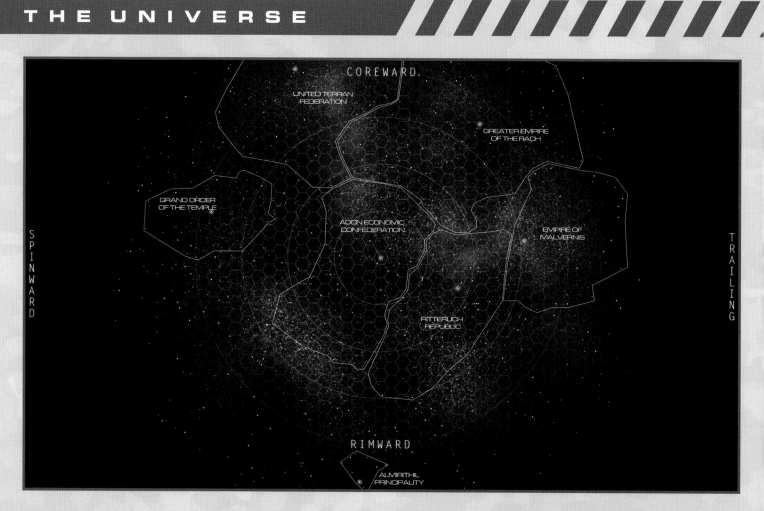

The Empire of Malvernis

The Inquisition has long held sway over the people of Capella for more than a millennia. Led by the Grand Inquisitor, the Malvernians have used their ascension to space as a means of bringing the Word of Khardullis to all those they encounter.

The Greater Empire of the Rach

The Rach Clans, led by their emperor the Kaharach, have long been the most aggressive of any of the known galactic races in the galaxy. Frequent border clashes and incursions are common along all of their shared borders.

The United Terran Federation

Humankind was the last of the known galactic races to reach for the stars and have suffered since making first contact with the Rach Empire, including the razing of Terra in 2181. A state of war remains between the two races, resulting in frequent clashes along their shared border.

The Grand Order of the Temple

An offshoot of humanity, the Templars left Terra after the construction of the first human Compression in secret with the intention of establishing their own galactic-state. With the arrival of the Rach, the Templars revealed their existance and with the support of the Adonese, helped the rest of humanity push the Rach back during the onslaught of the Vela Wars.

Other Galactic Groups

There are many other interstellar and interplanetary groups that exist outside the major galactic states. While not as large in scope, they all play vital roles in modern society:

Independents

Many star systems have been settled throughout the galaxy that have forsworn any allegiance to a galactic state, choosing to remain independent, typically for political or religious reasons, and go it "alone".

While some worlds remain exclusive to one race or another, many others have a mixed population base that can result in less than harmonious situations from time to time.

Prospectors

Lured by the chance of a quick fortune, modern prospectors comb through space in search of a promising location to lay claim to and mine the riches it may contain.

Unlike the large mining collectives, prospectors tend to keep their operations small-scale, hopefully beyond the notice of any potential competition or government interference. The majority of prospectors have very little training and rely on a lot of luck as they attempt to unearth the "mother lode".

Labor Unions

The majority of the galactic working-class, especially in the

THE UNIVERSE

less restrictive star-nations, don't always trust their employers to necessarily have their best interests at heart. For that reason, many of these workers have banded together to form labor unions and guilds capable of standing up for the rights and interests of their members through a variety of means.

Corporations and UCORs

The majority of corporations in the galaxy operate under a legal charter provided by their respective government within the confines of a single jurisdiction.

An Uncharted Corporation (UCOR) moves outside the normal control of an organized government. Typically massive conglomerates, the UCOR's have established their own monopolistic markets in areas they hold as "sovereign territory", possessing their own private armies and ignoring any laws or regulations that may exist as they sell their goods and services to anyone with the funds to buy.

Universal InterGalactic Communication Command

The UICC was founded in 2195 by Rika Brn'So, an Adonese industrialist who recognized the need for interstellar communications that would allow information to be passed from system to system throughout the galaxy.

Today the UICC's ComNet is the largest and most far-reaching communications network in the galaxy with transmitting stations in every galactic state. Since it's inception, the UICC has strived to remain an independent and neutral party, outside the normal animosities one faction may have for another, focusing on supplying secure and reliable communications throughout the stars.

Traders, Cartels, and Smugglers

Traders and smugglers, often in conjunction with one or more UCOR's, move throughout the galaxy bringing a variety of goods and services to the highest bidder. While the larger trade cartels move legitimate cargo within the borders of a galactic state or between allied trading partners, many smaller operators remain in the shadows, dependent on a fast ship and a bit of luck while transporting goods and contraband, trying to stay one step ahead of legal authorities and tax collectors.

Mercenaries

Mercenary companies are in service throughout the galaxy, fighting for anyone willing to pay their price. From one-man assassins and small strike teams to multi-brigade strength forces, mercenary companies can be found willing to complete almost any task required.

One interesting note concerning many of the more prolific mercenary companies is their diverse make-up troop- and equipment-wise as compared to the rest of the galaxy, making it quite common to see soldiers from so-called "enemy" races fighting side by side.

Breakers and Salvagers

The scavengers of the universe, breakers and salvagers scour the worlds and space lanes for anything they can turn into a fast profit. Battle zones and abandoned facilities are favored locations for both groups to ply their trade. Whereas breakers tend to be more formal in their activities, purchasing the rights to scrap a particular object or location, salvagers cruise the space lanes looking to "tear" down anything they can claim salvage rights to in a strange "finders, keepers" sort of mentality.

Pirates

In stark contrast to mercenary companies are the pirates of the galaxy, making up for their lack in structure with their brazen contempt of any legal or military force. Operating from secret havens across the stars, pirates will attack anywhere they sense an easy win and a reward worth the risk of death or capture.

REBECCA WORLEY

Daughter of Richard Worley, leader of the Black Rose pirate band.

The Technology of War (2269)

Dr. Theodore Wynn

ArSa Press, Vega

Introduction

The collective races of the galaxy have been fighting amongst themselves and each other for centuries and with each successive conflict the quest for new and improved technology continues. The basic need though for ways to get into the fight faster and kill the enemy quicker than they can kill you has remained unchanged since the dawn of warfare.

Combat Assault Vehicle

While each galactic state has continued to refine the staples of any modern military: infantry, combat vehicles, and aircraft, along with space-based weapon platforms of various designs and tonnages, it is the Combat Assault Vehicle or CAV that is the pinnacle of modern combat technology. A relative newcomer to the vast array of weapon systems being deployed throughout the galaxy today, the CAV is a culmination of several technologies fused together to provide the ultimate fighting machine.

Able to negotiate almost any terrain type and operate in even the most hostile and extreme environments, these humanoid shaped behemoths can weigh as much as 150 tons and stand over 30 feet in height and deliver a force projection previously unknown to any fighting force.

A multitude of CAV designs are in service with every military organization and faction in the galaxy.

Combat Assault Vehicle Classification

CAVs are classified by their chassis size: Small, Medium, Large, Extra-Large, and Super. Four-legged CAVs (known as Quads) are also available.

CAV: Small Chassis

Small chassis CAVs range in weight from 25 to 49 tons and serve mainly in reconnaissance roles across the battlefield. They are also responsible for seeking out other small chassis CAVs, reducing the enemy's ability to scout ahead.

Many small chassis CAVs are equipped with advanced electronics to direct the fire for artillery assets. Their above-average speed allows them to maneuver to avoid engaging larger units, as they are not designed to take a lot of punishment in a stand-up fight.

Approximately 15% of all CAVs are small chassis models.

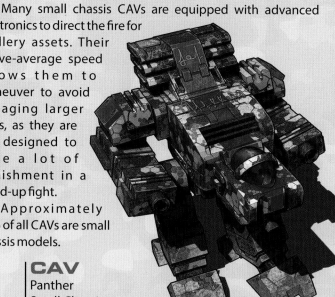

CAV
Panther
Small Chassis
The Ritterlich Republic

CAV: Medium Chassis

Medium chassis CAVs range in weight from 50 to 75 tons and typically serve as skirmishers, harassing the flanks of the enemy as they engage heavier units. They retain much of the speed of a smaller CAV but have improved armor and combat capabilities.

Medium chassis CAVs also provide a platform for many specialty roles that don't need to be in the forefront of a fight, such as indirect fire, engineering, and fire control.

Approximately 30% of all CAVs are medium chassis models.

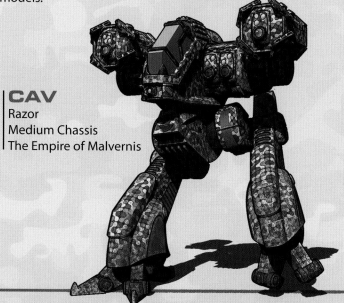

CAV
Razor
Medium Chassis
The Empire of Malvernis

CAV: Large Chassis

Large chassis CAVs range in weight from 76 to 100 tons and are the workhorses of every major military force. They are the best mix of speed, armor, and firepower to close and engage an enemy force.

Approximately 25% of all CAVs are large chassis models.

CAV
Halberd
Extra-Large Chassis
The Grand Order of the Temple

CAV
Tyrant
Large Chassis
The Greater Empire of the Rach

CAV: Extra-Large Chassis

Extra-Large chassis CAVs range in weight from 101 to 125 tons and are the heavy-hitters of a strike force. They sacrifice some speed for more armor and weapons, but maintain sufficient mobility to allow them to range out from a central deployment zone.

The extra-large chassis is also capable of being equipped with light artillery weapons and larger missile and rockets arrays for massive barrage-fire attacks.

Approximately 20% of all CAVs are extra-large chassis models.

CAV
Ogre
Super Chassis
The Adon Economic Confederation

CAV: Super Chassis

Super chassis CAVs range in weight from 126 to 150 tons and are the largest CAVs currently in production. Because of their slow speed, super chassis CAVs are generally deployed to areas requiring improved defensive capabilities or as a part of a protracted siege.

Approximately 10% of all CAVs are super chassis models.

HISTORY

The first purpose-built CAV, the Predator, was manufactured by the KDM company in 2207 for the Ritter army.

The Predator dramatically departed from the conventional design theories at the time for a weapons platform. While the Adonese and Malvernians had been experimenting with what was basically an armored deck on top of a traditional armored vehicle chassis, the Predator possessed a "torso" that could rotate a full 360 degrees mounted to a pair of articulated "legs" (hence the term walkers). The torso contained an enclosed cockpit for the pilot along with booms from both sides that contained multiple hard-points to attach weapons to.

The first Predator to see actual combat came during the Cygnus War in 2208. The Ritter deployed several of the machines during their assault on the Malvernian world of Cygnus. While several of the machines suffered massive system failures, a few did manage to contribute to the fighting by helping to exploit breaches through the enemy lines, throwing the Malvernian rear areas into chaos, unable to quickly respond to these new weapons of war. The rest of the universe took note and by the end of the war, the great CAV arms race had begun throughout the galaxy.

CAV development advanced quickly after Cygnus as data from the war was analyzed and new designs tested.

By 2240 the machines being manufactured were more inline with the CAVs most people are familiar with today.

During the Pictor War in 2242, the Rach unveiled the Tyrant, a model still in use. The Tyrant was the first CAV to use energy weapons only as its main armaments, solving the problem of re-supplying the vast amounts of ammo earlier designs had required. This has led to other more specialized designs for fire support and suppression tasks as new technology comes online. ∎

Combat Vehicle

While the CAV is the predominate fighting platform of choice on the modern battlefield, it is often the combat vehicle that serves as the backbone of most armies. Serving in a multitude of roles, combat vehicles are cheaper to build and maintain as well as requiring less training to use. As a result, combat vehicles are ideal for use in low-intensity conflicts and as auxiliaries to CAVs.

Combat vehicles are also classified by chassis size—Light, Medium, Heavy, and Extra-Heavy—as well as their mode of travel: Wheeled, Tracked, Hover, or Anti-Grav.

Combat Vehicle: Light Chassis

Light chassis vehicles range in weight from 5 to 20 tons. With their greater speed, light chassis vehicles tend to be recon-type models, unarmored personnel carriers, and other specialized utility vehicles.

Approximately 30% of all vehicles are light chassis models.

Combat Vehicle: Medium Chassis

Medium chassis vehicles range in weight from 21 to 40 tons, allowing for more armor and equipment without sacrificing too much top speed. Armored personnel carriers, self-propelled artillery, light tanks, and anti-aircraft vehicles tend to dominate this chassis size.

Approximately 30% of all combat ground vehicles are medium chassis models.

Combat Vehicle: Heavy Chassis

Heavy chassis vehicles range in weight from 41 to 60 tons and can carry the punch to knock out lighter CAV. The addition of heavier armor also improves their survivability on the battlefield. Heavy chassis combat ground vehicles are primarily encountered as main battle tanks and other forward combat types.

Approximately 25% of all vehicles are heavy chassis models.

Combat Vehicle: Extra-Heavy Chassis

Extra-heavy chassis vehicles range in weight from 61 to 80 tons and are similar in role to the super chassis CAVs in providing a strong defensive unit to secure and hold a static location. While slow and lumbering, extra-heavy chassis vehicles are faster than their behemoth brothers and are preferred for prolonged sieges due to their massive weapon arrays.

Approximately 15% of all vehicles are extra-heavy chassis models.

Combat Vehicle: Wheeled

Wheeled combat vehicles feature two or more wheels and use a powered drive train to turn at least one of them to move.

Wheeled vehicles offer greater mobility than a tracked vehicle and are more maneuverable in dense urban terrain.

Combat Vehicle: Tracked

Tracked combat vehicles use a series of continuous treads driven by two or more gear wheels to move. The larger surface area of a tracked vehicle allows for a greater distribution of weight, allowing it to traverse soft ground with a less likelihood of becoming stuck. The aggressive traction provided by tracks also allows the vehicle to "climb" over fallen trees or rubble, but can be very damaging to paved surfaces.

Combat Vehicle: Hover

Hover combat vehicles use a cushion of air, provided by blowers and retained by an armored skirt, to elevate themselves above the surface. A large volume of air, slightly above normal atmospheric pressure, is required to produce this lift. The skirt allows the vehicle to travel over small obstructions without damage, but can generate a large amount of "dust" that can be easily seen by an enemy force, reducing the chance for surprise.

Additional engines, generally mounted to the back, provides thrust to propel the vehicle. Some craft use a duct system, allowing some of the lift air to escape from the back to push the craft

Combat Vehicle: Anti-Grav

Anti-grav combat vehicles use a diametric drive to power blocks of negative and positive mass, causing them to alternate "falling" towards each other, pushing the vehicle in one direction or another. While anti-grav vehicles require larger breeders and more power to operate as compared to other vehicle types, they can go longer and farther as well as being extremely quiet.

DESPOT
Extra-Heavy Vehicle Chassis
Fakk Khun Saikoan "The Blood of Heroes Regiment"
The Greater Empire of the Rach

THE UNIVERSE

TSUISEKI
Heavy Chassis Aircraft
The United Terran Federation

Aircraft

Most aircraft found over the battlefield are designed to provide close air support or transport for the ground forces below. Aircraft pilots are a cocky lot and are all too aware of their projected life expectancy. Advances in open-shaft drives, ducted fans, and other vertical maneuvering technologies allow aircraft to remain close at hand while being able to move quickly as the battle evolves.

Aircraft are also classified by chassis size: Ultra-Light, Light, Medium, Heavy, and Ultra-Heavy.

Aircraft: Ultra-Light Chassis

Ultra-light chassis aircraft range in weight from 5 to 10 tons and tend to be very specialized in their design with a single purpose in mind, such as advanced warning systems or stealth recon models.

Approximately 10% of all aircraft are ultra-light chassis models.

Aircraft: Light Chassis

Light chassis aircraft range in weight from 11 to 15 tons. This type of chassis is typically used as lightly armed security models for low-threat areas and as supply aircraft.

Approximately 20% of all aircraft are light chassis models.

Aircraft: Medium Chassis

Medium chassis aircraft range in weight from 16 to 30 tons and are used in a multitude of mission roles. The majority of ground support, transport, and interceptors use this chassis type.

Approximately 35% of all aircraft are medium chassis models.

Aircraft: Heavy Chassis

Heavy chassis aircraft range in weight from 31 to 50 tons. This aircraft type is the heavy hitter of air-based attack craft and typically carries a number of anti-armor weapons.

Approximately 20% of all aircraft are heavy chassis models.

Aircraft: Ultra-Heavy Chassis

Ultra-heavy chassis aircraft range in weight from 51 to 75 tons. While some militaries have used this chassis type as an attack craft, its slow speed makes it an easy target from the ground.

The ultra-heavy chassis is predominately used as an armored transport due to its massive air-lift capabilities.

Approximately 15% of all aircraft are ultra-heavy chassis models.

KRAKEN-B
Medium Chassis Aircraft
Fakk Khun Saikoan "The Blood of Heroes Regiment"
The Greater Empire of the Rach

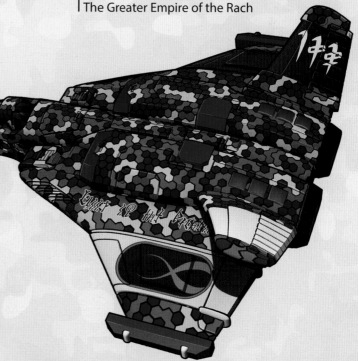

FACT

The Rach Kraken-B is in actual terms an aerospace craft, equally capable of operating in the atmosphere of a planet or the vacuum of space. It's twin vectored-thrust drives provide propulsion while an internal gyroscope is tilted in one direction or another to provide the torque necessary to basically spin the craft in place.

Aerospace fighters are extremely fast and the Kraken-B is no exception, blazing a path across the battlefield as it searches for a target. As with any craft of this type, it's main drawback is the need for fuel, which it can consume very quickly. ■

A New Kind of War

Every aircraft, CAV, and combat vehicle consists of seven basic systems, with slight variations based upon their origin and design. While most combat-capable machines possess these same base systems, their order of importance is an area of great debate. It is the crucible of war that will decide who is right and who is wrong.

Power

Without power the universe as we know it would cease to exist and while there are multiple methods for providing the power needed by the masses, the primary three used for propulsion in combat craft are:

Fusion

Fusion systems provide starships, space stations, and the vast majority of cities throughout the galaxy with power. These systems are large and complex in their operation and require massive amounts of upkeep to keep them functioning.

Breeders

Breeders are the workhorse energy source for anything smaller than a starship or city and larger than personal electronics. The smallest breeders require an area roughly 30cm by 10cm by 10cm (not including the T-Gel cells). Such small breeders provide barely more energy than some HCC batteries, but the lifespan is the advantage. With even a mere fist-sized T-Gel cell, a small breeder can run for days.

The largest breeders are, of course, used in industrial or military hardware like CAVs, large civilian transports, and small atmospheric flying craft. T-Gel is inert and breeders are considered very safe. Nevertheless, it has been documented that, if a breeder is severely damaged or ruptures mid-cycle, it can result in a very large instantaneous electrical discharge. The principal of a breeder is fairly simple even though, like fusion, the actual technology involved is quite advanced. A breeder has two storage tanks (called cells) attached to it. One cell is empty, and the other cell is filled with T-Gel (a substance primarily derived from Tyburinium ore). For safety and handling purposes, T-Gel is dyed a bright, almost phosphorescent blue and scented with an additive that makes it easy to identify. The breeder requires an initial electrical charge, provided by a battery, to start the chemical process. Once begun, T-Gel is cycled through the breeder as it is converted to Z-Gel in a process that creates electrical energy. Z-Gel is then converted back into T-Gel and the process continues. The energy created by the breeder during this conversion process is used to provide power to any attached devices. Very little matter is actually lost during a breeder's conversion cycle, but after roughly 20 cycles the T-Gel cell needs to be replaced.

Breeder cycle times vary based on the size of the breeder, but generally a cycle is about an hour for small portable breeders and a day or more for the larger breeders. Recent advancements in molecular refinement are helping to increase T-Gel conversion efficiency and dramatically boost breeder output.

HCC Batteries

High Capacity Chemical (HCC) batteries vary in size, from nano applications to extremely large starship applications. They are rechargeable and we use them in nearly every personal electronic device we own. Most personal weapons use HCC batteries where needed. Additionally, HCC batteries are used to initiate breeder reactions and provide us with electrical backup power in the event of a problem. Depending on how quickly electrical energy is being used, an HCC device can last an entire day of regular usage or for mere seconds of intense discharge.

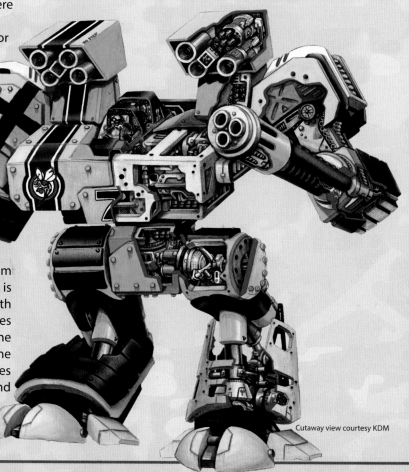

RHINO
Super Chassis CAV
The Ritterlich Republic
The Yellow Jackets Mercenary Company

Cutaway view courtesy KDM

Bellar Joints

Chances are you use bellar joints every day, even if you don't realize it. These frictionless, computer-controlled electromagnetic joints are found in everything from cargo doors and wheels to artificial limbs. While we may take them for granted, the military certainly does not. If it were not for bellar joints, the massive war machines known as CAV would not exist.

With the average CAV using over one hundred bellar joints, they have almost the same range of motion and the dexterity of a humanoid body. Bellar joints give CAVs speed and mobility unparalleled on the diverse battlefields found throughout the galaxy. Bellar joints also provide the CAV with the ability to rotate shoulders and elbows, bringing their weapons to bear in the blink of an eye without imposing any unnecessary G-forces on their crew.

Armor

The most effective armor is not a sheet of thick DuraSteel, but rather layers of specially designed composite materials that provide protection by controlling the disintegration of the armor itself as it stops the incoming attack. The structure of modern armor usually consists of a fitted outer ceramic layer to blunt and wear down the projectile of a kinetic attack and dissipate the heat of any energy-based attacks.

The next layer is a honeycomb-like flexible composite material designed to support the outer ceramics as well as provide a heat sink to further bleed off heat. The third layer is made up of woven fibers to consume the remaining energy of a kinetic attack. The final layer consists of an anti-spalling dampening material designed to keep pieces of the armor from breaking off and damaging any internal components.

Internal Systems

Immersive Heads-Up Display (IHUD)

Both the pilot and the weapons systems operator wear a helmet that fully encases their head, providing life support, communications, and a virtual-reality immersion heads-up display. The helmet delivers a wireless connection with the onboard computer systems as well as a redundant direct-wired connection as an emergency backup.

The IHUD allows a wearer to "see" through the craft they are on with a computer-generated display located on the inside visor of the helmet. Sensors on the gloves of either crew member allow for the user to interact with the heads-up display and control any of the on-board systems or weapons, rotating the viewpoint of the battlefield in the user's direction regardless of the current orientation of the CAV or combat vehicle they are riding in.

Combat Suit and Interface Harness

Pilots are often seen wearing their military-spec combat suits, complete with colorful insignias and combat award patches, even when off duty. Combat suits are designed to provide the wearer protection from extreme g-forces as well as exposure to vacuum or extreme temperatures. A combat suit forms airtight seals with a user's gloves, boots, and helmet to prevent exposure to any outside neurotoxins or radiation, while embedded nanites remove any liquids or solid wastes from inside.

The interface harness built into the back of the suit connects to the cockpit chair to keep the wearer securely fastened during movement and combat. Hard-wired connections also allow the monitoring of vitals and the introduction of pain reducers or stimulants as needed.

The suit allows plenty of mobility both in and out of the cockpit, permitting the wearer to access the cockpit controls without binding up.

CAV Cockpit Controls

Most CAVs use a two-joystick/pedal combination for maneuvering in conjunction with the IHUD. Joysticks can be moved from side to side to better fit the particular style of the pilot and can have any buttons programmed to perform particular functions as well.

Joystick One is referred to as the throttle and maneuvered forward or backward to control the speed of the machine.

Joystick Two controls the torso movement and firing of weapons. Twin pedals on the floor enable the turning of the machine and are used to help steady the machine as well.

Repair

Robotic Micro Engineers (RMEs)

You've probably seen a vid-feed of a damaged CAV or combat vehicle covered in a foamy substance. That foam is the lifeblood of a combat machine's automated repair system. It is used to transport the Robotic Micro Engineers (RMEs), which are the incredibly small nanobots that do the actual repairs, to the damaged area of the machine. Reserve tanks along a CAV or combat vehicle's internal chassis ensure that all major locations have instant access to RMEs, while a network of hoses allow a pilot to transfer foam from tank to tank as needed in the field. While the system is mostly automated and knows which vital systems to repair first, an operator can pull up a 3-D model of their craft and view the details of any damage. He can then give specific directions to the RMEs or their cousins, the Electronic Micro Engineers, which are used to repair internal damage to a machine's electronics.

Adaptive Thermal Camouflage

Adaptive thermal camouflage is used on aircraft, CAVs, combat vehicles, and even powered armor to help them blend into their surroundings more naturally. Thousands of small, interlocking panels make up the outer "skin" of a system using this technology, and can be rapidly heated and cooled to match the outside temperature or mimic the thermal signature of another object, such as a small car or a rock.

These panels are also treated with a special polymer containing paramagnetic iron oxide that can be programmed to project any color or pattern on a system's exterior. By using an electric current to adjust the spacing of the oxide's crystals, the level of light reflection is affected and thus influences the color or design a person sees.

Weapon Systems

While a variety of weapons systems are commonly deployed throughout the militaries in the galaxy, they all fall into one of the following basic types:

Energy Weapons

Energy weapons fall into two distinct categories: Photonic and Non-Photonic.

Photonic energy weapons use atoms to produce a beam of

energy to damage a target. Laser and Particle Bolt Guns, as well as Ion Disrupters, are all examples of photonic weapon systems.

Photonic energy weapons move at the speed of light, making evasion of an accurately aimed shot virtually impossible. With no need of ammunition and a sufficient power source, photonic energy weapons are not limited by the number of times it can be used. As a result, CAVs and combat vehicles with these types of weapons are favored when based in a remote location or during operations behind enemy lines where resupply tends to be limited.

Non-photonic weapons use magnetic energy to propel a shaped projectile down the barrel of the weapon. Magnetic accelerator cannons (MAC) are examples of non-photonic weapon systems.

Firing at over 3500 meters per second, non-photonic weapons release massive amounts of kinetic energy and heat upon impact. By firing at such high velocities, these weapon types have greater range and are not affected by gravity (bullet drop) or wind drift to the extent more conventional firearms are. Add to this their ability to fire in a vacuum or non-oxygen environment, and they are a very deadly weapon.

Laser-Bolt Gun

A laser-bolt gun (LBG) is an energy weapon powered directly from a model's onboard breeder. Unlike industrial-grade versions that produce a constant and focused stream, weapon-grade bolt guns use a condenser to collect charged particles and, when triggered, fire a compressed "bolt" of energy. This effect increases the damage potential of the weapon exponentially over a conventional beam.

Particle-Bolt Gun

The particle-bolt gun (PBG) was developed to provide a heavier energy weapon for the battlefield, sacrificing range for a more powerful energy stream.

The weapon works by "ripping" atomic particles apart in the main condensing chamber. This reaction is focused into a bolt of electrically charged, high-energy, neutral hydrogen atoms that moves in a straight line at near the velocity of light to its target.

The beam will burn through most power armor with little or no resistance, reducing the person inside to blackened husk. A person killed by a particle bolt is commonly referred to as a "briquette." Even the thick armor plating of a combat vehicle or CAV can be burned through with a strong enough beam.

The main drawback to the weapon system is that the atmosphere of a planet quickly degrades a bolt as it travels to the target. Naval versions of this weapon system in space do not suffer from this degradation and are very effective weapons for ship-to-ship combat.

Ion Disruptor Cannon

The ion disruptor cannon (IDC) is designed to damage or destroy onboard electronic systems on a target. The IDC ionizes hydrogen gas atoms within an acceleration chamber and releasing this stored energy when fired. The effect appears as a "ball" of glowing energy racing through the air, impacting on the intended target and generating a "lightning storm" of released energy along the surface of the target.

Ion disruptor weapons have prevented the widespread use of combat-capable robotic troops and several weapon manufacturers are experimenting with plasma weapons based on disruptor technology.

Magnetic Accelerator Weapons

Magnetic accelerator weapons are the heavy hitters of every major modernized fighting force. Using alternating rings of negative- and positive-charged magnetic energy, these weapons are capable of penetrating even the most advanced armored materials or hardened structures using only kinetic energy.

Magnetic accelerator cannons (MAC) fire a solid core penetrator rod made of a hardened metal alloy (depending on the manufacturer; duralloy steel is commonly used) in a super-conducting ceramic casing called a SABOT. The SABOT surrounds the penetrator rod to allow it to be fired down the barrel of the MAC at hypersonic velocities. Once the round leaves the barrel, the SABOT falls away, allowing the penetrator to continue on to its target.

When used in a close-quarters environment such as a city, the back pressure of larger MACs have been recorded shattering windows and causing light structures to collapse.

A variant of the MAC is the magnetic rotary accelerator cannon (MRAC). Originally designed as an anti-aircraft defense system, MRAC weapon systems continue to see widespread deployment throughout the galaxy because of its high rate of fire. A MRAC can literally burn its way through an armored target as round after round strikes.

The unique placement of the alternating magnetic rings generates the field around the barrel as it rotates into a firing position and releases the round. The weapon uses a tremendous amount of power and ammo to feed this multiple-barrel configuration, resulting in smaller caliber weapons and decreased penetrating power. What it lacks in punch, though, is made up by the sheer amount of rounds going down-range.

Propellant Weapons

Propellant weapons, while lighter and more efficient than those seen in every galactic nation in the past, use the same basic technology as the first Chinese guns made on Terra during the 12th century. An explosive charge in the weapon forces a projectile down the barrel, ejecting it at high speed at the target. Besides traditional auto-cannons and machine guns, guided missiles, rockets, mortars, and artillery are all examples of propellant-type weapon systems.

While many propellant weapons have the explosive

charge encased within their "shell", case-less ammunition has become a popular option, using a solid propellant formed around the round to provide the explosion needed to launch it down the barrel toward the target. Other weapons systems use a liquid propellant, stored onboard the combat machine, to fire the round as needed.

The main drawback to propellant weapon systems is their larger size and—as a result of the combustion needed to propel a round toward a target—the inability to function underwater or in an airless environment.

Auto-Cannons

The auto-cannon is a projectile weapon with a larger caliber than most machine guns, typically in the 20mm to 100mm range, using hypergel-propellant filled shells. With the aid of an auto-loader, auto-cannons fire a burst of high-explosive armor piercing (HEAP) ammo at a high rate of fire. HEAP is a point-detonating ammo type that can be used successfully against any armored target, requiring no power from the combat machine they are mounted on, decreasing the space needed to equip them.

The rotary auto-cannon (RAC) is a variant of the common auto-cannon that uses multiple rotating barrels (generally three to six) to further increase the rate of fire of this weapon type. The caliber of these weapon systems is typically smaller to make up for the immense amount of ammo needed to sustain this system in combat.

Machine Guns

Machine guns are fully automatic weapons that fire smaller-caliber rifle ammunition at a very high rate—typically several hundred rounds a minute—from an ammunition belt or large-capacity magazine. Machine guns are typically used as an anti-infantry weapon or against lightly armored vehicles or structures.

Guided Missiles

A guided missile launcher fires a single laser or radar-guided missile at a target, using a small charge to clear it from the launcher away from attacker before engaging its ramjet engine for propulsion. Once launched, the guided missile projectile deploys a set of small fins to stabilize it and prevent spinning, which can reduce the effectiveness of the shaped-charge explosive warhead.

The guided missile's internal targeting system directs the projectile to the desired target, attempting to avoid any counter-measures and strike a point where it is most vulnerable.

Cruise missiles are larger versions of the typical guided missile, capable of delivering a wide variety of very deadly payloads, including Super Thermex, a nanotech explosive compound on par with tactical nuclear devices.

Rockets

Unlike a guided missile, rockets do not require any additional targeting assistance beyond the user picking a point on the HUD and pushing the launch button, relying on multiple warheads to saturate an area around the desired target to increase the opportunity for a successful hit.

Rockets use solid fuel propellants for acceleration, resulting in a winding smoke-trail behind them as they arc through the air, eventually falling back down toward their target. As a result, rockets have a shorter effective range than most guided missiles and a smaller warhead to increase the number of rockets that can be fired at once.

Mortars

While similar in appearance to their centuries' old cousins, the modern mortar has more in common with a missile launcher than the tubes originally developed during the Siege of Grave on Terra in 1673 (TSD).

Mortars allow infantry to attack without exposing themselves to enemy fire. The crew determines the general area of the target and fires the round into the air. The round will travel vertically in order to clear any surrounding terrain, and then plunge back to the ground in the direction of the target, staying low as it seeks an aiming point. The proximity to the ground generates a humming sound that has caused troops to refer to incoming mortar rounds as "hummers." Once the round has arrived in the designated area it will go "active", searching for a target-lock to home in on and detonate. Because of its low altitude and speed, an incoming mortar round is very hard to intercept.

Artillery

Artillery fires a large caliber propellant-based round that is capable of hitting a target several kilometers away. Modern self-propelled artillery uses inertial navigation systems and satellite positioning (if available) to provide its own on-board fire control. This allows the individual guns to remain on the move, avoiding counter-battery fire while still delivering accurate and timely fire on-target.

The standard "dumb" round used by most military forces is a high-explosive (HE) projectile and is a bursting round providing fragmentation and blast effects. Other ammo types are available for more specialized targeting as well as rocket-assisted artillery, increasing the range exponentially.

Flamethrowers

Generally considered an anti-infantry weapon, a flamethrower will "spray" an area with a burning liquid gel designed to "stick" and burn at very high temperatures. Only total immersion under water (or anything that will cut off the oxygen supply), specialized fire-fighting foam, or time will put out the flames.

THE UNIVERSE

HISTORY

Excerpt from:
My Legion, My Life (2260)
Sgt Legionnaire Dexter Tidwell
Global Publishing, Antares

The Captain and I had been back at the battalion CP for a meeting. After grabbing some hot chow we headed to our forward section, checking the HUD for a short cut. Deciding a trail on the very edge of the display might work, we set out to find it and follow it back. We were making pretty good time, chatting across the com about getting back to the "world" soon when we heard the shriek of the incoming round.

Both of us had heard our fair share of the things over the last few months, but this one seemed to be louder and last longer than any others before. As the two of us froze, staring at each other, the noise just got louder and closer, seeming to last forever before it hit a flooded field off to one side. Dirt and red-hot fragments pelted our armor as we both finally dove for the deck. Glancing up, I saw the Captain holding up his arm, hand flat.

"Stop?" I asked. "Here? HERE, SIR?"

Motioning again for me to follow, he jumped up and ran toward the crater as it quickly filled up with water from the field. Sliding down one edge as he landed on his side, the Captain explained his plan over our comlink after he found a good spot to rest on.

He figured the round was just a probing shot, looking for a lucky hit as there were no friendly units stationed in this area and we just happened to be around. He doubted there would be a second shot anytime soon and probably not at the same spot (he hoped). So we would wait a bit and head out again.

Later we stopped by an artillery OP, located on the ridge behind our own area, to report on what we had seen (and heard) on the way in.

It turned out what we had heard was the Rats' (Terran slang for the Rach) new SP152 that had been shelling the whole mountain trying to get a shot in on the battalion HQ. Apparently they would only shoot once a day, not risking a counter-battery taking out their new toy.

The enemy's wariness continued until the first armistice, our own boys unable to ever get a good fix on the single tube. They wanted it really bad, but just never managed to run it down. It must have been really well camouflaged as even the sats and fly boys couldn't find it. The funny thing is they never hit a damn thing with it. In fact, the closet thing they ever came to hitting anything was me and the Captain! Go figure.■

Intelligence Briefing 2268-818: The United Terran Federation

The Evolution of Modern Battle Armor
Published 08.18.2268 TSD (Terran Standard Date)
Ronald Hawkins, Analysis Technician Class B

Leonardo da Vinci (1452–1519), described the first use of chemical weapons in a shell launched against a ship of the period, containing arsenic and sulfur dust. Moving ahead to World War One on Terra and the widespread use of chemical weapons following this conflict, military planners have long sought a system that would allow the infantry soldier to continue to operate effectively in such a lethal environment.

By the end of the 20th century, many nations fielded full-body protective suits for their troops that consisted of layered materials to absorb any chemical agents before they reached the wearer inside. These suits tended to be very uncomfortable and could only be worn for short times before needing to be replaced. They were also easily torn and provided no ballistic protection; definitely a minus in an active fighting environment.

In response to a worldwide Ebola epidemic the United States Military began replacing their venerable MOPP (Mission-Orientated Protection Posture) suits in 2016 with the new HEPP (Hazardous Environment Protection Posture) suits. While bulkier and still vision-impaired for the wearer, the HEPP suits were equipped with a fan system that moved filtered air through the suits to reduce heat and the associated humidity

caused by perspiration. Operational life for the suits was also extended and the outer layer was constructed from Kevlon III ballistic cloth. Lightweight, Kevlon III gave the wearer some protection from small arms fire and was more resistant to tearing.

As US and NATO forces began operations in 2036 to push Latin American forces out of the southern United States, some units were deployed with all-new SAVIOR body armor. Fully enclosed like a HEPP suit, but designed for constant use, SAVIOR body armor provided plating across vital areas of a soldier's body and contained an ablative material to disperse laser-based weapon attacks. The suit's helmet was equipped with thermal- and infrared-viewing screens and improved listening devices.

The next major leap in personal protection occurred in 2065 with the invasion of South America by the New Republic of Texas. The Texans landed in South America and quickly routed the Consortium troops based there wearing armor that incorporated an interior load-assist "skeleton", similar to those used by commercial power lifters in factories and shipping yards across the solar system. Soldiers were now fully enclosed by armor and could carry a heavier load of weapons and gear. While the suits were slow and choppy in movement, the Republic troops were virtually unstoppable and the rest of the world, taking note, rushed to catch up.

Advances in technology and materials allowed the continued refinement of powered armor. As artificially created beings were used more and more throughout the solar system, many advances made for them were adapted for use in powered armor. Artificial muscles, smaller computers, and the ability to "link" a man to the armor he wore—allowing thoughts to control functions of the suit—added incredible functionality to the suits.

Since the Vela War of 2176, the power armor in use today by the Federation has remained virtually unchanged. New plastics and metal alloys have allowed suits to get stronger and lighter while weapon systems, trying to keep up with technical improvements in defense, improved as well.

Today's powered body armor suit is made up of three basic systems, each system a layer within the suit with a specific purpose and function. Small variations exist from manufacturer to manufacturer, but the overall design remains the same.

The first layer is a permeable Neoprane suit covered with dozens of small sensors/transmitters. A network of small tubes runs throughout the Neoprane layer, carrying a special fluid that the suit can heat or cool as needed to control the temperature of the wearer.

The second layer of the suit is made up of hundreds of small metal interconnected rings, something similar to the chainmail worn by ancient knights. Manufactured from the alloy Veronimon, a highly conductive and lightweight material, this layer of rings rest on top of the sensors located in the first layer of the suit. As a soldier moves his arm or leg, the sensors in the first layer send a signal that is detected by the Veronimon rings, which is used by the suit to amplify the desired motion. The effect is almost instantaneous and allows for a smooth, unimpeded flow of motion. The Veronimon layer also acts as a "cushion" to help distribute the force of any impact away from the body of the soldier inside.

The final layer of the suit is the armor itself. Made up of layers of composite and ablative materials, modern body armor is one of the most protective devices ever built for the infantry. The armor layer has an internal powered "skeleton" made up of several Bellar Joints that performs the actual movement of the suit and carries the weight, allowing the wearer to remain active for some time before tiring. The powered frame can also be locked or frozen by the wearer, which is often done so a soldier can sleep without fear of falling over.

Power armor can be environmentally sealed for short times with an internal air reservoir and can be easily modified for outer space or underwater operations.

In summary, modern power armor is one of the greatest advancements in military history. Careful consideration should be used when engaging an armored foe without an appropriate counter-measure. No other equipment in the vast arsenal of military weapons is as sufficient and versatile as a power-armored force. End.

The Technology of War (continued)

Infantry

The life of an infantryman on the battlefield has always been brutal and bloody with the focus of weapon technology on how to kill the enemy soldier as fast and efficiently as possible. That basic truth remains unchanged in the 23rd century.

The modern infantryman is equipped with a wide array of weapons and electronics designed to keep them in the fight longer, doing their job no matter what hostile environment they may find themselves in. While cheap to equip and field (as opposed to CAVs or combat vehicles), massed infantry can be very lethal. With the addition of armored carriers, infantry have even more mobility and flexibility in a chaotic combat zone.

Infantry are classified by the type of armor they are equipped with—Light, Heavy, and Powered—as well as their mode of travel: Foot, Mounted, Mechanized, or Jump.

Infantry: Light

Light infantry make up the majority of the troops fielded by most modern militaries, and are the cheapest to maintain as part of a standing army.

Light infantry typically wear standard battle dress, with the addition of a helmet and an armored vest or jacket, and carry light weapons, such as an assault or pulse laser rifle.

Approximately 50% of all infantry are light infantry and typically make up the majority of a faction's reserve and defense forces.

Infantry: Heavy

Heavy infantry, having received more training and access to heavier weapons and armor, make up most of an army's career soldiery.

The use of heavier, non-powered ballistic plate armor, while offering improved protection over vital areas, sacrifices some mobility on the battlefield.

Approximately 30% of all infantry are heavy infantry.

Infantry: Powered

Powered infantry are the elite of the ground-pounder corps, wearing fully enclosed, articulated power armor. Powered infantry receive more specialized training in taking on armored vehicles or CAVs and close-quarters battle (referred to as Grenadiers).

Powered armor dramatically increases the overall speed and stamina of the grunt as well as allowing them to operate in even the most hostile environments.

Approximately 20% of all infantry are powered infantry.

Infantry: Foot

Foot infantry are their own transportation, putting one foot in front of the other, marching to battle. Foot infantry tend to be used as garrison troops or other static positions where a less mobile defensive force is required. Most reserve soldiery are foot infantry and a planet can quickly position thousands of lightly armed foot soldiers when needed in an emergency situation or attack.

Infantry: Mounted

Mounted infantry are typically equipped with personal transport vehicles—hover/anti-grav "skimmers" or motorcycles—allowing them to move quickly across the battlefield. Mounted infantry will typically maneuver as close as possible before dismounting from their "rides" before engaging their target.

Infantry: Mechanized

Mechanized infantry are assigned to armored personnel or infantry fighting vehicles, riding inside to allow a degree of protection from enemy fire. Mechanized infantry will dismount from their "taxis" in order to carry out their attack while their combat vehicles provide covering fire.

Infantry: Jump

Jump infantry are equipped with jump or anti-grav packs, allowing them to make short hops to clear any adverse terrain below. Jump infantry can also use their jump-packs to "launch" themselves out of an aircraft in flight and land safely on the ground.

Infantry: Combat Medic

For centuries, the combat medic has been there to provide life-saving triage on a wounded soldier on the battlefield. A soldier will fight harder and take risks they might not typically make knowing somewhere close is a combat medic ready to come to their aid.

While not every unit may have a medic, many militaries do provide for one when they are in combat, giving them the encouragement they need to hang in there and push on for victory!

Infantry Combat Weapon Systems

While infantry-based weapon systems have seen a multitude of evolutions over the last thousand years, the last three centuries have yielded a variety of weapon systems that allow a soldier to truly become an army of one. Today's modern infantryman has sufficient firepower to engage a multitude of targets with a decreased logistical need.

Assault Rifles

The assault rifle is the standard-issue infantry weapon in use by all modern militaries. While the definition of what is an assault rifle has broadened with the advent of new technologies, the requirement to deliver accurate and sustainable fire at a target in a variety of environments remains at the forefront of a successful design.

Assault Rifles: Propellant

Propellant assault rifles, while lighter and more efficient than those seen over a half-millennium ago, use the same basic science in their use: an explosive charge in the weapon forces a projectile down the barrel, ejecting it at high speed at the target.

Assault Rifles: Flechette

Flechette assault rifles use a cartridge full of fin-stabilized "spikes" that spread out at high velocity when fired. While the damage at short range from these types of weapons is devastating, the projectiles are easily de-stabilized in flight, causing them to tumble wildly and rapidly decreasing their effectiveness.

Assault Rifles: Needlers

Needlers use a spool of Iridium or Tungsten wire that is fed into the firing chamber of the weapon as the trigger is pulled. Small pieces of the wire are cut (approximately 25mm in length) and sent down the barrel of the weapon through magnetic energy at hyper-velocity speeds. The rate of fire for a needler assault rifle can approach 5,000 "rounds" per minute on some models.

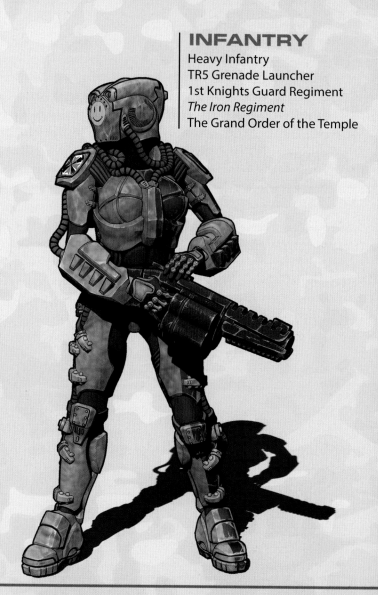

INFANTRY
Heavy Infantry
TR5 Grenade Launcher
1st Knights Guard Regiment
The Iron Regiment
The Grand Order of the Temple

Magnetic Accelerator Rifle

Magnetic accelerator rifles use the same basic tech as their larger MAC cousins and are typically assigned to power armored troops as their primary weapon system. Tripod-mounted versions are also available for use by light infantry as a crew-served weapon.

Pulse Laser Rifle

Portable solid-state laser systems work by generating plasma in energy pulses fired at a desired target and releasing the energy upon impact. With no report or muzzle flash, all that is seen is the effect it has on the target area. Their near-perfect accuracy and line-of-sight range made them seemingly the ideal weapons platform.

After their initial deployment, the drawbacks of laser weapons became apparent. If not properly maintained, the delicate parts of the weapon can lead to a loss of beam intensity, overheating, and a failure in its ability to regulate energy use. Smoke and fog also can lead to a loss in power of the beam, and the weapons have little impact on heavily-armored targets.

Within a few years of their initial deployment, most militaries had phased out laser-based weapons, though they remained popular with large game hunters, favored for the quick kill they provided with minimal damage to the tissue of their quarry.

Military-grade laser weapons have seen a resurgence over the last century as improved technology has made them more effective, their lack of ammo requirements making them a favorite of many cost-conscience mercenary units. Police and security forces also prefer laser-based weapons, as they allow a pulse beam to be used to generate an intense shockwave upon impact rather than the classic burn-through, allowing for the ability to stun or paralyze a non-armored target for a non-lethal alternative.

Anti-Armor Weapons

Most man-portable anti-armor weapons use a HEAT-type warhead to penetrate the armor of a target due to their ease in construction and overall effectiveness. Anti-armor weapon systems function by detonating a high-explosive shell at a specific distance and focusing the blast into a high-speed jet to punch through armor.

The firing tube is typically reusable for multiple firings and is armed by simply inserting the new round into the front of the launch tube. Upon firing, the projectile will deploy a set of small fins to stabilize it and prevent spinning, which can reduce the effectiveness of the explosive.

Anti-Air Weapons

Shoulder-fired surface-to-air missile, requiring a single operator, are used by infantry to engage air-based targets. Using a combo infrared and ultraviolet seeker-system to lock-

on to a target and once fired, will engage its solid-fuel based rocket motor to home in, closing the distance to the target at over Mach 3.0, before using a proximity or impact fuze to detonate. The weapon systems control module can be attached to a new rocket tube to allow multiple firings in a short amount of time.

SMART Weapon Systems

Unlike earlier "point and shoot" targeting systems, an operator equipped with a SMART modified weapon system "sees" what the weapon sees. A sensor suite is added to the electronics of the operator's powered armored suit to allow their HUD system to synch with the onboard transmitter installed on a SMART weapon system.

As an operator moves the weapon, a crosshair will appear on the HUD, showing exactly where a round will hit if fired at that moment. SMART systems adjust for current weather and wind conditions, and are ideal for sniper use, theoretically providing for a 360-degree arc of fire. Due to the expense of the system and the constant need of calibration needed to maintain targeting, SMART systems are not a standard-issue item.

Note: *The installation of a SMART sensor suite inside the body of an operator is also possible, displaying the targeting information directly onto the optic nerve of the user through the use of a cybernetic implant.*

THE UNIVERSE

Interplanetary (Sub-Light) and Interstellar (Faster-Than-Light) Space Travel

The Adonese were the first to travel among the stars with their initial discovery of the compression drive. Since that time, each of the other known races have developed their own compression drive technology. While naming conventions may vary from race to race, the Terrans referring to it as a Hyperdrive and the Rach a Stardrive, each uses the same basic principle to provide interplanetary and interstellar travel.

During interplanetary travel at sub-light speeds, a compression drive focuses subatomic energy particles (known as quanta), forcing them through aft-mounted nacelles that "push" a starship through space in constant acceleration. Once it reaches the halfway point of its trip, referred to as the "apex turn", a starship will "flip" and use the same acceleration to slow down, coming to a stop as it reaches its final destination. Most acceleration is kept in the 1 to 2 G range to keep a trip comfortable for the crew, but faster speeds are capable, a high-G burn, for short times.

The compression drive is also used for faster-than-light travel (FTL), requiring a much higher level of power consumption that exponentially increases with the amount of mass being moved, creating a "fold" or tear in space (referred to as "fold space") that a ship can enter, emerging later at a destination light years away. Exact calculations are required to make a jump to the desired location with any degree of accuracy; the longer the jump the greater chance for error.

The effect of Hyper-Disparity, also known as the "shakes", becomes more acute with longer jumps. Hyper-Disparity is a result of time spent in fold space and is made worse by an out-of-tune compression drive or a misaligned jump.

Hyper-Disparity can cause

Janet's Fighting Ships of the Galaxy 2273–2274

A Note on Modern Space Combat

To understand a starship's role in a planetary raid or assault you should also have a working knowledge of modern space-based naval combat doctrine as it applies in the 23rd century. Much of the theory applied to that of the wet navies from over 300 years ago has carried over to present-day ship-to-ship combat.

Space combat is limited to relative space, as once a starship enters fold space the distortion on time and distance (which increases the closer you are to a gravity source, hence why a starship has to move away from a planet or other large object in space to enter fold-space) makes detection and targeting impossible. Commercial shipping tends to stay to known routes that are safe of any unwanted gravity influences. Starships are designed with fail-safes to drop a ship out of fold space if any strong gravity sources are detected. There has been some talk of devices that create strong gravitomagnetic fields capable of forcing a starship out of fold-space, but to date have not been confirmed.

Starships operate in coordinated task forces as a general rule, each ship-type responsible for a specific duty and using tactics based on a concept known as "defense in depth", hopefully destroying an enemy well before it reaches the main body of the group.

Frigates and destroyers, along with fighter patrols, form an outer screen around the task force, scanning for any threats or enemy craft. The next layer is made up of heavy and light cruisers whose main function is to intercept any enemy craft or missiles before they reach the centralized main body of the fleet, made up of battleships and carriers.

When attacking, starships will typically begin with limited salvos of capital missiles at extreme range to test the defenses of an opposing force and the chance of scoring a lucky hit while the torpedo bombers and their fighter escorts gather to wait for the enemy to close-in, avoiding being overwhelmed by the close-in anti-ship missile capabilities of a massed fleet.

At long range, the salvos become more intense in an effort to exhaust the defensive missile stores of an enemy ship and increase the chance of a critical hit. Medium range finds the fighting becoming a swirling mass of missiles, torpedoes, and attack craft, with ships finally firing their cannons as the ships draw closer and closer.

Space Combat: Weapons

Missiles

Missiles come in two basic varieties—Anti-Ship and Anti-Missile—and are the first weapon-types generally used when engaging a spaceship; both missile types using Super Thermex-based warheads with proximity sensors, powered by magneto plasma dynamic (MPD) thrusters. An attacking starship will use its own sensor systems to lock onto an enemy target, firing a spread of missiles in an attempt to saturate a defender's defenses, directing them for as long as possible before switching them to their own onboard systems for their final attack run, exploding as close as possible to the target. While a direct hit will destroy most smaller ships, a close-in explosion is more likely, vaporizing armor panels caught within the blast and rupturing a ship's hull, exposing the inside to dangerous decompression and the crew to the radiation of deep space. This explosion can also produce spallation—large chunks of the interior of the hull coming loose, producing additional damage to the inside of a ship. This effect has led to most space forces referring to anti-ship missiles as "maces" (a medieval weapon that damaged by blunt force impact).

X-Ray Lasers

While technically a missile sub-munition x-ray lasers, commonly referred to as "flails", are nuclear-based missiles launched toward an enemy ship that once in range, will detonate and use the explosion to pump out over 100 million megajoules of x-rays. The missile's warhead contains multiple laser rods in various angles of projection that focus the x-rays into beams emitting from both ends of a rod. While no beam is independently aimed, the number of beams being generated makes a hit on a nearby starship likely. The amount of energy released in the directed beams will burn through the armor and hull of most starships in an attempt to damage critical internal systems onboard.

Torpedoes

Designed primarily as capital-ship killers, torpedoes carry smaller warheads than a typical anti-ship missile, but are larger in overall size to carry their own internal compression drives. As with a missile, an attacking ship will lock onto its target and launch one or more torpedoes, each one equipped with a low-level AI that pilots it toward an enemy ship. The use of an onboard AI allows the torpedo to be less susceptible to any jamming attempts or other types of "spoofing", communicating with other near-by torpedoes to actively work together and come at a target on differing vectors and increase the chance of a direct-hit.

The AI will use the torpedoes' compression drive to make small jumps as it closes with a target, coming out only long enough to make any corrections in its trajectory. This makes a torpedo very hard to intercept, especially at longer ranges, and lends to their nickname "hoppers".

severe psychological and physical reactions, including death. Although numerous chemical and medical treatments have been tested, nothing has been found to counter these adverse reactions other than time spent back in real space, and as a result ships usually make several smaller jumps to complete a voyage. ■

Dynamic Stream Jump Stations

With the discovery of naturally occurring "folds" in space, typically found within a star system's gravity well, the Adonese began looking at the possibility of building permanent jump stations. While many of these folds were temporary and would vanish after a short period of time, others were found to remain stable and connected to folds in other star systems.

Dynamic stream portals could be positioned inside these stable folds and aligned with another portal at the other end, allowing a starship to "jump" through without the time-consuming calculations normally required.

Over 180 jump stations exist today throughout the galaxy and are used by commercial and military ships alike, connecting major systems to one another and are heavily guarded. ■

STARSHIP

Destroyer
"Asagari" Class
Mitso-Ta
United Terran Federation

Built: 2265-
Class: 62 in service; 8 building
Displacement: 12374 tons
Dimensions: length 458 ft; beam 118 ft
Number of Decks: 8
Propulsion: 4 ZRK-8D Imaidegaw Fusion Drives
Armament: 12 Class D Yumiya Capital Missile Launchers (72 carried); 12 Hiya Anti-Missile Launchers (180 carried); 10 Class A Shuriken Naval Particle Accelerator Cannons; 22 Ryuujin Magnetic Accelerator Cannons.
Electronics: HSZ-16 Sagasu Space/Air Surveillance System; WZK-02 Gigan Search/Fire Control System; DZK-1226 Keiro Navigation System.
Shuttles: 2 Kashima Transport Shuttles; 4 Goryouho Drop Attack Craft.
Compliment: 250 crew and 25 Federation Fleet Marines.

Naval Particle Accelerator Cannons (N-PACs)

Made up of charged proton particles generated by a linear accelerator, particle cannons fire a pulsed-beam capable of penetrating a spaceship's armor. The beam travels near the speed of light (about .9 relativistic) and will release a tremendous amount of energy inside a ship should it manage to breach the hull, "frying" anything caught near the entry point.

The beam of a particle cannon expands the further it travels (since the similarly charged protons in the beam repel one another), causing it to disperse, limiting the range of even the most powerful N-PACs. Particle accelerator cannons are typically mounted along the port and starboard side of a starship in "banks" and used for close-in fighting.

Ion Disruptor Cannons

Ion cannons are used to disrupt incoming torpedoes by scrambling the onboard AIs. Absent the effects of atmosphere, space-based ion weapons generate a larger area of effect than their earth-based versions. The massive shielding located on spaceships prevent them from being affected by ion attacks.

Rail Guns

As particle cannons are ineffective when fired from space into an atmosphere and Super-Thermex missiles raining down on a planet's surface can result in indiscriminate destruction and civilian causalities, a starship will typically be equipped with one or more rail guns for attacking stationary or planet-based targets.

Made up of two electrically charged "rails" that generate a very strong magnetic field, a rail gun will use this field to propel a conductive projectile the length of the rail, accelerating it at hypervelocity speeds (approximating over 200km per second, relative) towards the desired target.

Damage from a rail gun projectile is produced through the release of kinetic energy generated by the velocity of the round, with larger rounds approaching the damage output of a small nuclear warhead without the radiation fallout normally associated with such a weapon.

Magnetic Accelerator Cannons

Naval versions of the standard "coil" mass drivers, these weapons are used for close-in point defense weapons

ALL THE SANDS OF HELLSPIRE

18 November.2274
Hellspire
The United Terran Federation

► The orange-red dust blew through the open inner-hatch, swirling silently across the floor ahead of Sergeant Legionnaire Leroy "Slam" Ferris as he entered the barracks. Across the room, Legionnaire Danny Garnier sat, playing cards, pausing only to mutter a silent curse under his breath. Despite the double airlock to the trooper's quarters, the dirt always found a way in, infiltrating into every corner of the buildings that made up the United Terran Federation base known simply as Outpost 12.

"Garnier!" Ferris shouted in the low baritone voice of the squat body of the platoon leader. He was a typical non-commissioned officer—a hulking brute with little education and even less manners, at least in the eyes of the men and women under him.

Danny did his best to ignore Ferris, focusing on the three ace cards in his hand, keeping a straight face as he tossed in his bet, hoping to sucker in the other soldiers sitting at the table. Across from him, Danny's bunkmate, Mike "Koz" Koslewski, looked up over Danny's shoulder across his own hand of cards at the approaching sergeant and knew that this game was about to come to an abrupt end.

Ferris drew closer, weaving through the bunks toward the card game, his anger rising as Danny continued to ignore him. Finally, standing behind the soldier, both fists placed firmly on his hips, Ferris boomed.

"Legionnaire Rich Boy, a moment of your time... please!"

Danny turned his head slightly, acknowledging the Sergeant's presence, but remained staring at his cards, hoping the Sergeant would take the hint and just bugger off. In a flash Danny was off his chair and sprawled on the floor of the bunkroom. Looking up at Ferris, Danny saw the Sergeant glaring down so hard it seemed as if the

non-com's eyes were going to pop out of his head and roll across the floor.

"What the hell did you do that for?" Danny demanded innocently as he sat up, wiping the blood off his mouth where he had bit his lip from slamming the floor. With entire galaxies of stars still floating across his vision, it was hard to focus on the Sergeant just yet.

"Because, you little puke, I've figured out that there are only two ways to get your attention on this Godforsaken dustball. One is to just shoot you, which—in spite of my feelings—the brass tells me is not a good use of military resources. The other is to whack you up alongside that worthless nut of yours. So get on your feet and come to attention now, Legionnaire!"

Danny jumped up, wishing the other troopers would say something, anything, and come to his aid. They all turned back to their cards, finishing the hand without him. Silently cursing their cowardice, Danny knew he was on his own and decided he would just have to convince this moron of a Sergeant to go pick on someone else.

"I didn't do anything," Danny told Ferris.

"How right you are, soldier. I just looked at the maintenance log on your CAV. I thought I told you to pull maintenance on it this morning?"

"I did!"

Ferris poked a scarred finger into Danny's chest, almost knocking him to the floor again. "No, you didn't. You paid someone else to do it for you."

"So, what's the difference? It's done, isn't it?"

"Legionnaire Rich Boy, it's your responsibility to make sure it's done right. You never know when that machine will save your worthless hide in a tight spot, so it's your job to keep it clean—absolutely spotless. Joints full of sand make you slow. Slow makes you dead."

Danny made a loud huffing noise, clearly exasperated with the Sergeant. "The service manual clearly states that my CAV only needs to be serviced once a month by a certified technician, which has been done."

"Wrong again, Garnier; your daddy's corporation says it needs to be serviced once a month and your daddy is wrong… dead wrong. Machines don't work worth jack if they ain't maintained on a daily basis, and this dustball of a planet makes it even worse. That's something I bet he forgot to tell you when he enlisted you in the ranks to make a man out of you, didn't he?"

"You leave my father out of this," Danny said, reaching up to rub the sore spot on his chest where Ferris had jabbed him.

Ferris slammed Danny's hand back down hard. "I told you to brace, mister, and that means don't move. You want to kiss the deck again?"

Danny quickly came back to attention but silently promised it was only a temporary victory for the Sergeant. A single word from Danny to his father would ensure that Ferris's next duty station would make Hydra seem like Paradise Lost. Danny smiled at the thought.

The air was expelled from his lungs as Danny fell back to the floor, doubled over after the blow Ferris struck him with in the stomach.

"See what that stupid smirk buys you now, Rich Boy? I already know what you're thinkin' before you think it. You're planning to call up Daddy so I get busted. Well, guess what, trooper? Your daddy doesn't care and sure as hell doesn't want to talk to you. He put you in the army to make a man out of you

and the last thing he wants to hear is a bunch of pissing and whining."

Ferris paused for a second, "And to make sure, I removed all of your call privileges for a month. You ain't talking to anybody but me, trooper! Now get on your feet and stop acting like some corp-exec excuse of a soldier!"

Struggling to his feet, Danny stood up and came back to attention.

Ferris moved in, sticking his face right in front of Danny's; his breath reeking of the boiled cabbage the Sergeant was so fond of eating.

Barely audible to Danny, Ferris whispered. "Okay, Rich Boy, here is the deal. You've got perimeter patrol tonight."

"Patrol?" Danny shouted out. "Patrol where?"

Grinning with the realization he had the soldier's attention now, the Sergeant shot back, "Out to Hill 103 and back for a little sightseeing."

"Are you nuts?" Danny asked. "That place is crawling with Rats. Go ahead and throw me in the brig, 'cause I'm not going out there… and certainly not by myself."

"Oh, you won't be alone, rich boy. Legionnaire Koslewski has already volunteered to join you."

Koslewski groaned from behind Danny, confirming that this was the first time the other soldier heard of his "volunteering."

Koslewski was a skinny kid from some backwater fringe world that was still coming to terms with the fact that bathing was something you should do more than once a year. He had only been in the army a little longer than Danny and always sent his paycheck back to his family. Nice enough guy, but his demeanor didn't exactly inspire confidence.

"No offense, Koz," Danny said over his shoulder without turning his head, "but I'd prefer the brig."

"It would seem to me, rich boy, that you don't have much of a choice in the matter," Ferris said. "Plus, what would

the other guys think if you let Koz go out there and get all shot up by his lonesome?"

Sweat began building up on Danny's forehead. A week in the brig would be bad enough on this rock—at least he would still be alive—but alive to face what? Danny knew that you never let another soldier down, not even a slummer like Koslewski. Danny looked back into the amused face of Ferris and could feel the eyes of the other troopers around them staring, waiting for the answer, his answer. No choice.

If he refused, Legionnaire Danny Garnier would be a pariah for the rest of his service, no matter where he went. Worse, if Koslewski got hurt or killed, Danny knew that he would be cornered somewhere on a dark night and that would be the end, period. The military didn't think too kindly of a soldier who tanked on his mates, and being in Recon only added to the mentality. Recon considered itself to be the elite of the elite and went to great lengths to make sure no one cast a shadow on that image.

"Well, Sarge, now that I've had a sec to think about it, I'm sure Koz and I will manage just fine," Danny smiled.

Ferris arched an eyebrow, "You sure about that, rich boy?" Danny thought he caught disappointment in the sergeant's response.

"Yeah, Sarge."

"Yes, what?"

"Yes, Sergeant Legionnaire Ferris."

"All right then, you two get suited up and report to me for your briefing. You got 30 mikes before you leave," said Ferris as he turned to leave back through the same door he came through earlier, leaving Danny standing at attention. Danny just stared at the sergeant's back as he walked away, his mouth aping a sentence as he tried to think of something, anything, to tell Ferris in hopes of changing his mind, the three aces of his winning hand lying scattered on the floor at his feet.

Checking that his comlink was open only to Koz, Danny keyed the mic located on the inside of his combat helmet. "This patrol doesn't have a thing to do with sand in my ride, not a freaking thing. He knows I'm corp and he's just jealous. I can't help who my parents are."

Danny could tell that the scrubbers inside the cockpit of the CAV were having problems keeping the air fresh as he caught the smell of his own sweat. He was sure that he had just changed them or, correcting himself, paid someone to change them. He just needed to calm down, he kept telling himself.

The patrol left the outpost and the protection it provided. Ringed by mines, gun emplacements, and a full Turma of CAVs, Outpost 12 was a very lethal piece of real estate on Hydra. Situated at the narrow end of Kushma Canyon in the southern hemisphere of the planet, the base protected an area the Rach liked to use to advance on other sectors of the planet.

"Don't matter no how, does it?" Koz's voice crackled through. "We're here and he's back there. Let's just get out there and get it done."

"You are such a wimp," Danny shot back.

"Why you calling me a wimp? I'm just telling you like it is."

"Because you let that garbage-breath idiot push you around."

"Me? Danny-boy, you're the one who got stuck on this patrol for screwing up. I'm just here because I helped you."

"You didn't have to tell Slam you were doing the maintenance on my ride, did you?" Danny pointed out.

"I didn't tell him nothin'."

"Then how in the hell did he find out?"

Koz chuckled over the link, "He didn't tell you?"

"You told him, that's what I know." Irritated by Koz's laughter, Danny demanded, "Okay, then how did he

Two hours later, Danny dug the front "toes" of his Starhawk V CAV, into the hard ground, watching the red and orange dust drift away on the constant blowing wind of Hydra, marching on towards Hill 103. God, he wished he could be on some beautiful beach, digging his real toes into warm, white sand. Doing that here would have broken them off from the extreme cold. Danny stomped down his CAV's other foot to make himself feel better, hoping to take his mind off his current situation.

From the aft seat of the Starhawk, Legionnaire Thomas Mays could only watch and grimace as Danny swung the CAV into a steady pace out into the desolate desert surrounding the base. As a Weapons System Officer (WSO or "Wizzo" as it is pronounced), the older Mays had only been with Danny a couple of months and was still trying to figure out what made the kid tick. Danny seemed like a decent pilot and that went a long way with Thomas as he had no desire to end up a grease spot on some god forsaken rock. Thomas looked back to his radar screen and made sure he had a good lock on the other Starhawk following them out of the bay, piloted by Koz and his Wizzo Kathy Voight.

know if you didn't tell him?"

"Your CAV was too clean, Corp. Slam knew right away you wasn't the one pulling maintenance on it."

"Well, drek, you didn't have to do such a good job then, did you?" Danny whined.

"'Get it spotless!' That's what you paid me for," Koz sputtered out while still laughing.

"Shut up! I am so sick and tired of hearing you laugh all the time about everything."

"That's a funny way of saying you screwed up," Koz answered. "Besides, he gigged me because I didn't get my own ride clean enough for him after working on yours all that time. So I guess I'm just laughing at both of us."

Danny couldn't think of a good answer to that and decided to just let it slide. It was time to check in back with the base anyway and he changed over to the company net.

"Command 12, this is Bravo Two-Niner, do you copy? Over."

"Bravo Two-Niner, this is Command 12. We have you in the clear. Over," the CommTech back at the base responded.

"Command 12, we have entered the valley and are proceeding to Hill 103 as ordered. Over."

"Affirmative, Bravo Two-Niner. Continue to follow the vector as ordered. Report any enemy activity, but do not engage. Over."

"Roger, Command," Danny answered. "Bravo Two-Niner out."

"Command 12 out."

Danny squelched the link and switched back to the private net he shared with Thomas. "We've got 10 klicks of pretty flat ground ahead of us before we get to the hill. I say we might as well enjoy the scenery on our way out."

"Not a chance," Thomas answered. "Let's make some speed."

"What for? We can see for a hell of a long way. No Rat is going to sneak up on us in this crap. Acres and acres of flat land and scrub, most of it no more than

a meter or two high—the wind sees to that," Danny said.

"Because, if I was an Rach looking to ambush two stupid and slow enemy scouts I would make sure it was exactly where they wouldn't be expecting it. Or did you sleep through that part of training?"

"Maybe."

Thomas just sighed into his mic, "Just keep your eyes open, Corp."

Danny stared out the view screen and checked the ground ahead of him. Nothing but sand and dirt in every dull, boring and, incessantly tedious color of the universe, the only relief some black outcroppings of basaltic rock frosted with frozen carbon dioxide.

"And?" Danny prompted when Thomas didn't continue.

"And let's maintain radio silence for a bit and make some tracks. Okay?"

"Sure thing," Danny agreed and switched off the link. Both CAVs eased into a steady, ground-eating trot, the pilots watching the ground ahead and their wizzos checking their radar for any sign of the enemy. They kept all of their sensors on passive but their passage kicked up dusty orange-hued clouds that the wind lifted to the sky. Danny cursed the damnable planet for the thousandth time for showing their position so clearly.

He topped those curses with several for Thomas for making him so nervous about Rach soldiers lying in ambush for them. Up until this patrol, Slam had kept the newer guys, like himself, closer to the base and always in force. The danger had still been there, but with the base backing them up it was negligible. This was the real deal now.

Danny checked to make sure all of his weapons were online and showing green across the board. Knowing he was in a good machine made him feel slightly better.

The Starhawk V was manufactured by SyRaM for the Federal forces and was in wide use as a recon and support CAV.

Its twin rotary MACs and Federal Ordnance Hunter missile system gave it quite the punch for an 87-ton machine. Better-than-average speed and armor made it a favorite of Fed pilots.

A good machine for sure, Danny thought to himself, unless the damn thing malfunctions. Surely Koz did a good job like he said, but did he do it well enough? The earlier dressing down by Ferris echoed in his head.

"Damn!" Danny swore as he pulled up on the controls to stop the CAV. Koz had pulled ahead earlier and had suddenly made an abrupt stop and seemed to be scanning the horizon in front of them. Danny tried to find what Koz had spotted but all he could see were endless waves of sand.

Koz rotated the top of his CAV to face Danny. As the CAV turned towards him, Danny spotted the indicator on his HUD that Koz was trying to establish a direct laser link to him. A laser link was line of sight only but it couldn't be intercepted. Obviously Koz was afraid someone might pick up their conversation.

"Danny," Koz spoke after the link was confirmed. "I'm pretty sure I saw something ahead down in the sand. It's not showing up on my sensors but I caught movement."

"So what do we do?" Danny asked.

"I'm sending over the spot that I think it's at about 100 meters out. Circle around to the left and I will go right—let's catch it between us."

"What if it's a bad guy?"

"We will cross that bridge when we come to it. The download is complete so let's move."

Danny complied, but swore silently as he swung the Starhawk out to the left. He wasn't at all sure that Koz hadn't just imagined something, but better safe than sorry, he guessed.

"Thomas, Koz thinks he saw something out there, anything on the box?" Danny checked with his wizzo.

"Nothing is showing so far Danny but I'm double checking now." Thomas answered.

Danny watched Koz on his HUD to make sure he wasn't outdistancing him… Danny didn't want to get to the spot first.

A couple of minutes passed as the two CAVs moved forward and Thomas still did not see anything on his sensors but he didn't dare switch to "active" this far out. He thought he saw a shape once or twice in the swirling sands but he just couldn't be sure.

Suddenly Koz sped up and yelled over the radio link for Danny to move in and cover him. Startled by the sudden shouting, Danny triggered a salvo of fire at the location Koz had marked on his map and the rotating cannons fired a stream of slugs into the spot, kicking up sand and debris into the air as Koz yelled over the BattleNet to cease fire. When no return fire came, both CAVs moved forward around a small outcropping of lava rocks overlooking the sands below.

Half-buried in the sand was a Rach CAV, a Vanquisher by the looks of it, a large portion of its front torso blown away. Hanging out of the blasted wreckage was the upper portion of the pilot, the combat suit and the flesh it protected long since torn away by the blowing sands of the planet. The body rose up and fell back with the passing winds and Danny realized it must have been the movement Koz had seen.

"Well, it doesn't look like we can claim credit for this one," Thomas said. "Hydra is definitely not good for one's complexion."

Koz snorted, "His loss."

"Yeah…his loss." Danny responded.

"I suppose," Koz answered. "This your first deader?" he then asked.

"Yeah. So?"

"It don't seem to be bothering you any. I've seen plenty of death back home in the streets, but I figured rich boys would, well…."

"Well, what?" Danny asked.

"Puke, run screaming the other way, pretend it wasn't there—whatever it is that rich people do. I just didn't expect you to crack a joke about it is all."

Danny shrugged his shoulders, a reaction lost to Koz sitting in the other CAV. "It's not like it's one of us. My father always said the only good Rach is a dead Rach."

"That's cold-blooded, man. Ain't no way to die, out here all alone. You got lifer-makings, you know that? No wonder Slam likes you," Koz smirked.

"Don't you ever say that again, slummer! Don't you ever say that again."

Seemingly with the mere mention of his name, the sarcastic voice of Ferris broke across the company net, drowning out any response that Koz might have tried to make. "Girls, we're glad you're stopping to fix your makeup, but I would appreciate a report when you can spare the time."

"Sorry, Command 12," Danny responded, ignoring the bait offered up by the sergeant. "We found a wrecked Vanquisher out here, looks like it's been here awhile. Over."

"Any markings, Bravo Two-Niner? Over," Ferris got more businesslike with the mention of an enemy unit.

"None that we can see. The sand picked it pretty clean. We can confirm one KIA. Looks to be a scout, probably was out doing the same thing we are. Over."

"Any others?" Slam asked, his voice more civil now. "Over."

"None that we can see, Command 12, but like I said, it's been here awhile, over," Danny responded.

"Strange, the Rach are pretty good about salvage and recovery being so far away from their normal supply lines. You boys better shag your asses out of there. Over."

"Well, I guess we'll never know what it was doing out here," Danny said.

Slam responded, "Maybe…but leave a tag on it for an Intel team to investigate later. Over."

Danny slapped the key to drop a GPS marker from the back of his CAV's leg and made sure it was transmitting. Keying his mic he asked, "So, now what? Can we head back? Over."

"You wish, Two-Niner. Get back on your vector and continue the patrol. Keep your eyes open for any of that Rach's buddies. Out." Danny was sure he heard a chuckle come across the net as Ferris ended the transmission.

"Affirmative, Command 12, Bravo Two-Niner out," Danny answered and switched back to their local link. "Great,

just when I thought we could call for a dust-off and ride back to base."

"No such luck for us, Danny-boy...and now comes the fun part: The Kush," Koz shot back.

The Kushma Canyon stretched across the southern hemisphere of Hydra like a giant slash. Nearly five times larger than the Grand Canyon back on Earth, the Kush was made up of twisting turns and massive pillars that reached into the pinkish sky of the planet. The Rach used the maze of the canyon to infiltrate units farther into the planet from landing zones they controlled at the southern pole.

Both pilots moved away from the wrecked Vanquisher and started down the long slope that would bring them to the canyon floor. Moving more cautiously than before, Danny swung the upper torso of the Starhawk back and forth scanning the walls to both side of them in the distance.

Thirty minutes later brought them to the top of Hill 103. Though not much more than a hump on the floor of the canyon, the hill was situated in a spot that allowed an observer to see a wide cross-section of the canyon before it turned and followed a new direction for several hundred kilometers.

"Damn!" Danny swore in astonishment.

Koz echoed his sentiment, "She's a big one, ain't she?"

"I saw it from the air when they brought me in to the base but looking out the shuttle window didn't do it justice."

"Not even close," Koz agreed.

Before them the valley stretched off toward the dusty blue-pink horizon, the walls rising high up into the air. Side canyons like the one they just traveled down, massive in their own right, forked out at random intervals along both sides. Danny had never seen anything so big in his entire life. It seemed like the great expanse would never end.

Finally he decided it was impossible to comprehend the sheer size of it all and focused on the icy browns, blacks, and reds that defined striations in the cliff walls. It was then that Danny noticed wispy clouds of fog rolling out of one of the side canyons ahead of them.

Clouds of carbon dioxide vapor, Danny guessed. Down in the canyons the wind was not as bad and the CO_2 was bunching up in the canyon floor.

It was an eerie sensation watching the fog, even more so when a dull red light flashed from inside the gas, disappearing as quickly as it appeared.

Danny started to back down the hill and quickly signaled Koz to do the same. Both CAVs squatted down on their haunches to lower their profile and put the hill between them and the approaching fog.

"What's up, Danny?" Koz asked once a secure laser link was established.

"I don't think that fog is natural," Danny responded.

"What do you mean?"

"I mean I think we just made contact. They must be using smoke-generators or something to mask their approach from the sat-birds."

"You sure?" Koz seemed doubtful of the rookie.

"My eyesight may not be as good as yours, but I know a man-made light when I see one."

"All right, all right, call the boss."

Danny quickly switched over to the company net, "Command 12, this is Bravo Two-Niner. Say again, Command 12, this is Bravo Two-Niner. Over."

"Bravo Two-Niner," the base acknowledged. "Go ahead. Over."

"Command 12, we've got major bad guy action coming up through the Kush. Over."

"You have a count yet, Bravo Two-Niner? Over."

"Negative. They're laying smoke down pretty heavy to cover their approach; I would estimate a pretty good force though to go to that kind of trouble. Over."

"You sure? You better not be yanking my chain rookie," Ferris had obviously taken over the radio back at the base and radio procedure be damned. "Where the hell is Koslewski?"

"Then I would like to report I just saw a bunch of naked dancing girls down here and they asked me to tell you they think you're a real hunk of a soldier, Sarge," Danny snapped back, upset because no one seemed to believe him.

"Can the crap, rich boy," Ferris answered. "Just report what you see and stay calm."

"I am calm!" Danny shouted over the link, cursing himself for contradicting what he was saying. He moved the CAV up just a bit to get a better visual on the fog, hoping to see something—anything—to confirm his earlier sighting. The fog only seemed to keep moving forward as if it had a mind of its own.

"Thomas?" Danny pleaded. "You see anything?"

"Wait one, I'm looking...there!" Thomas switched over to the company link to transmit. "Command 12, I confirm the enemy sighting."

"Affirmative, I'm starting to get massive returns on the sensors." Kathy, Koz's wizzo added.

"Roger that, Bravo Two-Ten," Ferris seemed all business again. "Got a count?"

"Hard to tell through the smoke and our passive sensors still are not showing anything," Kathy answered. "I saw at least three CAVs and a bunch of crunchies (slang for power-armored infantry), so at least a squadron, Sarge."

Danny felt relief rush through him from the vindication of what he saw. He was certain Slam would have made sure he never lived that one down.

"Affirmative. Okay, boys and girls, let's make sure they know that we know they are out there. Artillery is on the way and they need a track."

"Sighting now," Danny confirmed. Simultaneously, he and Koz activated their TargetLock TAG systems and began to aim at the floor of the canyon in front of the advancing enemy troops. They both "painted" a spot on the ground with the invisible beams, a small dot on their HUDs the only indication of the area being painted. The system was foolproof as long as none of the enemy machines crossed the beam. If they did, sensors would alert them to the attack beforehand.

Across the radio link both pilots heard a single word, "Splash!"

The response was impressively quick and with virtually no sound, just the blossoming of high-explosive rounds far beyond their position behind the hill, the shock waves of the impacts shaking the ground and dispersing the smoke into oblivion. Round after round dropped onto the spots the two had targeted. The Rach soldiers and their machines, those that still could, scattered in a vain attempt to hide from the raining death.

"I guess that got their attention," Danny quipped, amused with his newfound sense of death-humor.

Ferris spoke this time across the net, "Uhh, Bravo Two-Niner?"

"Yeah?" Danny asked.

"Has it occurred to either of you idiots that the bad guys are gonna start wondering how those rounds were so accurate?"

"Already on it, Sarge," Koz cut in.

"Oh, shit," Danny said.

Koz had already risen up enough so he could start backing the Starhawk up the way they came earlier. Danny followed suit and they moved behind a couple of pillars about half a klick back from their earlier objective. Now out of sight where the attack took place, both CAVs rose up to their full height and carefully surveyed the area around them.

"Which way now?" Danny wondered out loud.

"I'm thinking we need to find a spot to hole up for a while. They might try to get ahead of us for an ambush, figuring whoever is out here will try to scoot

back to base ASAP." Thomas answered.

"Well maybe up that other side canyon there then," Danny said and twisted his upper-torso in the direction he was thinking of. The ground had started to shake again.

"I guess base is really calling in the heavy stuff now they have the position," Danny told Koz. "That ought to keep them busy for a bit."

"Save it, Danny, that's not ours."

Danny moved to one side of the pillars and looked back in the direction they retreated from. Large geysers of dirt and rock erupted from Hill 103 and more blasts seemed to be moving in their direction.

"How the hell did they know we were there?" Danny asked. "We need out of here fast; these guys are too good."

"Yeah, it's like they know where we are now," Koz agreed as they began moving both of their machines toward the side canyon Danny had pointed out. "I mean it's like—oh crap!"

"What? What?" Danny demanded.

"Did you switch your TAG off?"

"What?"

"Your targeting laser, did you remember to turn it off?"

Danny checked his status board as they continued to move through the rocks and pillars around them. He felt his heart sink down to his stomach; the indicator showed that both his TAG lasers were active. Frantically he jabbed down on both of their control switches and the indicator flipped over to stand-by mode.

"Of all the damned stupid things I could have done," Danny cursed as he dashed from one pillar to the next. "I'm so sorry, Koz."

Koz moved in behind him at the next pillar. "I did it too, Danny," Koz sounded winded over the link. "Our mistakes are going to get us killed."

Shockwaves shook both CAVs and rocks pelted against their armored skin as a new wave of blasts landed closer. The Rach had gone to active sensors now and the powered-up targeting

lasers helped them locate the Fed scouts they knew had to be out there.

"I hate this," Danny moaned. "I hate screwing up. I hate being out here. I just hate it all!"

At the same time a more rational part of Danny's brain was taunting him. "The real reason you hate it, Danny-boy, is that you just messed your pants and isn't that several kinds of embarrassing?"

To shut up the voice in his head, Danny shouted to Koz, "We have to get the hell out of here. If we sit any longer they are going to start dropping shells right on our head. Let's shake and bake and run for it."

"Anything," Koz agreed.

Pivoting his CAV, Danny took off from behind the pillar they had been sheltering behind. He hadn't gone ten steps when it seemed like a giant hand reached down and picked him up, throwing him violently back down against the ground. Laying prone now, Danny kept his eyes closed and felt the warm trickle of blood move down across his face from where his helmet had cut into his forehead from the impact.

Like there is anything to see, Danny thought. He slowly opened his eyes and looked around the cockpit of his Starhawk. Red lights were flashing everywhere and he thought he heard air hissing in the background. Dust seemed to be floating around him now in a constant slow-motion pattern.

Danny started to giggle. Not that he found anything particularly amusing; he just started to giggle. Danny wanted to call for help but nothing seemed to come out. His voice just seemed to be lost, a thousand miles away and it didn't want to come back.

"Well, up yours!" Danny cursed. For god's sake, make up your mind!

Still staring at the dust, he wondered now why some idiot was screaming his name over and over and he wished the moron would just stop shouting. Danny knew he should be doing something but just couldn't seem to remember with all the noise.

As the effects from the enemy artillery strike wore off, Danny finally managed to get his wits back about him. Looking at his status board, both legs of his CAV were gone and he was leaking air; this ride was going nowhere. Behind him Thomas kept yelling, "Danny!" over and over, trying to get his pilot back into the fight.

"Thomas I'm good," Danny finally answered. "This ride is shot though."

Both men were wearing their life-support still suits. Danny reached up to grab the two emergency cylinders of air he was equipped with from an inside wall. Attaching one to the intake of his suit, he locked down the front of his helmet and blew the emergency escape hatch. Releasing the straps that still held him to his chair, Danny reached up and grabbed the edge of the open hatch, pulling himself up and out. Crawling across the downed Starhawk, Danny jumped to the ground, falling as he hit the hard ground below. Danny lay there, gathering his thoughts. Thomas landed right next to him and reached down to help him up.

The appearance of the CAV behind his wizzo quickly roused him back into action as a giant three-toed foot struck the ground. Danny looked up to see the cockpit of the machine centering on the two of them, both arms swinging into firing position. Danny knew from his briefing he was looking at a Rach Tyrant. A thirty-foot-tall bundle of wires and metal ready to destroy anything its pilot identified as a threat, which at this moment, Danny knew, was him and Thomas.

It could crush him like a bug, it could slice him in half, it could kick him a klick away with its foot, it could..." "Stop it!" Danny told himself. It could kill both of them any damned way it pleases so just stay still. Danny knew it was stupid advice as he thought it. The CAVs sensors would tell Danny was alive but

he just couldn't think of anything else to do.

The Tyrant just stood there, seeming to be studying him. Probably trying to decide which way he was going to kill the two Federation soldiers, Danny thought; how cheerful we are now.

The CAV suddenly turned and began to walk away from where Danny still lay with Thomas standing over him. That was too easy, Danny said to himself, and began to roll away from his downed CAV. Danny's instinct saved his life as the enemy CAVs starboard arm turned and unleashed a wave of energy

from its Laser Bolt Gun, striking the ground where he had been laying only moments before. Shards of rock pelted him as adrenaline kicked in and surged through Danny's body, urging him to his feet as he came up running. I'm alive! I'm alive! So intent with making good his escape, Danny didn't even notice the smoking boots sitting on the ground next to the blast zone.

Fear kept Danny running in whatever random direction his feet took him. It was then that Danny found his voice again and prayed the radio in his CAV was still working to forward his signal to the company net.

"Help!" he shouted into the mic of the helmet. Danny hated the pleading, childish sound of it, but he couldn't stop. "Oh, sweet Jesus, help me! Please help me!"

When his pleas got no response, he switched to cursing everything he could think of. Finally, exhausted, he stopped and fell to his knees.

"Command?" he asked. Still more silence.

"Command...Slam...Thomas…anyone? Answer me, damn it! Where are you? Don't leave me out here!" No answer.

Danny could feel the blood crusting on his face as he looked around. He didn't see the enemy CAV anywhere but he knew the Rach had to be all around him.

Danny tried to calm himself as he attempted to raise the base again on the radio, "Command 12, are you there?"

It was then that Danny noticed the link to his onboard radio was not activated. He'd forgotten to open a channel in his blind panic. They couldn't answer because they had never heard him. He'd had been yelling to himself the whole time. Activating the link, he tried again. "Command 12, this is Bravo Two-Niner...are you there?"

"Bravo Two-Niner, this is Command 12," it was Ferris still on the net. "Where the hell have you been? I told you to keep giving us updates on the enemy movement. Now what is..."

"Shut up!" Danny interrupted, the sound of the sergenat's voice giving him new courage. "Slam, my CAV is wrecked and I'm on foot. I can't find Mays and this place is crawling with Rats. A Tyrant just tried to fry me!"

Ferris laughed over the link, "A few enemy shells and you're having delusions. Now calm down and tell me what the two of you are doing out there."

"Damn you to hell, Slam. I'm telling you it nearly blasted me. I don't know what your read-outs are telling you but I am now a pedestrian and totally lost."

Ferris's tone got serious again.

"What the hell have you guys got into out there? Where's Koslewski?"

"Hell, I don't know," Danny said as he started to low-crawl towards some rocks for cover. "I took a direct hit and when I came too he was gone."

"Well the board is still showing you both active but he isn't answering any calls."

"So what do I do now?" Danny asked.

"You find you a hidey hole and wait for the cavalry," Ferris advised. "I think you guys have stumbled across a major assault force and that's the best I can do for now. Good luck, corp. Command out."

All alone again, Danny thought...now what? Danny knew he needed to get somewhere safe and hunker down quick. He didn't have the oxygen to hike too far and, after checking his pistol, definitely not the ammo to shoot his way out. Checking back over the top of the rocks he was hiding behind, Danny caught sight of several Rach infantry spreading out along the direction he ran from. With rifles ready, the soldiers in their power armor marched forward slowly as they searched the landscape for him like hounds on a hunt. Where the hell is Thomas he thought to himself.

Good discipline, Danny thought with reluctant admiration. The soldiers were keeping their distance from each other now to reduce an artillery round from taking them all out, their helmets swiveling back and forth.

Danny swore silently as two of the soldiers began moving toward the rocks he was hiding behind. He didn't think they knew he was there yet by the pattern they kept moving in. Sooner or later they were going to come to this side of the pile and....

What the hell am I going to do now? Danny asked his inner voice. Danny knew that in a couple of minutes he was going to be dead or headed to an Rach interrogation unit, which was as good as dead, just at a later date.

The two soldiers kept moving closer and Danny made his decision. He made sure a round was chambered in his pistol and he braced himself, ready to jump up and open fire. Hopefully, this would be over quick.

Just as Danny started to move, both soldiers turned and looked back in the direction they had come from. It was then that Danny saw Koz's Starhawk come running out, it's rotary MACs firing a steady stream of shells.

"Koslewski! You dumb slummer bastard!" Danny yelled as he jumped up and started pumping 11mm rounds into the backs of the two soldiers who had almost discovered him. After both of them dropped to the ground, Danny ducked back behind his rock and watched Koz go to work.

The guns of the Starhawk cut down soldier after soldier as they scattered to get away from the CAV. Danny thought Koz seemed to be moving almost in slow motion, like he was running through mud. The artillery barrage that destroyed his CAV must have damaged Koz's as well, Danny guessed. Then a horrible thought entered his mind, one he didn't want to even consider: What if Koz hadn't got his machine cleaned, free of the sand Ferris had yelled at him about? Koz said he hadn't had time to finish his earlier and now when he really needed it, the machine was failing him. Danny prayed that it wasn't his fault.

Koz continued to fire on the Rach, moving away from Danny's position, almost like he was trying to draw the enemy away from him. Danny hoped Koz made a run for it. He dared not try to call on the radio for his partner without giving away his location.

What should I do? What can I do? Danny thought as he slumped down behind his rocks, unable to keep watching. He had no weapon to speak of and was alone, there was still no sign of Thomas, without any way to get help from the base. That's when Danny heard the thundering of massed rocket fire. Hoping that help had finally come,

Danny scooted back up to look. What he saw filled him with horror.

A pair of Rach Dictators had moved up the canyon floor to support the infantry being blasted by the Federation CAV. As they cleared the edge of the canyon wall that led to this section, they locked onto the enemy machine and let loose salvo after salvo of rockets. Large chunks of armor flew off the Starhawk as it collapsed under the massed fire. Their mission done, both Dictators returned to the column moving further up the canyon.

You bastard Koslewski! Danny shouted in his mind, as if he could will the thought into the slummer's mind. Don't die for me! Don't you dare die for me! I don't want to owe you, Koz, not for this.

Danny's plea seemed to have the opposite effect. He watched as several Rach infantrymen moved up on the wreckage of Koz's downed CAV. Koz jumped out of the machine and pumped a full clip into the closest Rach, who crumpled under the withering fire. Out of ammo, Koz spun in place as a round from another soldier's rifle impacted his shoulder and knocked him down. Danny saw one of the enemy infantrymen start waving his arm, signaling for the others to cease fire. Kathy's body remained slumped over her console in the back of the Starhawk's cockpit.

The soldier that ordered the hold moved toward the spot where Koz knelt hunched over. Pulling out a long sword from the sheath slung across his back, the Rach activated the power switch, thumbing up the grid across the blade until it turned bright blue as it vibrated with energy.

Danny sucked in his breath as he watched the soldier turn Koz's head to expose the neck and, after raising the blade, slice downwards. Danny couldn't hear it but he just knew that the bastards were laughing.

Seconds later, the triumphant Rach waved the other soldiers to follow him

and they moved out to join their advancing column as it moved towards the base, the hunt for Danny forgotten in their blood-drenched victory.

Hours passed and Danny still sat in the spot behind the rocks where he watched Koz die when Sergeant Ferris found him. Unable to will himself into action, Danny hadn't moved. Slam stood over him, nudging him with his foot.

"Garnier? You still alive in there?"

"Yeah," Danny finally managed an answer.

"We found Koslewski and the rest."

"He drew them away from me and...they chopped off his head."

The sergeant remained silent for several seconds before answering. "Saved your life, huh?"

"Yeah."

"You know that for sure, Garnier?"

"Yeah. I mean I think so. The Rach were coming right at me and he came running in and started blazing away."

"I see," Ferris said. "Let me ask you something, Garnier."

"Yeah?"

"Were there a lot of Rach here?"

"Damn straight, sergeant."

"So Koz just might have been in deep drek with nowhere else to go, just like you."

"Maybe...I don't know."

"That's exactly right, Garnier, you don't know. I don't care if Koslewski tried to save your rich boy ass or not. You want to know what I do care about?"

"What, sergeant?" said Danny as he finally stood up from the ground.

"He went out like a soldier in Recon should. Balls to the walls, no quarter asked and none given and that's what counts."

Danny's shoulders sagged under the meaning he thought Ferris was inferring. "I tried, Slam, I wanted to help him but I just hid behind the rocks here."

The sergeant's reply surprised Danny. "Garnier, what could you do? Your CAV was destroyed and that pea-

shooter is just about useless. You did your job. Now guess what the most important thing is?"

"What's that?" Danny asked in confusion.

"You're alive, Garnier. You didn't let your buddies down and from all indications you did your job. That's all that matters out here. The war killed Koslewski and the rest. You lived and there isn't a thing you can do about it except keep fighting until someone tells you that's it over."

Danny carefully considered the sergeant's words for a moment. "Sarge, when we get back to base I would like to call my father."

The usual contempt Slam had for Danny returned instantly. "You want out now, rich boy?"

"I want to talk to him about the CAVs that his company produces."

"And what are you going to tell him?"

Danny turned away from Ferris and stared into the distance at the wreckage of Koz's Starhawk. "I'm going to tell him that they're all wrong about how to maintain these things and might have gotten a good man killed today. His son may be next. He'll understand that."

"I'll bet, but you still haven't answered my question, rich boy. You want out of this man's army?"

Danny stood up straighter, "No, Sergeant Legionnaire Ferris, I do not want out of this 'man's' army."

The sergeant grunted his approval of Danny's response and Danny realized that simple sound meant more to him than all the words of praise his father had ever given him.

"Alright, Garnier, let's get out of here," Ferris ordered. "When we get back to base, have a medic check you out."

Danny obeyed and moved towards the shuttle that had come out to find him and Koz, the turbo fans kicking up clouds of dust as it idled on the ground.

"Damn all this dust," Danny swore as he walked on, "Damn it all." ■

FINIS

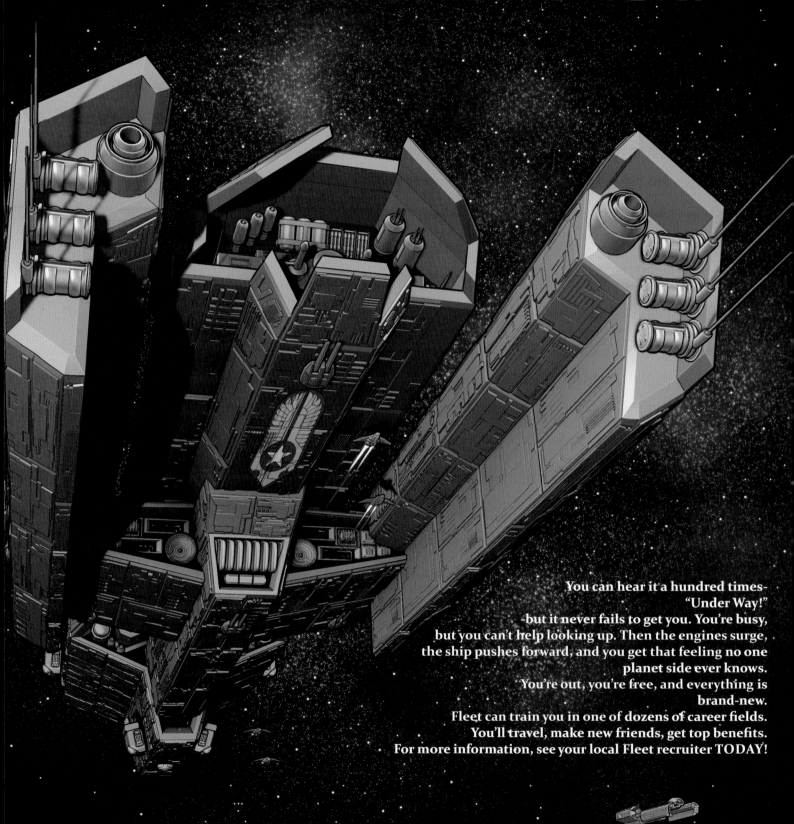

HUGHES
M A R I E T T A
Land Systems

CRUSADER

Crusader is a platform that adapts new technologies while minimizing development time and cost. This superbly engineered and battle-tested design continues to meet the challenges of new and emerging threats associated with the next generation of warfare.

ABOUT THE VEHICLE

The Crusader Combat Assault Vehicle is built to confront and destroy enemy forces using unrivaled firepower, maneuverability and shock effect. With its four Thunder Strike II particle-bolt cannons, the Crusader can engage a variety of targets, including armored vehicles, personnel and even low-flying aircraft. A heavy exterior armor provides outstanding protection to its crew of two.

CRUSADER
Features & Specifications

SIZE/WEIGHT

Length - (Guns Forward) 160 in
Width - 180 in
Height - 360 in
Curb Weight - 94 tons
Ground Pressure - 15.4 psi

PERFORMANCE

Maximum Speed - 40 mph (Governed)
Cross Country - 40 mph
10% Slope - 35 mph
60% Slope - 8 mph
Acceleration (0 to 20 mph) - 7.2 sec
Maximum Trench Crossing - 15 ft
Vertical Obstacle - 120 in
Power-to-Weight Ratio - 21.6 hp/ton
NBC System - 200 SCFM - Clean Cooled Air
Electronics/Crew Cooling - 25,600 BTU/hr
Cooling 14 KW Hydraulic

POWER TRAIN & SUSPENSION

3000 HP Notlin 250 Breeder
Flint 10C1 Power Cell
HM3 Mercon Chassis

FIRE SUPPRESSION

Automatic Fire Detection/Suppression

CREW

2 man

ARMAMENT

Target System - Nh6 Line-Lock II
Main Armament - (4) Thunder Strike II 25kw
Particle Bolt Cannon

For More Information Contact Your Local Sales Office

CONCEPTS

There are a few general concepts players should have an understanding of while reading these rules for the first time and the procedures for handling any rules disputes.

Sportsmanship

While miniature gaming simulates the violence of war between conflicting sides, players should always remember that it is just a game. Players should strive to maintain a level of sportsmanship at all times in every aspect of the game. Games like CAV: SO are designed to provide entertainment and friendly competition, so maintain a good attitude and have fun!

Resolving Rules Issues

No set of rules can include every possible situation that may arise during a game. While we have tried to cover as many contingencies as possible, something will come up that has not been discussed in this rulebook.

If this happens, players should attempt to work out an amicable solution to resolve the situation and keep the gaming moving along. If an agreement cannot be reached quickly, roll for the resolution. Each player rolls 1d6 and the person with the highest roll decides the outcome, rerolling any ties. This resolution will remain in effect for the remainder of the game and applies to any further instances should they arise.

After the game ends, players can take more time to discuss the rule(s) in question and decide how best to handle the same situation in the future. Feel free to contact us as well with any questions or concerns. CAV: SO is a game that is always improving and your feedback will only make it better.

Models, Squads, and Force Groups

In CAV: SO the term "model" refers to any single-based miniature in use during a game session or—in the case of infantry figures—multiple figures mounted on the same base.

The squad is the basic level of organization in CAV: SO and is made up of two or more models of similar form or function. Models in a squad activate at the same time and complete all of their actions together.

A force group is a combination of all the squads in play during a game session belonging to a single player or team.

Force Group Example

Model Basing

To help facilitate easier game play, it is recommended that all CAV: SO models are mounted on a base. The addition of a base aids in stability and will assist in measuring distances. It is suggested that a hex-base (6 sides) is used as this shape is ideal for determining base-to-base (B2B) contact and model facing.

Base-to-Base Contact

Certain actions by a model during a game require it to be in base-to-base (B2B) contact with another model (friendly or enemy). A player must declare their intent to move a model into B2B contact at the beginning of their activation, before any movement is made. B2B contact is determined by bringing any point of a model's base into contact with any point on the base of the other model. If a model is sized to prevent actual contact, move the model in as close as possible. B2B contact with another model immediately ends the current move action of a model. Models may perform any other action(s) when in B2B contact with another model (friendly or enemy), including moving away from B2B contact provided neither model has initiated or has been part of a **close-combat** assault.

Aircraft models in flight can never be in B2B contact.

Model Basing & B2B Example

FIELD NOTES

Close-Combat

The modern battlefield is a symphony of high-tech gadgets and fire and forget weapons, making it sometimes easy to forget the brutality of what war really is.

Close-combat in CAV:SO is not hand-to-hand combat per se, though it is an element of what transpires when two enemies collide up close. Close-combat attempts to simulate the chaotic nature of close quarters fighting as both sides seek an opportunity to outmaneuver and over-power an opponent.

For now, understand that close-combat is typically not the preferred method of attack for most model-types and once initiated, both sides remain locked in combat, fighting to the death or one side attempts to break and retreat. ∎

THE RULES

Model Facing

A model's base is used to determine the facing of every non-infantry model (infantry models have no facing). For models using a hex base, the flat side closest to the "front" of a model, is considered its front facing. If a model does not have a hex base, make sure everyone playing understands what is considered the front of the model. The exact facing of a model is very important when determining its perspective in relation to its current location on the game board, allowing the controlling player to direct any actions it may make during an activation in the correct direction.

Scale and Measurements

Models for CAV: SO are 1/180th figure scale, with each inch of the gaming surface representing approximately 15 feet (4.57 m). All terrain should be sized accordingly to compliment the miniatures available for CAV: SO and players will find that "N-Scale" sized terrain (available for model railroading) is a good fit for use in CAV: SO.

Any distance values in CAV: SO (such as movement or ranges) are in inches. It is recommended that rulers and/or tape measures be used when making any measurements. All measurements are made from and to the edge of the base of a model from the side facing the direction in question.

Turns

In CAV: SO the flow of a game is dictated by turns. Each turn represents a period of "real time" in respect to the game universe, but the actual time of a turn during a playing session will vary as players activate and conduct the various actions for each of their squads.

Each turn is broken down into three rounds to better manage the flow of events during a game.

A Note on Scale and Time

While CAV: SO tries to follow many real-world thoughts and processes, it must be remembered that it is just a game. As a result, some abstractions must be made for the sake of playability. So don't get hung up worrying about physics or other mechanics and just have fun!

The Dice

CAV: SO uses three types of dice, a six-sided die (abbreviated as d6), a ten-sided die (d10), and a twelve-sided die (d12), to generate random numbers or track the results of actions during the game.

Most events during a game require rolling two six-sided dice (2d6) and adding the results together to generate a number range of 2–12.

Various game situations may require a **situation modifier** or the addition (+) or subtraction (-) of an amount, expressed by a number or notation after the die roll indicated.

For example, 2d6+2 indicates that a "2" will be added to the total amount rolled on two six-sided dice.

A ten-sided die (d10) is used when making a drift roll to determine the direction and distance of an attack that misses its intended target area.

A twelve-sided die (d12) is used to track the current damage level of a model during the game and is placed behind each model on the playing surface.

Types of Dice Rolls

To determine the success or failure of any action during the game, one of the following three methods will always be used as described below:

- **Target-Point Roll:** A target-point roll requires a player to roll 2d6, adding or subtracting any applicable modifiers. If the final result is equal to or greater than the given target point value, it is a success. The amount a target-point roll succeeds by is often important and is referred to as the margin of success (MoS).

- **10+ Roll:** The 10+ roll is a variant of the target-point roll and while a player will still roll 2d6, a "natural" roll of 10 or better is always a success regardless of any (-) situation modifiers.

- **Opposed Roll:** The opposed roll requires players from both sides to each roll 2d6, applying any situation modifiers to their own die roll. The player with the highest modified roll is the winner. In the case of a tie, the player that initiated the action wins.

Note: *Make sure when rolling any dice that the results can be seen by everyone playing the game. Take care not to damage or move any miniatures and/or terrain while rolling. Should one or more dice fall off the game table, re-roll both to determine the final result.*

Critical Failure and Success

Anytime a 2d6 dice roll is called for during the game and a "2" is rolled, it is considered a critical failure. A roll of "12" is a

FIELD NOTES

Situation Modifier

Situation modifiers are used in CAV:SO to provide a bonus (+) or a penalty (-) to a die roll and represent a variety of game situations that can affect the overall success of a desired action.

A situation modifier is expressed as a value after the indicated die roll type, the amount being added (+) or subtracted (-) from the actual roll. ■

critical success.

Critical failures always result in an automatic failure for whatever is being determined by the roll and may have additional consequences as detailed throughout these rules.

A critical success is not an automatic success, but does allow the player to roll an additional 1d6 and add that to their dice roll as a (+) situation modifier.

Game Markers

CAV: SO uses various markers to represent certain events or actions that have transpired during play and are placed on the surface of the gaming table next to the model. Copies of the game markers used to help keep track of these events can be downloaded to print from at:

www.talon-games.com/downloads

Rounding

When rounding any fractional numbers in CAV: SO, values of .5 or greater are always rounded up to the next whole number and values of .49 or lower are always rounded down.

The Data Card

Every model in CAV:SO has a unique data card that displays the capabilities and stats for its use during a game.

The following list is provided as an overview of the data card; specific terms and concepts are detailed later in the game rules.

Printable data cards can be downloaded for free at:

www.talon-games.com/downloads

❶ Model Name: The specific name and variant (if applicable) of the model being described.

❷ Model Type: The specific type of model (CAV, combat vehicle, etc.) being described.

❸ Model Task: Every model has an

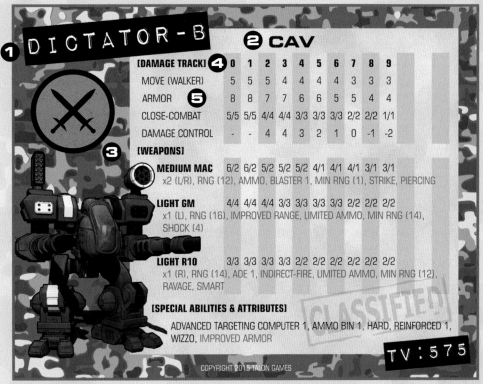

❶ DICTATOR-B   **❷ CAV**

[DAMAGE TRACK] ❹	0	1	2	3	4	5	6	7	8	9
MOVE (WALKER)	5	5	5	4	4	4	4	3	3	3
ARMOR ❺	8	8	7	7	6	6	5	5	4	4
CLOSE-COMBAT	5/5	5/5	4/4	4/4	3/3	3/3	3/3	2/2	2/2	1/1
DAMAGE CONTROL	-	-	4	4	3	2	1	0	-1	-2

[WEAPONS]

MEDIUM MAC 6/2 6/2 5/2 5/2 5/2 4/1 4/1 4/1 3/1 3/1
x2 (L/R), RNG (12), AMMO, BLASTER 1, MIN RNG (1), STRIKE, PIERCING

LIGHT GM 4/4 4/4 4/4 3/3 3/3 3/3 3/3 2/2 2/2 2/2
x1 (L), RNG (16), IMPROVED RANGE, LIMITED AMMO, MIN RNG (14), SHOCK (4)

LIGHT R10 3/3 3/3 3/3 3/3 2/2 2/2 2/2 2/2 2/2 2/2
x1 (R), RNG (14), AOE 1, INDIRECT-FIRE, LIMITED AMMO, MIN RNG (12), RAVAGE, SMART

[SPECIAL ABILITIES & ATTRIBUTES]
ADVANCED TARGETING COMPUTER 1, AMMO BIN 1, HARD, REINFORCED 1, WIZZO, IMPROVED ARMOR

CLASSIFIED

TV : 5 7 5

COPYRIGHT 2015 TALON GAMES

---

assigned task it performs as part of a squad. These symbols denote what task the model being described has been assigned:

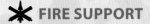 **ATTACK**

⚹ FIRE SUPPORT

♘ RECON

FLIGHT

▲ TRANSPORT

★ SPECIALIST

❹ Damage Track: The damage track of a model is a series of columns that represent the amount of damage the model being described can take before being destroyed.

As a model takes damage (moving left to right) its effectiveness degrades, the values under the current track being used to determine any game-based results. Once a model has received more damage than it has damage tracks left, it ceases to function and is removed from play.

❺ Model Movement Value & Class: The movement value is how far the model being described may move, in inches, across open terrain during a single action.

The movement class refers to mode of transportation a model uses when it does move (foot, wheeled, etc.).

Armor Value: The armor value of the model being described is used as a target point by an attacker when making a combat roll during a ranged assault combat action. This value is a representation of how hard a model is to damage.

Close-Combat Value: The close-combat value of the model being described is the base number to use when making an opposed roll for a close-combat attack.

Two values are provided, one for hard targets and one for soft targets.

Damage Control Value: Many models have the ability to make limited field repairs during combat in an attempt to bring damaged systems back online. Using the repair action, the model being described will make a 10+ roll, adding the current damage control value to the roll as a (+) situation modifier.

6 Weapons Data: This section details the weapon systems the model being described is equipped with.

This description includes the type of weapon system, using the following abbreviations:

AC	Autocannon
AR	Assault Rifle
AT	Anti-Tank Weapon
CM	Cruise Missile
FAS	Field Artillery System
FT	Flame Thrower
G	Grenade
GL	Grenade launcher
GM	Guided Missile
IDC	Ion Disruptor Cannon
LBG	Laser Bolt Gun
LBR	Laser Bolt Rifle
MAC	Magnetic Accelerator Cannon
MAR	Magnetic Accelerator Rifle
MG	Machine Gun
MRAC	Magnetic Rotary Accelerator Cannon
M	Mortar
P	Pylon
PBG	Particle Bolt Gun
RAC	Rotary Autocannon
R	Rocket
SAM	Surface-Air Missile Launcher
SMG	Sub-Machine Gun

Additionally the ranged assault value (RAV) of each weapon system is included. This value, one for **hard targets** and one for **soft targets**, is added to a successful combat roll to determine if the attack has penetrated the armor value of the intended target.

The higher a weapon system's RAV, the more likely it is able to inflict damage.

Also included are the number of weapon systems of each type on the model, their mounting location, the base short range, and any SAs the weapon system may have.

Mounting Location Abbreviations:

ALL
(T)	Turret
(N)	Not Applicable

CAV
(F/B)	Front and/or Back Torso
(L/R)	Left and/or Right Arm

VEHICLE
(F/B)	Front and/or Back Hull
(L/R)	Left and/or Right Hull

AIRCRAFT
(F/B)	Front and/or Back Fuselage
(L/R)	Left and/or Right Wing

7 Model Illustration: To help players identify the model being described an illustration has been included on each data card.

8 Special Abilities & Attributes: SAs represent any special attributes the model being described may possess.

9 Threat Value: The threat value of the model being described is used a numerical rating that helps define the overall "worth" of a model, allowing a comparison from one model to another of its relative strength.

The threat value is used when building a player's force group in an attempt to create a more evenly matched game.

FIELD NOTES

Hard & Soft Targets

Hard and soft targets refers to a specific special ability or attribute a model may have as part of its description.

Special Abilities and Attributes (SA) are used in CAV:SO to help make a model more "unique" and provide a means to highlight different capabilities or equipment a specific model-type may have. A SA will generally improve a model's performance but may also provide for a limitation or specific rule that may affect the model during play.

A model with the SA: *Hard* is considered a hard target, which is a military term for an heavily armored or well defended installation. Examples of a hard target include all CAVs, heavier combat vehicles, bunkers or other reinforced buildings and structures.

A model with the SA: *Soft* is just the opposite, lightly defended or armored, examples of which would be all aircraft and infantry, light combat vehicles, and standard buildings and structures. ∎

DICTATOR-B CAV

[DAMAGE TRACK]	0	1	2	3	4	5	6	7	8	9
MOVE (WALKER)	5	5	5	4	4	4	4	3	3	3
ARMOR	8	8	7	7	6	6	5	5	4	4
CLOSE-COMBAT	5/5	5/5	4/4	4/4	3/3	3/3	3/3	2/2	2/2	1/1
DAMAGE CONTROL	-	-	4	4	3	2	1	0	-1	-2

[WEAPONS]

MEDIUM MAC 6/2 6/2 5/2 5/2 5/2 4/1 4/1 4/1 3/1 3/1
x2 (L/R), RNG (12), AMMO, BLASTER 1, MIN RNG (1), STRIKE, PIERCING

LIGHT GM 4/4 4/4 4/4 3/3 3/3 3/3 3/3 2/2 2/2 2/2
x1 (L), RNG (16), IMPROVED RANGE, LIMITED AMMO, MIN RNG (14), SHOCK (4)

LIGHT R10 3/3 3/3 3/3 3/3 2/2 2/2 2/2 2/2 2/2 2/2
x1 (R), RNG (14), AOE 1, INDIRECT-FIRE, LIMITED AMMO, MIN RNG (12), RAVAGE, SMART

[SPECIAL ABILITIES & ATTRIBUTES]

ADVANCED TARGETING COMPUTER 1, AMMO BIN 1, HARD, REINFORCED 1, WIZZO, IMPROVED ARMOR

CLASSIFIED!

TV: 57.5

Building Your Force Group

To create a force group, each player will need to first choose the faction they wish to play and decide the threat value pool to use. These two factors will determine what kind and how many models a player may use during the game.

Faction Affiliations

By 2274 the vast majority of explored space is under the dominion or direct-influence of seven major star-nations and the military forces they control. While there are many other independent worlds and smaller states spread throughout the galaxy, they tend to avoid the intrigue of interstellar politics, focusing on regional or local issues, using planetary defense militias and/or mercenaries for any security needs.

Supplying an army that moves from planet to planet is a colossal undertaking made even harder by the wide variety of equipment and weapon types contained in each individual military. The logistics alone makes even the most experienced quartermaster cringe when a new supply request form is presented.

To ease this supply burden, captured equipment is generally destroyed or sold in the open market. As a result, each star-nation may only choose models for their force group that bears their faction affiliation. Specific scenario rules may allow this requirement to deviate from time to time.

When selecting a player's force group, every faction in CAV: SO has an associated tactical briefing. Each tactical briefing details the organization and equipment available (also known as the Table of Organization & Equipment, or TO&E in military jargon) for a particular faction to help prevent creating an unrealistic and unbalanced force group within the CAV: SO universe.

Faction Doctrines

A force group made up of models that all have the same faction affiliation may choose to use a faction doctrine during a game. A faction doctrine is a unique "perk" based on the fighting style and training techniques used by a faction on the battlefield. A faction may have more than one doctrine but may only choose one to use during a game. The doctrine must be declared before deploying any models. A faction doctrine must be applied to all elements of a force group and are included as part of the tactical briefing for each faction.

Independent Factions

Independent factions cover a wide variety of military organizations outside the traditional faction set-up. Independents represent mercenaries, pirates, local planetary defense forces, corporate security forces, and many more. These groups typically field a variety of model types that have been purchased, salvaged, and/or looted. As a result, an independent force group may choose to use any model, regardless of it's faction affiliation.

Threat Value Pool

As detailed earlier, every model in CAV: SO has an assigned threat value (TV) that provides a numeric "rating" based upon a model's overall offensive and defensive capabilities, and how it compares to others models in the game. The higher the threat value, the more effective a model can be.

While the threat value system has been designed to provide a balanced numerical system to define the capabilities of a model, there are many factors that cannot be incorporated into any point system. Terrain, superior numbers, and the skill and/or luck of a player are just a few of the factors that could affect the outcome of any battle.

The threat value pool (TVP) is the maximum number of threat value points that each side can spend when designing their force group. The number of points used for the threat value pool is an amount agreed upon by both sides. It is suggested that players keep the threat value pool limited to no more than 3000 TV points when starting out. As they become more familiar with the rules and the flow of the game, this amount can be increased.

A side may spend less than the agreed-upon threat value pool, but never more.

Force Group Selection

Squad Types

The squad is the basic unit of play in CAV: SO and any number of squads can make up a given force group. Squads are divided into two types: primary and secondary. When creating a squad, a player will need to determine what type of squad to build as this determines the number of and the **task** of the models that can be included within that squad.

A force group cannot have more secondary squads than primary ones.

Primary Squads are:

> *Attack*
> *Infantry*
> *Mechanized Infantry*
> *Specialist*

Secondary Squads are:

> *Fire Support*
> *Flight*
> *Mortar*
> *Recon*
> *Transport*

FIELD NOTES

Model Task

As part of a squad, every model has a role or task assigned to it, telling you what the model is designed to do best during a fight and where it "fits" in as part of a squad.

A model may have more than one task. ∎

THE RULES

Primary Squads

Attack Squad

The attack squad is the basic armored combat unit in CAV: SO. It is typically where the firepower of a force is grouped and is able to sustain the greatest amount of damage before being knocked out of a fight.

- An attack squad must begin play with four to six CAV and/or combat vehicle models. At least 75% of the models in the squad must have the model task of attack, with the remaining models (if any) having the model task of fire support or recon.

Example: *An attack squad with four models will have at least three with the model task of attack; five models will have four and six models will have five.*

- Models with the SA: *Bulky* count as two models when determining squad size and transport capacity (if any).

Infantry Squad

Infantry squads are the foot-slogging grunts of the galaxy and make up the majority of military and defense forces. Although slow, infantry squads are capable of massed attacks that can overwhelm the defenses of most other single model types.

- An infantry squad must begin play with four to twelve **infantry models** with the model task of attack.
- Models with the SA: *Bulky* count as two models when determining squad size and transport capacity (if any).

Infantry Model Basing Example (x5 models)

FIELD NOTES

Infantry Models

Infantry models are unique in CAV:SO as each model will typically contain more than one figure. When we refer to an infantry model, we are talking about a single "base", regardless of the actual number of figures mounted on it. ∎

Mechanized Infantry Squad

Mechanized infantry are equipped with their own armored vehicles to provide transport and limited fire-support during combat. Mechanized infantry can maintain a more rapid level of movement, as compared to normal infantry, but are less effective when fighting from prepared defensive positions as they depend on their mobility when on the attack.

Mechanized infantry require more supplies and a large proportion of their manpower is regulated to crew and technicians to maintain their vehicles.

- A mechanized infantry squad must begin play with four to eight infantry models with the model task of attack.
- Up to one model per infantry model with the task of transport. These transports do not count towards the squad model limit.
- Models with the SA: *Bulky* count as two models when determining squad size and transport capacity (if any).

Note: *An infantry squad may not contain more than one class of armor.*

Also, a squad with one or more models with the Task: Transport must use the same model type (example: all combat vehicles).

Specialist Squad

Models found in a specialist squad perform a variety of missions or roles outside the usual combat squads that may be needed for a particular mission.

- A force group may only contain one specialist squad. Any model with the SA: *Specialist* must be a part of this squad.
- A specialist squad must begin play with one to four models of any type and task designator.
- Up to one model per infantry model with the task of transport. These transports do not count towards the squad model limit.
- Models with the SA: *Bulky* count as two models when determining squad size and transport capacity (if any).

Secondary Squads

Fire Support Squad

A fire support squad provides up-close covering fire, directly and indirectly, to the other squads in a force group.

- A fire support squad must begin play with four to six CAV and/or combat vehicle models. At least 75% of the models must have the model task of fire support, with the remaining models (if any) having the model task of attack or recon.
- Models with the SA: *Bulky* count as two models when determining squad size and transport capacity (if any).

Flight Squad

A flight squad provides close air support for the ground forces.

- A flight squad must begin play with two models with the same model task designator (attack, fire support, or recon).

Mortar Squad

The mortar squad is the heavy-hitter of the infantry and the principle anti-armor component of an infantry force.

- A mortar squad must begin play with three to six infantry models and at least 75% of the models must have the model task of fire support. The balance may have the model task of attack or recon.
- Up to one model (any type) per infantry model with the task of transport. These transports do not count towards the squad model limit.
- Models with the SA: *Bulky* count as two models when determining squad size and transport capacity (if any).

Recon Squad

Recon squads are the eyes and ears of any force group and are often the first ones in a battle and the last ones to leave. They are also tasked with striking the flanks of the enemy and getting in behind their lines to strike command and communication assets.

- A recon squad must begin play with four to six CAV and/or combat vehicle models. At least 75% of the models must

have the model task of recon, with the remaining models (if any) having the model task of attack or fire support.

- Models with the SA: *Bulky* count as two models when determining squad size and transport capacity (if any).

Note: *For each recon squad a player may have as part of their force group (including any flight squads with the task of recon), a player may choose to skip a required squad placement during deployment at the beginning of a game.*

Transport Squad

Transport squads are used to move any models not equipped with their own transport.

- A transport squad must begin play with four to six models with the model task of transport.

Command, Control, and Communication Points (C3)

As the old saying goes, "No plan survives contact with the enemy".

Command, control, and communication points (C3) represent the ability of the leadership within a force group to try and adjust for these unforeseen events and attempt to lessen their severity through experience and tactical superiority.

The number of C3 points received by a force group is based on the number of squads (each squad in play provides one C3 point) as well as any bonus points provided by one or more specific SA, upgrades, and any scenario or tactical briefing bonuses.

Using C3 Points

Once the number of C3 points is determined for a force group, these points form a pool that can be used during the game to try and influence certain events. Each point may only be used once and only one point may be used during the activation of any single friendly squad each turn.

Spending one C3 point will allow a player to perform one of the following activities:

- Inspire: Add a (+1) to any single die roll.

- Seize the Initiative: Activate a single model from a squad that has not yet activated this turn and attach the model to a currently activated squad for the current turn only.

- Motivate: Grant a model one additional action point during its current activation for the current turn only.

- Rally: Remove the suppressed or stunned model state from all models in a single squad.

Force Group Specialization

As a player selects their base force group, they will want to anticipate the strategy and tactics that will be used by their opponent(s) in the upcoming battle. Models are chosen to compliment a player's style of play and as a counter to the ones chosen by the other side.

Force group specialization helps a player to personalize their force group even more, making it truly unique to that player.

Each force group will receive a bonus pool of threat value points equal to 20% of the designated threat value pool that may only used for purchasing force group specializations from the following:

- Battlefield Upgrades
- Battlefield Support Assets
- Battlefield Support Strikes

A player may also spend up to 10% of their base TVP to for additional force group specialization options.

Note: *See "Force Group Specializations" (pp. 128-141) within the appendixes section for more detailed descriptions.*

Getting Started

CAV: SO can be played a variety of ways but a typical game is for two players to match forces across an area that is referred to as the game-board, using the following rules for terrain selection or any set-up agreed on by all of the players prior to play.

Specific scenarios (p. 43) may also dictate a particular set-up as well.

Terrain Selection

A typical CAV: SO game should be played on a game board with an area measuring 48" x 48" at the bare minimum in order to allow plenty of maneuvering room for your models. A larger playing surface is recommended if you are using a large number of models on both sides.

When choosing terrain to set on your game board, you are limited only by the preferences and imagination of the players themselves. The most important part during set-up is to make sure any terrain feature is clearly defined and understood by every player before play begins. A terrain feature should cover an area with a diameter of around 3" at least; unusual shapes (the "kidney bean "or the "dog bone" seems to be war-game staples) can be used as well

A game board can be as simple as a sheet thrown over a few books to represent hills. Other terrain features can be added by cutting up construction paper or felt into the shape you want to define the borders of a certain terrain-type. Model railroad buildings, trees, and such are also available, as well as several commercially designed terrain systems that add a level of

realism to a game that is well worth the cost and effort.

The following system can be used to generate a random board set-up. Each side will roll 1d6+1 to determine the number of terrain features each team will place then, using the table below, roll 2d6 to select which type of terrain they may place.

TERRAIN SELECTION TABLE

Result	Terrain Type
2	Special
3	Water
4	Heavy Woods
5	Light Woods
6	Hill
7	Hill
8	Hill
9	Light Woods
10	Rough or Rubble
11	Structure
12	Special

ROLL 2D6

Terrain Type Descriptions

- Special: The special selection allows a player to place a "unique" item from the available terrain supplies on the game board. This could be a swamp/marsh area, a flowing lava stream, or any other terrain type not found on the **Terrain Selection Table**. A player may also choose any other terrain type from the selection table.

- Water: The water selection allows for a small pond, lake, river, or stream section. Multiple rolls can be added together (from both sides) to increase the overall area covered.

- Heavy Woods: The heavy woods selection allows for a "grove" of trees providing heavy cover. Multiple rolls can be added together (from both sides) to increase the overall area covered.

- Light Woods: The light woods selection allows for a "grove" of scattered trees or scrub providing light cover. Multiple rolls can be added together (from both sides) to increase the overall area covered.

- Hill: The hill selection should be used to allow a player to build a hill with one or more elevation levels on the game board. While there is no set limit on the size of the hill, players should avoid building their own "Mt. Everest" in the middle of the board without first consulting with the other players.

- Rough/Rubble: This selection allows for an area of rough terrain or one or more destroyed structures. Multiple rolls can be added together (from both sides) to increase the overall area covered.

• Structures: The structures selection allows for one or more non-battlefield asset-type structures to be placed on the game board. Multiple rolls can be added together (from both sides) to increase the number of structures, allowing for a larger city to be built. Players are encouraged to add roads for a greater degree of realism to the terrain set-up.

Scenarios

The following list comprises nine common scenarios that are found in CAV: SO. Both sides should agree upon the scenario being used. A set of mission cards are also available that can be used by players to randomly select a scenario. These cards can be downloaded for free at *www.cavhq.com* website and printed out by the players for use.

Each scenario-type has a brief description, any special rules required, the **deployment zone**, and the victory conditions needed to win the match.

Scenario One: *Stand and Fight!*
• Description: An all-out, winner-take-all brawl.
• Special Rules: None.
• Threat Value: Each side will receive an equal threat value amount when selecting their force group and both sides should have roughly the same number of models.
• Deployment: Standard.
• Victory Conditions: The battle continues until only one side remains, either through attrition or concession.

Scenario Two: *Time Stands Still for No One.*
• Description: A timed event, this scenario will force players to engage quickly and push for maximum damage before time runs out.
• Special Rules: Each side will secretly write down a number on a scratch piece of paper from 3 to 6 and keep it hidden for now. A 1d6 is then rolled, the value indicating the base number of turns the game will begin with. When the last turn is finished (based on the 1d6 roll), both sides will reveal the number they each wrote down, adding them together. This is the number of additional turns that will be played before the game ends.
• Threat Value: Each side will receive an equal threat value amount when selecting their force group and both sides should have roughly the same number of models.
• Deployment: Standard.
• Victory Conditions: The winner of the scenario is determined by side with the greatest amount of threat value points remaining.

Scenario Three: *Take that Hill!*
• Description: A classic "king of the hill" style battle for two sides. One side tries to hold the hill while the other attempts to push the defender off and take control.
• Special Rules: A large hill is placed in the center of the playing surface. Both sides should agree on a set number of turns to be played before the game ends.
• Threat Value: One side is designated as defender, the other as attacker. The defending force group will only receive 75% of the agreed upon starting threat value pool (rounding up) to pick their models from.
• Deployment: The defender will deploy first, placing at least 50% of its starting force group on the hill, the remainder anywhere on the gaming surface outside the attacker's deployment zone. The attacker will deploy next, using standard deployment after determining their starting side.
• Victory Conditions: If the defender has no surviving models remaining on the hill at the end of the final turn, the attacker wins. Otherwise, the defender wins.

FIELD NOTES

Deployment Zone

Regardless of the scenario being played or the required set-up for the battle, each player or side must have a designated starting edge before play begins, opposite of each other.

This starting edge is referred to as the deployment zone and is an area that runs the length of the game board along each player or side's starting edge, extending six inches into it.

If a scenario does not designate a specific area for the placement of models, each player or side will need to roll 2D6. The high roller (in case of a tie, re-roll until there is a winner) selects the starting edge for their deployment zone. ∎

Scenario Four: *Hold at All Costs!*

- Description: A small defending force attempts to prevent a larger attacking force from moving through their area in a flanking attempt.
- Special Rules: None.
- Threat Value: One side is designated as defender, the other as attacker. The defending force group will only receive 50% of the agreed upon starting threat value pool (rounding up) to pick their models from.
- Deployment: The defender will deploy first and may place any models from the middle of the gaming surface back to their deployment edge. The attacker will deploy next along the back edge of their deployment zone.
- Victory Conditions: If the defender destroys a number of models equal to or greater than its starting threat value pool, the defender wins. Any amount less than that results in a win for the attacker.

Scenario Five: *Headhunter!*

- Description: Both sides attempt to "take out" the force group commander of the opposite team first.
- Special Rules: Each team will secretly note their force group commander on a scratch piece of paper before play begins.
- Threat Value: Each side will receive an equal threat value amount when selecting their force group and both sides should have roughly the same number of models.
- Deployment: Standard.
- Victory Conditions: When any force group commander is killed, the battle ends, and the side with the surviving commander is declared the winner.

Scenario Six: *It's a Rescue Mission, You're Going to Love It!*

- Description: An elite rescue team has been sent in to extract a deep-cover spy, but has been discovered as they attempt to flee. Reinforcements have been sent in to complete the mission.
- Special Rules: A single model figure (separate from either side's force group) is used to represent this high-value target, designated as the VIP. To "capture" a VIP, a model needs only to "touch" the VIP, after which the VIP will move with the capturing model until it is "dropped" or the controlling model is destroyed.
- Threat Value: One side is designated as defender, the other as attacker. Each side will receive an equal threat value amount when selecting their force group and both sides should have roughly the same number of models.
- Deployment: Standard. The defender will place the VIP anywhere on their half of the playing surface, but no closer than 12" from their starting edge.
- Victory Conditions: The attacking force must capture the VIP and move with it in an attempt to exit from their starting edge and winning the game. The defending force may

also capture and move with the VIP once it has been moved from its starting position (by an attacker), but may not exit the board.

If the defending side destroys all of the attackers before they are able to escape with the VIP, they are declared the winner.

Scenario Seven: *Breakthrough!*

- Description: The front has fallen, trapping a group of attackers behind enemy lines. In an attempt to make it back to their operations area, they must fight a determined enemy set on destroying them to the last machine.
- Special Rules: None.
- Threat Value: One side is designated as defender, the other as attacker. The attacking force group will only receive 75% of the agreed upon starting threat value pool (rounding up) to pick their models from.
- Deployment: Standard. Defenders will deploy first.
- Victory Conditions: The attacking force will attempt to exit the map along the defender's starting edge. Play continues until either side is completely destroyed or all of the attacker's models have exited the board.

If any of the attacker's models survive to exit, add together the threat value amount of the models that exited with the threat value of any defending models they managed to destroy. If this amount is greater than the threat value destroyed by the defender, the attacker wins. If not, the defender is declared the winner.

Scenario Eight: *A Bridge too Far.*

- Description: A river crossing can often end up as an important objective as each side seeks to cross during a prolonged battle.
- Special Rules: During setup, a river is placed across the middle of the playing surface with a single bridge crossing it. The river should be deep enough to prevent CAVs from crossing it and be at least 8" wide.
- Threat Value: Each side will receive an equal threat value amount when selecting their force group and both sides should have roughly the same number of models.
- Deployment: Standard.
- Victory Conditions: Both sides are attempting to cross the bridge and exit as many models as possible off the opposing side's starting edge. Play continues until one side has no remaining models on the game-board.

The side that exits the greatest amount of threat value points wins the game.

Scenario Nine: *The Objective is...*

- Description: Often a battle is decided by who controls important features, such as a high-vantage point or an important building or road, at the end of the fight.
- Special Rules: A series of 1"x 1" squares should be

cut-out and marked with a number from 10 to 100, counted by tens (10, 20, 30, etc.). These markers should be turned upside-down and drawn by random, setting them on the playing surface at various spots that both sides have agreed on as being "important".

- Threat Value: Each side will receive an equal threat value amount when selecting their force group and both sides should have roughly the same number of models.
- Deployment: Standard.
- Victory Conditions: Both sides should determine the number of turns each side wants to play. At the end of the last turn, any marker with a model on it unopposed (no enemy model also on it) is considered captured for that side. Each side will add together the value for the markers they control, the side with the highest total value being declared the winner.

Pre-Generated Scenarios

From time to time we will offer pre-generated scenarios with unique stories and objectives, typically using a supplied model list, as part of a larger series of connected battles. These are intended to challenge you to try out something new or help move along the CAV: SO universe story line.

For more information, check out *www.cavhq.com* to see when these will be available for download.

Winning the Game

Most scenarios have specific victory conditions used when determining the winner of a match. Some scenarios may have secondary goals that may allow a side to claim partial success by meeting certain goals. A scenario that requires calculating the surviving threat value pool of each side to determine a winner uses three criteria to establish if a model can be used when making those calculations:

- Destroyed: A model that has no remaining damage tracks at the end of the last turn is considered destroyed and its threat value cannot be added to a side's remaining threat value pool when determining victory conditions.
- Retreat: A model that leaves the playing surface for any reason cannot return to the game and its threat value cannot be added to a side's remaining threat value pool when determining victory conditions.
- Mission Kill: Only the most fanatical members of a military force will fight "to the bitter end" in a battle, while the majority will seek to get away after they can no longer contribute to the fight. Any model that can no longer use the combat action or perform its primary task (transport, etc.) is considered a mission kill. Infantry models cannot be a mission kill.

Once a model has been designated as a mission kill, it must retreat from the playing surface at maximum speed to the nearest game board edge. Any mission kill models remaining on the game board at the end of the final turn cannot have its

threat value added to a side's remaining threat value pool when determining victory conditions.

Note: *Any unspent threat value points remaining from a force group's battlefield assets or support strike packages will be added to a side's surviving threat value pool when determining victory conditions.*

The Draw Deck

The draw deck is a deck of normal playing cards used to determine the order that squads from both force groups are required to activate during play. As a squad is activated, each model in the squad may perform any action allowed to it.

Generally, one force group will be designated "Red" and the other "Black" (if more than two force groups are fighting in the same fight, designate each side by suit). For each squad in a force group, one card of the appropriate color needs to be added to the draw deck. Once the deck is assembled, shuffle the cards and place them in a stack face down. Beginning with the first turn, simply flip over the top card to see which side is required to activate the next squad.

For small battles of 12 or less models per force group, the draw deck should be used to activate a single model to provide for a more balanced fight.

Recon Squads and the Draw Deck

Recon squads can be used by a player to "skip" a revealed card by declaring to discard the current card and return it to the bottom of the draw deck, allowing a new card to be drawn.

This "skipping" of cards can be used during initial deployment and during a turn later in the game.

Players may only discard one card per recon squad each turn. Players may choose to discard their own side's cards.

Adding Bonus Cards

From time to time, certain events or actions will grant the option of adding one or more extra cards of the appropriate color to the draw deck for a given side. Extra cards placed into the draw deck will increase the chance that the next card drawn will be the appropriate color for that force group, while other cards may be assigned to specific activities that can only transpire with the drawing of that assigned card.

Removing Cards from the Draw Deck

Whenever a given squad is removed from play, due to battle damage or assimilating into another squad through the regroup action, a card is removed from that force group's draw deck during the end phase of the current turn.

Any bonus cards are removed from the draw deck if the specific activity assigned to that card is no longer in play as well.

Deploy!

To begin deployment someone will need to shuffle the draw deck and place it face down on the gaming surface. Draw

the top card and turn it over, revealing the color or suit of which player must place one of their squads first. After the selected squad is placed, the next card is drawn and placement continues on until all of the squads in each force group have been deployed.

Delayed Deployment

Occasionally a scenario, squad type, or one or more SAs will call for delaying the deployment of one or more models in a force group until after the start of the game. Squads/model(s) that are not deployed add no cards to the draw deck until the turn they enter play.

Squads/model(s) that delay deployment are placed on the game board according to the instructions of the scenario, squad type, or SA. In the absence of any specific deployment location, the squad/model(s) will deploy inside that player's deployment zone.

Recon Models and Deployment

Any models with the recon task may choose to conduct a single move action before the beginning of the first turn once all of the models from both sides that are available for pre-game deployment are on the game board.

Playing the Game

Each player or side should have completed the following:

- Chosen the scenario to be played.
- Set-up the game board with terrain.
- Selected the models for each force group.
- Provided data cards for each model.
- Assembled the draw deck.
- Placed all of the models in their appropriate deployment zone.

The battle is ready to begin!

The Game Turn

A game of CAV: SO is fought in a series of turns with each force group alternating their activations of squads as dictated by the draw deck. Game turns continue until one side "wins" the game.

Any game effects with a duration of one turn remains active until the next activation of the model that initiated the event.

While each game turn can be a whirlwind of activity, the following sequence of play structures each turn into a series of phases performed in the indicated order until the game is over.

- **Start Phase:** Shuffle the draw deck, place it face down on the playing surface, and flip over the top card, indicating which side must activate their first squad/model.

- **Activation Phase:** Once the first card is flipped over from the draw deck, the color (or suit) of the card indicates the side that must activate their first squad (or model).

When the squad has performed all of its available actions, a new card is drawn and play continues. As a squad may only be activated once per turn, ignore any extra activation cards belonging to that player if there are no more squads to activate (special cards for specific activities may still be used). If all of the squads for each player have been activated, no more cards are drawn and proceed to the next phase.

- **End Phase:** After all of the squads have been activated, both sides should determine if the conditions for ending the game have been met and, if so, calculate any points as directed by the scenario and decide on a winner.

If the game continues, any special rules or scenario objectives that trigger an additional event to take place during the end phase now take effect.

Players will need to make adjustments to the draw deck for any squads that may have been eliminated from play or that regrouped into another surviving squad.

Remove any extra cards for each destroyed model that possessed any SAs granting an extra draw deck card and begin the next turn's start phase.

Action Points

Every model begins a game of CAV: SO with two action points (AP) to use each turn. Once a model has been activated, a player may choose to use a model's action points to perform one or more actions from the **Action List Table**.

Most actions require only one action point to perform and once an action point is used, it is gone for the remainder of the turn. Action points not used by a model during its current activation cannot be saved or transferred to another model and are lost.

At the beginning of a new start phase, all models have their action points reset.

Action Types

In CAV: SO there are three types of actions:

- Free Actions: Free actions are actions provided by a specific game rule that are allowed during a model's activation but do not require using a model's action points to use. How to use a specific free action will be included in their description.

- Repeatable Actions: Repeatable actions are actions that require spending one or more action points to use, but may be used more than once during a model's activation.

- Non-Repeatable Actions: Non-repeatable actions are actions that require spending one or more action points to use, but may not be used more than once during a model's activation. A model may use two different non-repeatable actions during the same activation.

Example: *A model, during its activation, could spend two action points to perform the target-lock action and follow it with the combat action as they are two different non-repeatable actions.*

Declaring Actions

The first step in performing one or more actions is for the controlling player to announce which actions a model is using to their opponent. Once the action(s) have been declared, you may begin to resolve them as allowed by these rules.

If multiple models in the same active squad will be performing one or more non-repeatable actions, the controlling player must declare the actions for each model before resolving any of them.

If an enemy model is destroyed before another model has had a chance to resolve their declared action(s), those actions are lost.

Example: *A player has an attack squad with four models in it and wishes to use the combat action for three of the models during the current turn/activation.*

All three models must declare their actions for the turn before resolving any of them.

Conducting a Special Action

A special action is a non-repeatable action that is unique to a specific model, generally as a result of a particular SA. Special actions will include, as part of their description, instructions on when and how to resolve it during play.

Resolving Declared Actions

Once a player has begun resolving any declared action(s), they cannot stop and change their declaration.

You are not allowed to pre-measure any distances on the game board until after you have declared your action(s). If you declare an action and then find you are unable to complete the action for any reason, you must try to perform as much of the action as possible, within the scope of these rules. If you are unable to perform any part of the declared action, that action is forfeit.

Option: *To help track which models have used their action points for the current turn, each model's d12 damage die can be placed in the front of each model at the start phase of a turn. Once a model's action points have been spent, move the d12 to the rear of the model's base to indicate its completion.*

Action List

Players have a range of actions to choose from and there is no set order in which a player must use their action points.

The following action list provides the available actions a model may use and the page number where a more detailed description can be found:

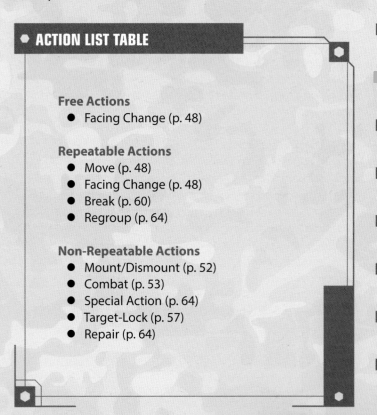

ACTION LIST TABLE

Free Actions
- Facing Change (p. 48)

Repeatable Actions
- Move (p. 48)
- Facing Change (p. 48)
- Break (p. 60)
- Regroup (p. 64)

Non-Repeatable Actions
- Mount/Dismount (p. 52)
- Combat (p. 53)
- Special Action (p. 64)
- Target-Lock (p. 57)
- Repair (p. 64)

THE RULES

The Move Action

The move action is used by every model in CAV: SO to change their position on the game board during play. A model's movement class, various types of terrain, and battle damage can affect the actual distance it may move in any given turn.

Typically, for each move action used, an activated model may move a number of inches forward in open terrain equal to the move value (MV) of a model's current damage track as detailed on their data card.

- 1 MV point equals 1" of movement.

Example: *A model that uses two action points to perform the move action with a MV: 8 could move forward 16" in open terrain.*

Facing

A model's facing is determined by the direction the "front" of the model is orientated on the game board. The facing of a model affects movement and a model's **firing arcs**. Infantry models have no facing.

Every player must be aware of what constitutes the front-facing side of a model in play to avoid any misunderstandings so take a minute before play and make certain everyone understands what is "front" on every model.

Facing Change

A facing change is used to change the orientation of a model's "front" from one direction to another. For each declared move action, a model may make one free facing change up to 90-degrees left or right.

Any additional facing changes will cost the model 1 MV each (regardless of the terrain type the model is currently occupying). A model can make as many facing changes as it wishes in a turn, provided it has the required MV available to do so.

Measuring Movement

To avoid moving too far (or short!) when conducting the move action, all measurements are measured from the "front" of every model's base, with the exception of infantry models.

An infantry model has no "front" per se, moving in any direction. When measuring for movement with an infantry model, use the edge of the model base facing the direction of the intended move.

A model using the move action is not required to move its full move value. If a model chooses to move a shorter distance when using a move action, it still requires one action point to be used.

Example: *A player declares they are using the move action for a model (MV: 8) to move towards cover, 4" away. After completing*

the desired move, *the player chooses to end the model's movement, discarding the remaining 4" of MV, still using one action point.*

Stacking

A model can only move next to or between other models and terrain where its base can physically fit. At no time may the base of one model overlap or "stack" another model's base unless:

- Both models are on differing elevation levels, such as different floors in a structure or one or more models in flight.
- Friendly infantry models do not block the movement of other models. Any friendly model may move through the area occupied by an infantry model as long as its move does not end in the same space.

If a model is not equipped with a base, use the width of the model plus ¼" on either side as a guide to the area it occupies during movement.

Firing Arcs

The current facing of a model determines the orientation of a model's firing arcs. Firing arcs are used during combat to determine which weapon systems can fire at a target. There are four firing arcs as detailed in the following diagram:

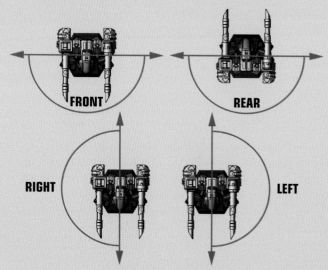

CAV models may rotate their firing arcs up to 90-degree left or right by twisting their torso. This is a free action that may be performed once per turn.

If a model has a turret, weapon systems mounted in that location can fire into any arc (360-degrees).

Infantry models do not have any firing arc restrictions.

Note that firing arcs extend to the edge of the game board and are only limited by the range of the weapon system being used. ∎

● TERRAIN EFFECT MODIFIER TABLE

Terrain Type	Movement Class						
	Foot	**Wheeled**	**Tracked**	**Hover**	**Grav**	**Walker**	**Air**
Open	1	1	1	1	1	1	1
Road/Paved	.5	.5	1	1	1	1	1
Rough/Broken	2	3	2	1	1	2	1
Rubble	2	4	2	NA	1	2	1
Light Woods	1	2	2	3	2	2	1
Heavy Woods	1	NA	3	NA	3	3	1
Swamp/Marsh	3	NA	NA	1	1	4	1
Water 1	NA	NA	NA	1	1	2	1
Water 2	NA	NA	NA	1	1	NA	1
Structure	1	NA	NA	NA	NA	NA	1
Hills	+1	+1	+1	+1	+1	+1	NA

Movement: Terrain Effects

The effect terrain may have on a model is determined by the type of terrain being traversed and the model's movement class. Terrain effect modifiers apply when any part of a model's base comes into contact with a given terrain type during the move action.

A model must pay the movement cost in MV for each full inch moved on the game board as detailed by the **terrain effect modifier table**.

Movement Class

The movement class determines how well a model can negotiate a given terrain type or obstacle that it may encounter while using the move action:

● Foot: The standard movement class of every army, their own two feet.
● Wheeled: Wheeled models move along on two or more wheels.
● Tracked: Tracked models employ two or more tracks to move.
● Hover: Hover models ride on a cushion of air, allowing them to skim over the ground beneath them.
● Grav: Grav models use an anti-grav generator to "push" up from the surface of the ground. By alternating the flow of this push they can propel themselves along as well.
● Walker: A walker model uses two or more articulated legs to walk across the ground.
● Air: Air models use a variety of engine types to keep them well above the ground, flying about.

Terrain Type Descriptions

The following is an overview and description of the majority of terrain types to be found on a game board and how they can affect a model while using the move action.

As detailed during game set-up, make sure that every terrain type is clearly marked by a boundary of some kind to designate the area occupied by it.

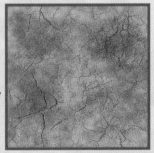

● Open: Open terrain is an area of the playing surface that provides unobstructed movement and vision to the model crossing it.

An open area represents firm ground that, while it may be slightly inclined, does not change elevation severely enough to impede a model's movement.

Examples of open terrain are grasslands, fields, and prairies.

● Road/Paved: A road or paved area is a prepared surface allowing for easier movement through other terrain types.

If a model spends their entire move action along a road or paved area, they do not have to use any additional MV for the other terrain types they may be moving through.

● Rough/Broken: Strewn with rocks and sharp drop-offs, an area that is defined as rough or broken slows down a model's movement significantly. More care must be taken with each footstep to avoid being thrown off-balance.

The ground is firm and does not change elevation significantly.

● Rubble: Large rocks, heavy undergrowth, and/or chunks of broken ferrocrete and twisted durasteel cover the ground below, making crossing these type of areas very dangerous.

● Light Woods: Light woods is an area of ground covered with scattered trees, hedgerows, and shrubs.

Light woods require a model to slow down, avoiding hitting a tree or making a misstep that could cause damage to their machine.

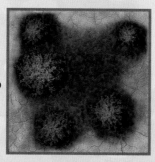

● Heavy Woods: Heavy woods is an area of ground covered by larger, more densely packed trees, slowing movement and obstructing vision.

Heavy woods require a model to spend more time navigating through the trees and the under-growth below.

● Swamp/Marsh: Swamps and marshes are muddy areas, typically with heavy vegetation, that restrict the movement of models as they move through the muck and mire.

Swamps and marshes are typically found in slow-moving or standing water.

● Water: Water is an area covered by oceans, seas, lakes, ponds, streams, or rivers.

Water is defined by:
depth 0 (less than 5' deep)
depth 1 (less than 10' deep)
depth 2+ (greater than 10' deep).

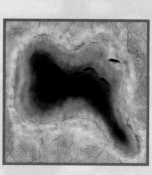

● Structures: Most non-hardened structures cannot support the weight of CAVs or combat vehicles and will collapse if these machines try to move through or over these areas, reducing them to rubble and risking damage from cave-ins and falling debris.

Larger structures, such as factories, warehouses, or armories with sufficient **elevation levels**,

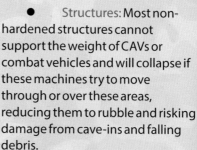

may have doors and floor space large enough inside for CAVs to enter and move around in.

For a more detailed description of structures, refer to that section (p. 65).

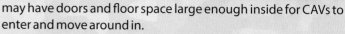

FIELD NOTES

Elevation Levels

Every model, structure, hill, and any other object or obstruction in CAV: SO is measured in elevation levels(E). Elevation levels are important during movement as they are used to determine if a model is eligible to move up or over a terrain type that raises above an adjoining area.

Each elevation level is ten feet tall. A model is only allowed to change one elevation level per 1" moved.

● **Hills:** A hill is a E1 terrain effect that raises above the surrounding terrain, sloping to a relatively "flat" summit.

A hill increases the terrain type being crossed by +1 MV whenever a model moves up one elevation level to the next. Going down does not incur any additional cost.

● **Obstructions:** Obstructed terrain, such as cliffs, sink holes, or large boulders, prevent any type of movement through it by ground-based models. ■

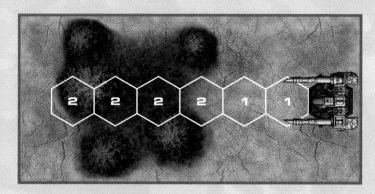

*Example: The above CAV model is trying to move from open terrain to the far side of a light woods terrain object. The first 2" moved would require 2 MV as it is still in open terrain but, once the model's base touches the light woods, it would spend 2 MV for **each** inch moved (as indicated on the terrain effect modifier table for a CAV model) . Each additional inch moved in the light woods area would also cost 2 MV.*

Combined Terrain Effect Types

Some terrain types can occupy the same area (such as an open area with a hill or light woods in a swamp), making it even harder to traverse. When this occurs, a model will use the terrain effect with the higher movement value and add an additional 1 MV for each extra terrain effect to determine the overall cost of moving through that area.

Example: The CAV model below wishes to move through an area occupied by a swamp and a light woods terrain object. The first 2" is open terrain, requiring only 2 MV to move through. The terrain effect modifier table indicates a swamp/marsh terrain object costs a CAV model 4 MV and a light woods 2 MV. Using the higher MV cost (the swamp) and adding +1 for the addition of the light woods, once the model's base touches the combined terrain area, each additional inch moved would cost 5 MV!

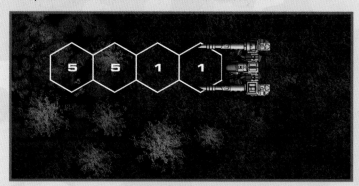

If a combined terrain effect area includes a road or other paved terrain object, a model will ignore any other terrain effect that may also occupy the same space as long as the model moves continuously on the road/paved terrain type.

In the event the MV cost to move only one inch surpasses a model's movement value for a single move action and the model is not prohibited from entering a particular terrain type, a model may always move forward 1" per move action spent, regardless of the actual cost in MV.

Other Movement Options

Moving Backwards

A CAV or combat vehicle model may only move backwards through the following terrain effect types by spending an additional +1 MV per inch moved in reverse.

- Open
- Road/Paved
- Rough/Broken

Any other terrain types permitted to that model require an additional +2 MV per inch moved in reverse.

Aircraft models or any other models with the movement class of air are not permitted to move backwards at any time.

As infantry models are allowed to move in any direction at any time, there is no need to spend any additional MV.

Going Prone and Standing-Up

A CAV model may use a single move action to "go prone" in an effort to avoid being seen. A model may not perform any other action type while prone except to stand back up.

A prone CAV model may use a move action to stand-up. Once a model stands-up, it may choose any direction to face and, if available, perform an additional action.

Additional information on how the move and combat action interact during play can be found under the combat section (p. 57).

MORE INFO

Destroyed Models!
CAVs, vehicles, and aircraft do not simply disappear from a game board when destroyed; they become fixed terrain obstacles upon their demise until the end of the game.

Use a "destroyed model" counter (or whatever token you may wish) to mark the model's final resting spot and treat the area as rubble for any other model that may wish to move through the indicated area at a later time. ∎

THE RULES

An infantry model may only use a charge once per activation and the bonus 2" can only be used to move in a straight-line toward the enemy model. The attempt to charge must be declared prior to any measurement.

If the MV bonus does not allow the infantry model to come into B2B contact with the enemy model, the charging infantry model is moved back to where it was at the beginning of the charge, ending the infantry model's activation for the turn.

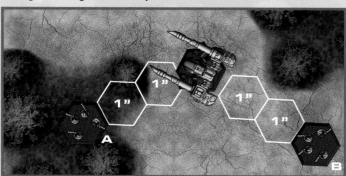

Example: *Infantry model A could use the charge bonus at the end of its normal movement to close the gap to the enemy, regardless of the MV cost, provided it moves in a straight line to the base of the other model only.*

Infantry model B would come up just short, ending its current activation and returning to current location if it attempted to do so.

Nap of Earth

Aircraft models may use a special movement type called "nap of earth" for very low-level flight to avoid being targeted by the enemy during a move action(s).

A player must declare at the beginning of the model's activation that it is flying "nap of earth" and will use an additional +1 MV for each inch traveled, twisting and turning as it maneuvers just above the "deck".

A model flying "nap of earth" may not be attacked unless:

● An enemy model that is currently set to **over-watch** and has the **SA: Anti-Air** may use its attack on the aircraft model provided it has a valid line of sight.

● The aircraft model ends it movement within 12" of an enemy model while flying "nap of earth" and a valid line of sight exists between the two models.

Note: *An aircraft model flying "nap of earth" may still use the combat action to attack an enemy model during activation.*

Infantry Charge Bonus

An infantry model may, at the end of a single move action (no remaining MV), declare a charge allowing it to move an additional +2" forward (disregard MV cost) to bring it into B2B contact with a enemy model.

The Mount and Dismount Action

Only models with the **SA: Transport** may be used to transport infantry. An infantry model in B2B contact with a transport model may use the mount action to load into the transport. Models are not required to be part of the same squad in order to load or transport.

FIELD NOTES

Over-watch

During a model's activation it may use the combat action to go on over-watch, allowing it to delay making a ranged assault until a valid target becomes available later in the turn, even during the other side's activation.

See (p. 58) for more information.

SA: Anti-Aircraft

The SA: Anti-Aircraft is a special attribute restricted to certain weapon systems that are more adept in targeting and hitting a moving target in the air.

See (p. 125) for more information.

SA: Transport

A model with the SA: Transport is designed to move infantry models across the battlefield as quickly as possible. Each rating level allows the model to transport one infantry model.

See (p. 125) for more information ■

The dismount action is used by an infantry model to unload from a transport and is placed anywhere within B2B contact with the transporting model. If there is no space available for the dismounting infantry models, the dismount is cancelled and the action is lost.

Note: *Infantry models may dismount directly into B2B contact with an enemy model.*

An infantry model may not mount and dismount from a transport model in the same turn.

If a transport model receives any critical damage while transporting one or more infantry models, each infantry model will take one point of damage as well. If the transport model is destroyed, then any infantry models currently mounted are also destroyed!

Motorized Infantry

Infantry models can also be equipped with specialized personal transport craft (Battlefield Upgrade: *Motorized*, p. 132) to allow for faster travel across the game-board surface.

These types of craft can include:
- Hover or Grav Skimmers
- Motorcycles

Note: *Infantry models with this type of transport are not required to use the mount/dismount action before conducting*

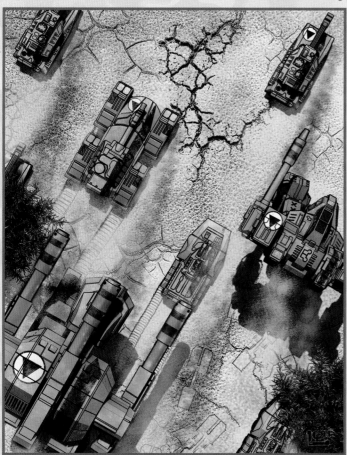

The Combat Action

The combat action is used by every model in CAV: SO to perform either a ranged or close-combat assault during their activation in an attempt to destroy the enemy.

Declaring Targets

Before resolving any combat actions, the attacking player must declare the following to the defending player for the entire activated squad:

- Which models are using the combat action during their activation.
- Which enemy models are being targeted.
- What kind of an assault is being attempted, ranged or close-combat.

Note: *Any assault using the combat action must be declared before any measuring is allowed. If a declared assault cannot be completed for whatever reason, it is an automatic miss and play continues.*

The Combat Roll

A single 2d6 die roll is used to determine if an assault has successfully "hit" a declared target and the damage done (if any) and is referred to as the **combat roll**.

- Ranged assaults will always use a target-point roll when making a combat roll, adding or subtracting any situation modifiers.
- A close-combat assault will always use an opposed roll when making the combat roll by both the attacker and defender, adding or subtracting any situation modifiers.

The Margin of Success

The amount a combat roll equals to or exceeds a required target-point or opposed roll number is referred to as the margin of success (MoS). The margin of success is used to determine the amount of damage (if any) done to a model from a successful "hit".

FIELD NOTES

The Combat Roll (definitions)

Typically you will see a combat roll annotated with the terms primary or secondary.

A primary combat roll is used when a combat action is specifically targeted at one model, such as a direct-fire ranged assault or a close-combat assault.

A secondary combat roll is used when a combat action results in one or models being targeted due to their proximity to the attack, such as a indirect-fire ranged assault using the SA: *AoE*.

Both terms are used to determine which situation modifiers may be applicable to a particular assault being rolled for as detailed throughout these rules.■

Ranged Assault

A ranged assault is used by a model to attack a target with one or more eligible weapon systems that it is not currently in B2B contact with. There are two types of ranged assaults:

- Direct-Fire (DF): A direct-fire ranged assault requires a valid LoS between the attacking and defending models.

Any weapon system without the SA: Indirect-Fire may be used as part of a direct-fire assault.

- Indirect-Fire (IF): An indirect-fire ranged assault does not require a valid LoS between the attacking and defending models.

Only Guided Missiles or a weapon system with the SA: Indirect-Fire may be used as part of a indirect-fire assault.

Note: *A model may only perform one ranged assault type when using the combat action during its activation.*
Other models in the same squad can choose to use different ranged assault types.

Line of Sight

The battlefield is a cluttered place, full of things that make seeing the enemy that much harder. When playing a game of CAV: SO you need to be aware of what you can (or cannot) "see" in order to attempt some actions. This is where line of sight (LoS) comes into play.

Checking Line of Sight

Every model or terrain object in CAV: SO occupies a set amount of space that is defined by the base of the model or terrain object that designate's its physical location on the game-board and the volume of space directly above equal to its current elevation level.

Common elevation levels in CAV: SO are:

- Infantry models (elevation 0)
- Combat vehicles (elevation 1)
- CAVs (elevation 3)
- Prone CAVs (elevation 1)
- Grounded aircraft (elevation 1)
- Light woods (elevation 3)
- Heavy woods (elevation 3)

To check LoS between two models, draw a straight line (a string works well for this) from the closest side of each model's base facing one another. If this "line" is free of any other models or terrain objects, then line of sight exists and both models can "see" one another.

If this line crosses certain terrain objects or other models, line of sight may be obstructed or blocked (see Cover).

Always remember the golden rule, "if you can see it, it can see you"!

Cover

During a ranged assault, other models and terrain objects may provide cover, partially obstructing or blocking line of sight between an attacking model and its target.

Before play begins, players should determine what on the game-board may be used for cover and the type of cover it is:

- Light Cover: An object designated as light cover provides a (-1) situation modifier. Example: *Light Woods*.

- Heavy Cover: An object designated as heavy cover provides a (-2) situation modifier. Example: *Heavy Woods*.

- Blocking Cover: An object designated as blocking cover prohibits a valid line of sight. Example: *CAV Models*.

Cover based situation modifiers are applied to combat rolls only and are only counted if:

- The total elevation level of the cover object is equal to or higher than the total elevation level of both models; or
- The cover object is adjacent (within 1") to the attacking or defending model's base; or
- The defending model is "standing" in the cover object, regardless of either model's total elevation level.

The total elevation level of a model is its base elevation level PLUS the elevation level of the terrain type it currently occupies.

Example: *A CAV model (E3) standing on a elevation 2 hill would have a total elevation level 5.*

Cover and Guided Missiles/Rockets

A ranged assault with guided missiles and/or rockets does not require a valid LoS before making the combat roll. As a result, an attack with these weapon systems will ignore any intervening cover with the exception of cover a defending model may currently be "standing" in.

Cover and Other Models

CAV, combat vehicle, and grounded aircraft models may be used for cover when located along the line of sight between an attacking and defending model. Aircraft models in flight and infantry models will never provide cover.

A CAV model behind a combat vehicle or grounded aircraft, in relation to line of sight, and is adjacent (within 1") will receive a light cover situation modifier.

Example: *A CAV model (E3) is behind a combat vehicle model (E1) and within 1" of it. While LoS is not blocked, the CAV would receive a light cover situation modifier to any attacker's direct-fire ranged assault if LoS tracked through the combat vehicle's base.*

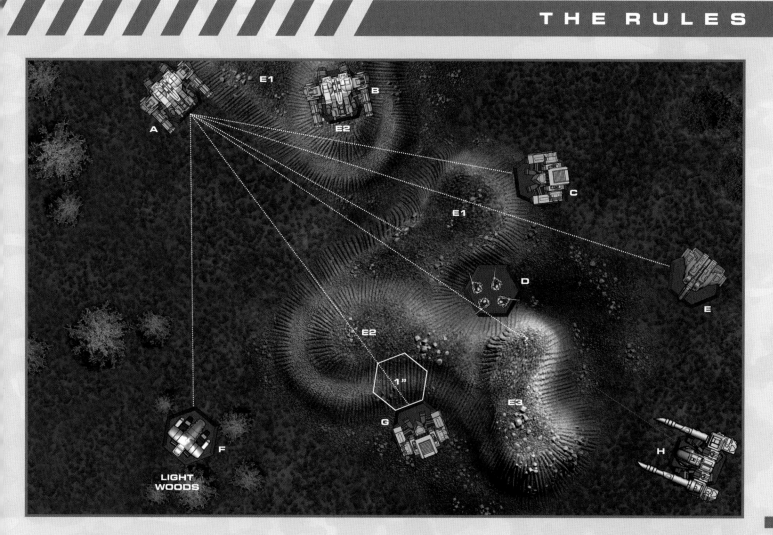

Cover and Line of Sight Diagram

The above diagram is used to illustrate many of the concepts discussed in relation to line of sight and cover:

- *CAV A has LoS to CAV C but will recieve a (-1) to any direct-fire ranged assault as C is adjacent to a E1 hill (light cover).*

- *CAV A does not have LoS to infantry D as it is adjacent to a E1 hill and has a total elevation level of "0".*

- *CAV A has LoS to aircraft E as it is in flight, ignoring any intervening terrain objects.*

- *CAV A has LoS to CAV F but will receive a (-1) to any ranged assault as F is inside a light woods terrain object.*

- *CAV A has LoS to CAV G but will receive a (-2) to any direct-fire ranged assault as G is adjacent to a E2 hill (heavy cover).*

- *CAV A does not have LoS to CAV H due to the intervening E3 hill and both models have a total elevation level of 3.*

- *CAV B has LoS to CAV H as it is on a E2 hill, bringing its total elevation level to 5 and H is not adjacent to the cover object, therefore ignoring the E3 hill completely.*

Range Bands

While the many weapon systems in CAV: SO have the ability to "shoot" a very long way, the modern battlefield is filled with a myriad of "hazards" designed to foil a successful attack. Constant jamming and electronic "viruses" are just a few of the more common targeting hazards an attacking model must deal with. Range bands are used to represent these hazards.

Every weapon system listed on a model's data card has its short range band value (RNG) displayed as a numeric value in inches. Each additional range band adds this same value to its overall total. To determine which range band to use, measure in inches from one model's base to the other, using the side facing one another and compare to the weapon system's RNG value.

Each range band provides the base target-point number used by an attacker during a direct-fire ranged assault combat roll. For indirect-fire ranged assaults, a range band will provide a situation modifier to the strike-point roll (p. 56) only.

Range bands are not used for a close-combat assault.

- Short Range Band: The short range band is equal to the base RNG value listed for each weapon system on a model's data card.

A **target point roll (6+)** is used when making a combat roll for a weapon system firing inside the short range band.

- Medium Range Band: The medium range band is equal to twice the RNG value listed for each weapon system on a model's data card.

A **target point roll (7+)** is used when making a combat roll for a weapon firing inside the medium range band.

- Long Range Band: The long range band is equal to three times the RNG value listed for each weapon system on a model's data card.

A **target point roll (8+)** is used when making a combat roll for a weapon firing inside the long range band.

- Extreme Range Band: The extreme range band is equal to four times the RNG value listed for each weapon system on a model's data card.

A **target point roll (9+)** is used when making a combat roll for a weapon firing inside the extreme range band.

Point Blank Range

Any direct-fire ranged assault at a target 3" or less will receive a (+1) situation modifier to any combat roll regardless of the range band indicated.

SA: Minimum Range

A weapon system with the SA: *Minimum Range* cannot be used for a ranged assault if the target is equal to or closer than the listed value regardless of the range band indicated.

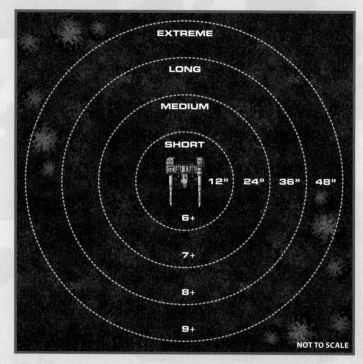

NOT TO SCALE

Example: A weapon system with a RNG 12 would use the following range bands:

- *Short 0-12"*
- *Medium 12.01-24"*
- *Long 24.01-36"*
- *Extreme 36.01-48"*

Strike-Point Roll

As already noted, weapon systems with the SA: *Indirect-Fire* do not require a valid LoS in order to conduct a ranged assault as they are used to target a specific area on the game-board as opposed to an enemy model. This desired target area is referred to as the strike-point.

After declaring the desired strike-point for an indirect-fire ranged assault, a player will then make a single strike-point roll (10+ roll), regardless of the number of weapon systems being fired, for each declared strike-point. Refer to the **Strike-Point Roll Table** to determine any situation modifiers that may apply.

Range band penalties are not applied to an indirect-fire ranged assault combat roll as they are applied to the strike-point roll as a (-) situation modifier, making it harder to hit the desired impact area. Cover based situation modifiers are not used for a strike-point roll.

A successful roll indicates the ranged assault has hit the desired strike-point. A failed roll results in drift (see below).

Unless otherwise noted, a model occupying the final strike-point location is subject to a secondary combat roll with a **target point roll (6+)**.

Strike Point Roll: Drift

The drift roll is used to determine the final point of impact for a failed strike-point roll.

To make a drift roll, the attacking player will roll one d10 as close as possible to the original strike-point location. The "point" of the d10 is used to indicate the direction of the drift, in relation to the initial strike-point location, while the number rolled is the distance in inches the ranged assault.

Range band penalties are also "added" to the number of inches rolled for by the drift roll, increasing the distance an attack has missed the initial strike-point location.

STRIKE-POINT ROLL TABLE

SM	Situation Modifier Description
+1/+2	SA: *Advanced Targeting Computer Rating*[1]
+1/+2	SA: *Active Phase Array*[2]
+1	SA: *Wizzo*
+1	Battlefield Upgrade: *Veteran Pilot*
+2	Battlefield Upgrade: *Ace Pilot*
+1	Battlefield Upgrade: *Semi-Guided*[1]
+1	Valid LoS to Strike-Point[3]
+1	Each consecutive turn firing at Strike-Point
-1	Per weapon system in Run N' Gun
-1	Long Range Band Penalty
-2	Extreme Range Band Penalty
-2	Model State: *Suppressed*

[1] Target-Lock or SA: *TAG* required.
[2] Applicable to Strike-Point Roll only.
[3] Not applicable to Bomb Run assaults.

ROLL 2D6

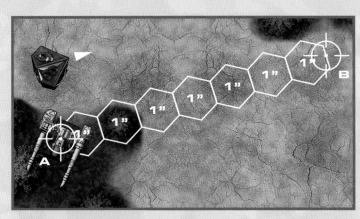

Example: An attacker is attempting an indirect-fire assault in the long range band at strike-point A. After missing the strike-point roll, the attacker has rolled 1d10 for the drift roll. The "point" of the die indicates the direction, the "6" the number of inches the attack has drifted, with an additional +1" added for the long range band. This results in a final strike-point 7" away at point B.

Strike-Point Roll: Critical Fumble

When making the strike-point roll, should an attacker make a critical fumble roll, the defending player is allowed to move the strike-point to any location on the game-board within the front firing arc of the model that made the attack.

This new strike-point is not allowed to violate the minimum range of the weapon system used and may not be farther than the maximum distance allowed by the extreme range band. The drift roll is then made based on the new location to determine the final strike-point.

SA: *Area of Effect (AoE)* and Indirect-Fire

A weapon system with the SA: *Area of Effect* has the chance to damage any target (friend or foe) caught within the effective area (in inches) as measured from the final strike-point of an indirect-fire ranged assault.

An attacking player will designate the model or desired strike-point for the indirect-fire ranged assault, making the required strike-point roll to determine the final impact point as normal.

Any model located in the AoE radius, measured in inches from the center of the final strike-point, of the weapon system(s) is subject to a secondary combat roll.

Ranged Assault and Guided Missiles

Guided missiles are special in CAV: SO as they can be part of a direct or indirect-fire ranged assault but require a model to first use the **Target-Lock Action** (or TAG) before making any combat roll.

Example: The Rach Dictator B CAV from our earlier data card example is equipped with two medium MACs, one light guided missile launcher, and one light rocket 10 launcher.

It may fire both of the MACs as a direct-fire ranged assault

provided a valid LoS exists to the target or the rockets (SA: *Indirect-Fire*) only as an indirect-fire assault (no LoS required). If there is an existing target-lock or TAG, it may also include the guided missile as part of either ranged assault type.

Ranged Assaults and the Move Action

A player may choose to combine the move and combat action (using both APs) in order to conduct a ranged assault at some point along the model's declared movement path.

When performing this double action, the controlling player will need to mark the desired location for their model to end its movement while placing the model in the location where the ranged assault will actually occur from. If the attacking model is damaged as a result of any defensive fire and does not have the available MV to complete its planned move, simply carry out as much of the move as possible and move the model to the new location. If the move value is lowered to a distance shorter than what has already been moved, the model is left at the current location.

Ranged Assault Sub-Types

The following sub-types of a ranged assault allow a model an alternative to the standard "point and shoot" combat action.

Ranged assault sub-types may not be combined:

Target-Lock Action

Every non-infantry model in CAV: SO is equipped with a basic targeting computer to increase their chance of hitting an enemy model. By factoring in such things as recoil, atmospheric conditions, and a target's movement, a targeting computer will calculate where a pilot should direct their fire for the greatest chance of success, displaying the information on the HUD.

- A player may choose to use the Target-Lock Action to "lock-on" to any single non-infantry model on the game board, allowing the targeting computer to refine the firing solution even more.
- A valid LoS does not need to exist to use the Target-Lock Action.
- A ranged assault that includes guided missiles must use the target-lock action before firing or the missiles will automatically miss.
- An enemy model that has been target-locked receives a warning signal, alerting them of the potential danger, allowing it to use the SA: *Counter-Measures* (p. 120) if available.
- A model equipped with the SA: *Advanced Targeting Computer* can also use the target-lock action to add the rating level of the SA as a (+) situation modifier to a direct-fire ranged attack or to improve the chance of hitting the desired target of an indirect-fire ranged assault (see strike-point roll, p. 56).
- A model with the SA: *EST* (p. 121) can "share" their target-lock with other models in the same squad as a Free Action each turn.
- A model with the SA: *TAG* (p. 124) uses the Special Action to "paint" an enemy model with a laser designator. ∎

Defensive Fire

A model that is the target of a ranged assault and has not yet activated during the current turn may choose to use defensive fire, allowing it shoot back at any one attacking enemy model with a direct-fire ranged assault (0 AP) at the end of the enemy model's activation.

A player must declare which model will use defensive fire before any combat rolls are resolved, using its current damage track when conducting its own fire, even if the model has been damaged or destroyed during the current enemy activation.

Defensive fire may not be used against a target that is farther away than long range (see range bands, p. 56) and receives no (+) situation modifiers when making the combat roll. A model using defensive fire may not use the combat action again for the remainder of the current turn.

Run 'N Gun

While similar to combining a combat action with the move action, a model using the run 'n gun sacrifices accuracy for more speed by combining two move actions with a single ranged assault, reducing their current MV by (-2) and any primary combat roll (-1) for EACH weapon used as part of the attack.

Exception: A model with a current MV of four or less will only reduce their MV by (-1) while weapon systems with the SA: Indirect-Fire will apply the (-) situation modifier for each weapon fired to the strike-point roll.

Salvo Fire Strike

A player may choose to use multiple weapon systems of the same type as a single massed assault, firing them in unison at the same target to increase their chance of a hit and inflicting damage. This type of ranged assault is referred to as a salvo fire strike and costs 1 AP to use.

When using a salvo fire strike, only multiples of the same weapon system type may be used for the assault. A model's remaining weapon systems may not be used when using the salvo fire strike option.

A player executing a salvo fire strike will make only one combat roll for the ranged assault, receiving a (+1) for each extra weapon system (beyond the first) used in the ranged assault.

An indirect-fire ranged assault using a salvo fire strike does not receive a multi-weapon bonus to the strike-point roll.

Example: A model making a ranged assault uses the salvo fire strike to fire four light laser bolt guns at the same target, adding a (+3) situation modifier to the combat roll.

Over-Watch

Over-watch costs 2 APs to initiate and allows a currently activated model to delay making a ranged assault until the later activation of an enemy model that moves into LoS.

During an enemy model's move, the player controlling the model in over-watch can request the enemy model to hold in place and proceed with its ranged assault, immediately applying any damage. Once completed, the enemy model can continue with its current activation (if able).

A model may remain in over-watch from turn to turn, provided it makes no other action, spending 1 AP to initiate a new ranged assault while in this mode.

Example: During model A's activation, the controlling player declares the use of over-watch, hoping to catch enemy model B moving out from behind a pile of rocks.

Later in the turn, model B uses the move action to head away from the pile of rocks and into the LoS of model A at "X". Before model B is able to finish its entire move, model A declares a ranged assault at model B, halting it in place until the combat roll is completed. If model B survives it may then complete its move, provided it has the remaining MV to do so.

Multiple Targets

A model may split its fire (or actions) among more than one target, provided that all of the targets are in the same firing arc. The attacking model will receive a (-1) for each additional model targeted beyond the first to any required die rolls.

Example: A model is attempting to shoot at three separate targets in the same firing arc, firing one weapon system at each during the current activation. Each combat roll will receive a (-2) to the die roll as a result.

Immobile Targets

A model conducting a combat action on any target that has been defined as an immobile (see model states, p. 63) will receive a (+4) to any combat roll.

SA: Ammo/Limited Ammo

While ammunition is not tracked during the course of a

firefight, a critical fumble during a strike-point or primary combat roll using a weapon system with the SA: *Ammo* or *Limited Ammo* may result in the model being "out of ammo" for that weapon system type for the remainder of the game.

Roll an additional 1d6, if the result is a "1", the weapon system has run out of ammo. A weapon system with the SA: *Limited Ammo* will run out of ammo on a "1" or "2" roll. Any other number is ignored and play continues.

The SA: *Ammo Bin* (or Battlefield Upgrade: *External Ammo Bin*) allows a model to ignore an out of ammo roll for each bin it is equipped with.

A model with the SA: *Resupply* may use a special action to reload the ammo of another model that it is in B2B contact with.

Ranged Assault Special Rules

Artillery

The successful use of artillery (also known as "hogs") within a game can break the advance of an enemy or dislodge them from a heavily defended location without exposing front-line troops to counter-attack.

While artillery is typically deployed as part of a battlefield support strike package, artillery models can also be used as part of a force group. It is recommended that all players agree to the use of on-board artillery as their use can change the normal flow of a game.

An artillery model (one or more FAS weapon systems) will always have the fire support task designation and have the same actions available to them as other model-types, but have a number of action and upgrades variations available to them.

Artillery models typically remain in the back, away from the front-line using indirect-fire ranged assaults to rain destruction from afar.

Artillery: Counter-Battery Fire

Counter-battery fire is a variant of over-watch that is used by an artillery model in an attempt to hit other enemy artillery after they fire.

Once an artillery model has been set to counter-battery fire, the model may choose a strike-point centered on an enemy model that has just conducted a standard artillery-based ranged assault and make an indirect-fire artillery ranged assault of it's own.

Artillery: Shoot 'N Scoot

An artillery model may use the run 'n gun option to perform their own version of this move known as the shoot n' scoot.

After an artillery model fires, it's exact location is known by every enemy model thanks to modern counter-battery radar and the BattleNet. To sit in one place is certain death for an artillery crew.

The shoot n' scoot uses the same combination of two move

and one combat actions for 2 AP but requires the model to conduct the ranged assault before any movement.

An artillery model using the shoot n' scoot option will reduce their current MV by 2 and will receive a cumulative modifier of (-1) for each weapon system used in the attack to the strike-point roll.

Artillery models using the shoot n' scoot cannot be the target of enemy models set to counter-battery fire.

Artillery: Counter-Artillery Fire

Counter-artillery fire is a set of weapons and fire-control networks designed to detect and destroy incoming artillery rounds in the air with pinpoint accuracy before they hit their target.

A player may assign a model with one or more rotary weapon systems to counter-artillery fire (2 APs), allowing it a chance to intercept ANY artillery-based ranged assaults with a final strike-point within their weapon systems maximum range. More than one model set to counter-artillery fire may attempt to hit the same round, provide all declarations are made before any die roll is made.

An intercept requires a 10+ roll with the following situation modifiers from the **Counter-Artillery Fire Modifier Table**, ending the artillery ranged assault on a successful roll.

A critical failure roll will cause the fire control network being used to "crash", going off-line for the remainder of the turn, preventing any further intercepts by any models.

A model will remain in counter-artillery fire until it's next activation.

COUNTER-ARTILLERY FIRE MODIFIER TABLE

SM	Situation Modifier Description
+1	Each additional weapon system
+1	Battlefield Upgrade: *Veteran Pilot*
+2	Battlefield Upgrade: *Ace Pilot*
+1	SA: *Wizzo*
-1	Long Range Band Penalty
-2	Extreme Range Band Penalty
-2	Model State: *Suppressed*

ROLL 2D6

Aircraft: Bomb Run

The bomb run is another variation of the standard run n' gun allowing combat aircraft equipped with one or more pylons to drop bombs on the area below their flight path.

During the aircraft's movement, a player may choose a strike-point directly below its path, receiving a cumulative modifier of (-1) for each weapon system used in the attack to the strike-point roll.

Should the strike-point roll result in a critical failure, the bomb(s) has become stuck on the bomb rack, preventing any further bomb runs for that model for the remainder of the game.

THE RULES

Close-Combat Assault

Most combat situations in CAV: SO are fast, brutal, and highly impersonal as combatants target each other from afar. A close-combat assault brings the enemy in close, making war much more personal.

Close-combat is not hand-to-hand combat per se (gun barrels make horrible clubs after all) but is more about the ability of a pilot or squad to outmaneuver an opponent up-close, bringing their weapons to bear at just the right moment and blasting them to bits!

Areas with confined spaces (such as building interiors and trenches) or lots of cover (thick forests or city streets) will see extensive use of close-combat assaults. Most models are not designed for this "to-the-death" style of combat, while others specifically seek out a defender to close with and overwhelm them in close quarters.

CAVs and infantry are by far the best model types to perform a close-combat assault, with CAVs' sheer size and heavy armor providing a formidable platform from which to launch a close-in attack while infantry are small and nimble making them hard to target as they look to exploit any weakness an enemy may have. The base close-combat value (CCV) of these model types reflects their ability to survive and master a close-combat assault.

Combat vehicles are at a severe disadvantage in close-combat, unable to act quickly with an enemy in such close proximity, while aircraft cannot participate in this type of attack at all—grounded aircraft are destroyed immediately if targeted by a close-combat assault.

Close-Combat Resolution

Close-combat begins with one or more activated models declare their intent to move into B2B contact with an enemy model and use the combat action to conduct a close-combat assault. Up to six attackers may choose to initiate a close-combat assault against the same defending model with one model being designated as the primary attacker and any others being referred to as support. Each supporting attacker will add a (+1) to the primary attacker's base CCV.

A single opposed roll is made for both the defending and primary attacking models, adding each model's current CCV (vs hard or soft) to their roll and any additional (+/-) situation modifiers as required. The model with the highest modified combat roll is the winner (see combat action resolution, p. 61).

Close-Combat: Break

Any model wishing to leave B2B contact after participating in a close-combat assault must use the break action first. The break action is a "tactical withdrawal" designed to minimize any additional damage while putting distance between itself and the enemy and requires 1 AP and a 10+ roll to succeed.

A model attempting to "break", after declaring their intent to do so, will use their current CCV (as applied to the enemy model from the close-combat assault) as a (+) situation modifier to the roll. The model will also receive a (+1) for each friendly model and a (-1) for each enemy model that remains in B2B contact from the earlier close-combat assault.

Example: *A defending model with a current CCV of +3 (vs SA: Hard) is trying to "break" from close-combat with two enemy CAV models (-2). Its total 10+ roll situation modifier is +1.*

A successful 10+ roll will allow the model to move away from the close-combat assault up to one-half of its current MV.

A failed roll results in the loss of the AP and the model remaining in its current location. The break action is a repeatable action, provided additional APs are available.

A model that has failed to break from its current B2B location will receive a (-1) situation modifier to any close-combat assaults for the remainder of the turn.

Combat Action Resolution

Resolving the combat action is a multi-step process that uses a single die-roll to determine if the attack "hits" and if any damage is done.

The model(s) that initiated the combat action is the attacker while the target model(s) is the defender.

Any combat actions are considered simultaneous and damage (if any) will not take effect until all combat actions have been resolved during the current squad's activation phase.

• **Step 1:** Any models wishing to use the combat action during a squad's current activation will declare their intent to do so, which model(s) they are targeting, and the type of assault being attempted.

Models conducting any ranged assaults will also declare which weapon systems are being used and any ranged assault sub-types they may want to use.

• **Step 2:** Any defenders wishing to use defensive fire will now declare their intent to do so along with the target and weapon systems they will be using.

• **Step 3:** For direct-fire ranged assaults check LoS while determining the range of the attack and any situation modifiers and/or SAs that may apply to the combat roll.

Ranged assaults using a weapon system with the SA: *Indirect-Fire* will now make any strike point rolls that may be required.

• **Step 4A (ranged assaults only):** The attacker chooses which ranged assault to resolve first. Once an assault has begun against a particular target, all ranged assaults are resolved before proceeding to the next.

A target-point combat roll is made for each ranged assault, adding or subtracting any situation modifiers, and comparing the modified roll to the designated range band target-point number. If the result is equal to or greater, the ranged assault is a "hit". If less, the ranged assault is a miss.

Note: *A natural roll of "2" on any ranged assault combat roll is an automatic miss and a critical fumble (if applicable).*

A natural roll of "12" on any combat roll is a critical success, allowing an additional 1d6 to be rolled, adding the result to the current combat roll.

• **Step 4B (close-combat assaults only):** An attacker chooses with close-combat assault to resolve first. If more than one attacker is involved in the same close-combat assault, one model is designated as the primary attacker and all other allied models are referred to as supporting attackers.

Both the primary attacker and defending model will make an opposed roll, adding or subtracting any situation modifiers and each model's CCV to their roll. The side with the highest modified combat roll is declared the winner (a tie roll results in a draw).

Note: *A natural roll of "2" on any close-combat assault is a critical fumble, allowing an opponent to roll an additional 1d6 and adding the result to their current combat roll.*

A natural roll of "12" on any combat roll is a critical success, allowing an additional 1d6 to be rolled, adding the result to the current combat roll.

• **Step 5A (ranged assaults only):** If the combat roll was a "hit", the attacker will add the margin of success to the RAV of the weapon system that was used. This combined value is then compared to the defender's AV. If equal to or greater, refer to the **ranged assault damage table (see p. 62)** and apply the result as indicated.

A lesser value, while still a "hit", indicates the defender's armor has deflected the attack, preventing any damage.

• **Step 5B (close-combat assaults only):** The winner of the opposed combat roll will use the margin of success for the close-combat assault and refer to the **close-combat assault damage table (see p. 62)** and apply the result as indicated.

• **Step 6:** If a model is destroyed before the completion of all combat actions directed towards it are resolved, the assaults are "lost" and cannot be reassigned to another target.

• **Step 7:** Once all of an attacker's ranged assaults are complete, the defender (even if destroyed) may now resolve any defensive fire ranged assaults that were previously declared.

• **Step 8:** Any model receiving one or more damage points during the current activation will now subtract the amount of damage from its current damage track, turning the d12 damage die to display the new damage track for each model.

If a model has no remaining damage tracks, it is destroyed and removed from play. Non-infantry models will place a destroyed model counter (see p. 51) to mark its final resting place!

CAV model(s) subject to a pilot check target-point roll will now do so and any model(s) affected by one or more model states (see other combat effects, pp. 62-63) as well as any critical damage, should place a counter next to the model as a reminder.

Note: *Unless modified by an SA, infantry models will only take one point of damage regardless of any margin of success rolled for.*

Infantry models are immune to any critical damage results.

THE RULES

RANGED ASSAULT DAMAGE TABLE

MoS	Result
0	One damage point to defending model
1	One damage point to defending model
2	One damage point to defending model
3	One damage point to defending model[1]
4	One damage point to defending model[1]
5	Two damage points to defending model[1]
6	Two damage points to defending model[2]
7	Two damage points to defending model[2]
8	Two damage points to defending model[2]
9	Two damage points to defending model[3]
10+	Three damage points to defending model[4]

CLOSE-COMBAT ASSAULT DAMAGE TABLE

MoS	Result
0	One damage point to both models
1	One damage point to losing model
2	One damage point to losing model
3	One damage point to losing model[1]
4	One damage point to losing model[1]
5	Two damage points to losing model[1]
6	Two damage points to losing model[2]
7	Two damage points to losing model[2]
8	Two damage points to losing model[2]
9	Three damage points to losing model[3]
10+	Three damage points to losing model[4]

[1] Pilot Check
[2] Pilot Check (-1) and model is suppressed
[3] Pilot Check (-2) and model is stunned
[4] Roll on critical damage table

CRITICAL DAMAGE TABLE

ROLL 2D6

Roll	Result
2	Breeder destroyed (model is disabled)
3	Breeder damaged (-1 AP)
4	Leg/Drive system crippled (1/2 MV)
5	Leg/Drive system damaged (-1 MV)
6	Model is knock-down and stunned
7	Model is knock-down and suppressed
8	Model is knock-down and stunned
9	Weapon systems damaged (-1 to any combat roll)
10	Targeting systems damaged (-2 to any combat roll)
11	Weapon systems crippled (all RAV/CCV 0/0)
12	Cockpit destroyed and pilot/crew killed

Other Combat Action Effects

Certain situations during play may arise that affect a model, resulting in additional damage and/or other restrictions and situation modifiers that may influence the successful completion of an action(s).

Model States

As a game progresses, a model may come under the affect of one or more model states. A model state is the result of a particular action made by that model or an attack/action performed against it by another model (friendly or enemy). A model can only be affected by any individual model state once per turn; consecutive model states of the same type do not stack.

The following is a current list of the model states available and their affect on a model during play:

● Burning: While most modern fighting equipment is designed to withstand intense temperatures, the effect of being covered in a flammable liquid and set on fire can make even the most seasoned veteran cringe with fear as well as interfering with any onboard sensor systems.

A model with the SA: *Hard* and the Model State: *Burning* will receive a (-2) to any die roll made by the model while affected by this state.

A model with the SA: *Soft* and the Model State: *Burning* will also take damage, receiving one damage point for each additional turn that the model remains (applied at the end of the model's next activation) on fire.

The Model State: *Burning* can only be removed by a model with the SA: *Fire-Proof*, moving into an allowed water terrain object, or allowing the fire to burn itself out (three additional turns).

- Disabled: A model with the Model State: *Disabled* is unable to perform any actions for the remainder of the game and if the target of an assault, will provide a (+4) situation modifier to an attacker's combat roll.

Infantry models are immune to the effects of this state.

- Disrupted: A model with the Model State: *Disrupted* is unable to perform any actions during the duration of this state. The Model State: *Disrupted* is typically the result of being hit by an ion disruptor cannon (see p. 112).

Infantry models and models with the SA: *Shielded* are immune to the effects of this state.

- Hacked: With the advent of modern nano-technology, the ease of introducing a malignant virus to a complex computer system became readily apparent. New countermeasures were required to protect a system from these "mini-hackers" and defend against their attempt to overwhelm their firewalls.

A model that has been "hacked" will receive a (-2) situation modifier to any die rolls it makes and a (-2) move value until the Model State: *Hacked* has been removed.

After a model has been "hacked" it may try to counter the affect during its next activation, using a special action to disable the attacking nano with a successful 10+ roll. Each additional turn attempted adds a (+1) situation modifier to the roll.

Infantry models and models with the SA: *Shielded* are immune to the effects of this state.

- Immobile: Any model or terrain object with the Model State: *Immobile* will provide a (+4) situation modifier to an attacker's combat roll (direct-fire) or strike point roll (indirect-fire).

Infantry models are immune to the effects of this state.

- Knockdown: A CAV model that fails a **pilot check** or that chooses to **go prone** receives the Model State: *Knockdown*. This state prevents a model from using the combat action and if the target of an attack, will provide a (+2) situation modifier to an attacker's combat roll.

A model must use the move action to stand-up to get back to its "feet".

Non-CAV models are immune to the effects of this state.

- Suppressed: A model with the Model State: *Suppressed* may not move in a direction that takes it closer to any enemy model, not moving if no direction is available.

A model with the Model State: *Suppressed* will receive a (-2) to any die roll made by the model while affected by this state.

A suppressed model will automatically recover from this state after spending one complete activation under its affect. A player may also spend one C3 point to immediately remove the Model State: *Suppressed* if available.

- Stunned: A model with the Model State: *Stunned* will lose all of its action points during its next activation as well as receiving a (-2) to any die roll made by the model while affected by this state.

A stunned model will automatically recover from this state after spending one complete activation under its affect. A player may also spend one C3 point to immediately remove the Model State: *Stunned* if available.

Taking Damage while Transporting Models

Should a model that is currently transporting one or more models receive a critical hit during combat, each model being transported will receive one damage point as well.

If the transporting model is destroyed, any models being transported are also destroyed.

Infantry in the Open

An infantry model squad that is "hit" for damage from a weapon system with the SA: *Ravage* and is currently located in open or paved terrain types will take double damage, receiving two damage points.

Dug-In Infantry

An infantry model squad can use a special action and "dig-in", ignoring the infantry in the open damage bonus, in any terrain type other than paved, swamp, and water.

Infantry models may also use the SA: *Pop-Up* after using the dug-in option provided they remain at the same spot they performed the action in.

FIELD NOTES

Pilot Check

CAVs are the only models required to make a pilot check, typically due to damage received during the combat action.

A pilot check uses a **target-point roll 6+**, adding or subtracting any situation modifiers called for. Quad CAVs always receive a (+1) situation modifier when making a pilot check due to their improved stability.

A model that fails a pilot check receives the Model State: *Knockdown*. If the target-point roll is a critical failure, the model will also receive one damage point.

Go Prone

A CAV model may choose to "go prone", generally in an attempt to avoid line of sight from an attacker. Prone models also receive the Model State: *Knockdown* and have an elevation level of one.■

The Repair Action

The ability of a crew to make a quick "fix" in the heat of battle is often the difference between victory and defeat. The majority of model types in CAV: SO can use the repair action to bypass damaged systems and restore limited functionality to destroyed ones using advanced microscopic repair nanites.

To make a repair, a player will declare their intent to use the repair action during a model's activation. The repair action uses a 10+ roll to determine if the attempt is successful, adding the model's repair value from its current damage track as a (+) situation modifier to the die roll.

A natural or modified result of ten or greater indicates one damage point has been repaired to the model.

The repair action is a non-repeatable action and cannot be used by a model without a repair value.

Lingering Damage

While field repairs or a quick patch by a medic can improve the functionality of a damaged model during a fight, the repair action cannot be used to return a model to 100% (damage track "0") after taking damage in battle.

Typically, once damaged, a model will have one point of lingering damage for the remainder of the fight.

Note: *A model with the SA: Combat Engineer and access to the Battlefield Support Asset: Level II Repair Module can repair lingering damage (see p. 139).*

The Repair Action: Critical Success

When using the repair action, a critical success roll will allow two non-lingering damage points to be repaired.

The Repair Action: Critical Failure

When using the repair action, a critical failure roll will result in one point of damage to the model attempting the repair.

The Regroup Action

During a battle, a squad may take casualties that degrade its ability to fight effectively as a unified force. The regroup action allows two damaged squads to join together, making a new stronger single squad.

To use the regroup action, both squads must have fewer models in them than the maximum amount allowed for their squad type. An active squad may only regroup with a squad on the game board that has not yet activated during the current turn.

At the beginning of their activation, the models in the active squad will declare a simultaneous regroup action, as well as indicating which squad they will be regrouping with. This second squad will now activate, conducting a simultaneous regroup action, combining into one new squad with each model having one remaining action point.

If the squads being combined contain model types and/or tasks that are not usually found together, the squad will become a specialist squad. While force group creation prohibits having more than one specialist squad in a force group, the regroup action allows for an exception to this rule.

Extra models (if any) that will not fit into the newly formed squad are removed from play immediately and count towards any victory conditions established by the scenario for the opposing side as if they were destroyed.

Remember to remove an initiative card(s) of the appropriate color from the draw deck at the end of the current turn for squads that regrouped.

The Special Action

The special action is a catch-all for any action granted by using a specific model type and/or a special ability or attribute.

The use of a special action will be detailed in the description of the function granting its use.

Example: *A model with the SA: Engineer may use a special action to attempt to clear a minefield on the game board during its activation (see p. 137).*

The Special Action: Jamming

Models with the SA: *Active Phase Array* or the SA: *ECM* (see pp. 118 & 121) can use a special action in an attempt to "jam" each other when activated, canceling the effect of the other's SA.

After a model declares they are using a special action and the target of their attempt, both models will make an opposed roll, adding the rating level of their SA to their respective die roll.

If the model attempting the jamming wins the roll, the opposing model may not use the effected SA for the remainder of the current turn. A loss indicates the attempt has failed and no further action is required.

Note: *A model with the Battlefield Upgrades: External Active Phase Array Pod or External ECM Pod cannot use the jamming special action and are automatically "jammed" (no roll) by a model declaring their intent to do so with the SA versions.*

Structures

While most commanders will typically avoid a fight in a built-up, heavy populated area, combat does happen. Block after block of buildings and long, winding streets and alleys provide a bevy of locations for the enemy to hide, limiting line of sight and the mobility of CAV and vehicle models.

The following represents a simplified system for including various structures on the game board.

Structure Types

Structures are divided into four types: residential, commercial, industrial, and hardened. Each type refers to the base damage it can receive before being destroyed (damage points) and the protection it provides (armor value). A typical structure section measures 30 feet by 30 feet (2"x2") and has an elevation level of one.

Larger structures (more sections) can be used, retaining the same armor value assigned to their type, but will have a larger damage point amount based of the area the structure covers (not elevation levels).

Example: *A base residential structure (2"x2") normally has a damage point amount of five and an armor value of two. By doubling the size of the structure (4"x2") and increasing its elevation level to two, the damage point total would increase to ten, but retain the standard armor value of two for being a residential structure with no additional changes for the second elevation level.*

Residential Structure
- Damage Points: 5
- Armor Value: 2
- SA: *Soft*

A residential structure is typical to any of the homes found on countless worlds across the galaxy. Mostly built of wood, brick, rock, or adobe, residential structures provide very little protection and only an infantry model can enter these type of structures without destroying them.

Commercial Structure
- Damage Points: 10
- Armor Value: 4
- SA: *Soft*

Commercial structures tend to be of more solid construction, featuring more ferrocrete and steel in their designs. Stand-alone stores, apartment buildings, and strip malls are typical commercial structures. Like residential structures though, only infantry models can enter these type of structures without destroying them.

MYGAR
Capital City
The Greater Empire of the Rach
Mohr and Vhas (moon)

Industrial Structure

- Damage Points: 15
- Armor Value: 6
- SA: *Hard*

Industrial structures cover larger buildings such as hi-rise apartment buildings, skyscrapers, warehouses, and factories. These type of structures are primarily built of durasteel and ferrocrete and may be several elevation levels tall.

Typically non-infantry models cannot move through industrial structures without first destroying them, but larger structures may include doors and interior areas large enough for CAVs and vehicles to enter.

Hardened Structures

- Damage Points: 20
- Armor Value: 8
- SA: *Hard*

Heavily reinforced, hardened structures are built to withstand a lot of punishment. Hardened structures tend to be only one or two elevations tall, but may have many more levels under ground, especially command centers or other important facilities. Hardened structures are also used as bunkers, equipped with one or more weapon systems for defense and may also feature ramps or steps to allow a model to "climb" to the top to be used as a firing position. While hardened structures can support the weight of even the heaviest CAVs, non-infantry models cannot move through a hardened structure without first destroying them if there are no doors and interior areas large enough for them to enter.

Structures: Damage Points

The damage points of a structure refer to its structural integrity and is a reflection of the amount of damage it can sustain before being reduced to rubble (0 damage points).

Each structure type begins the game with a set number of points that are tracked should they receive any damage. Regardless of the current damage points of a structure, its type will not change. An industrial structure with only 5 damage points remaining is still an industrial structure.

Structures: Elevation Levels

Every structure has an assigned elevation level and may act as blocking cover (regardless of type) when determining any line of sight measurements that may cross their location.

Structures: Movement

Infantry are the only model types allowed to move into, through, or onto a structure unless specifically designed to allow other model types access. Infantry models may spend 2 MV to move up or down floors while inside a structure. Models on differing floors ignore normal stacking limitations but may not enter a hardened structure during play that they do not control.

Other model types that attempt to move into, through, or onto a non-hardened structure will cause that section to immediately collapse, reducing it to rubble. Non-powered infantry models located inside a destroyed structure are removed from play while any other model type receives one point of damage.

Structures: Combat

Attacking a structure uses the same combat action to make a ranged assault only (no close-combat) and all structure types have the Model State: *Immobile*.

An attack that equals or exceeds a structures armor value will compare the margin of success to the **structure damage table** and apply the results as indicated.

Models inside a structure may fire "out" at an enemy model but are restricted to direct-fire ranged assaults only. An attacker may target a model inside a structure, but will add the current armor value of the structure to the defending model's armor value. If the model is damaged by the attack, the structure will also take one damage point.

STRUCTURE DAMAGE TABLE

MoS	Result
0	One damage point to structure
1	One damage point to structure
2	Two damage points to structure
3	Two damage points to structure
4	Three damage points to structure
5	Four damage points to structure
6+	Five damage points to structure (+ critical)

CRITICAL DAMAGE TABLE

Roll	Result
1	The structure is on fire and burning. +1 damage point per turn until destroyed.
2	Reduced structural integrity, reduce the AV by ½.
3	Reduced structural integrity, reduce the AV by 1.
4	Reduced structural integrity, reduce the AV by 1.
5	Reduced structural integrity, reduce the AV by ½.
6	The structure implodes and collapses into rubble (destroyed).

ROLL 1D6

The Adon Economic Confederation (AEC)

Background
Reaching for the Stars

While each of the known races of the galaxy would like to consider themselves the center for all others to revolve around, it is the Adonese that can make the claim to have traveled to another world first. While their own history is rife with conflict, the Adonese managed to reach a period of stability and cooperation that led to the construction of the first known compression drive and access to the rest of the galaxy.

With the discovery of each new world and the resources they contained, the discord and jealousy of the past grew anew, finally erupting into an all-out world war, the barbarity of which devastated the planet of Adon over a twenty year span. By 2065, the end of the Perrini Wars saw the overthrow of the crown princes of Hakir and Racheau and a new chance at peace while they rebuilt their shattered planet.

First Contact

As the Adonese moved further and further out into the galaxy, their first encounter with another race brought them into contact with the Ritter. A militaristic society, the Ritterlich Republic had already encountered another race, the Malvernians and had begun a rapid expansion of their space-based assets as a deterrent to any outside threats.

The Adonese, realizing that individually they were ill-equipped to fight an interstellar war, banded together as part of a mutual defense pact. Within the framework laid out by all ten signatories, the nations of Adon would form a united military force, the New Adon Defense Organization (NADO) and an economic collective under the auspices of the Adon Economic Confederation (AEC). With the Malvernians seemingly oblivious to the comings and goings of their galactic neighbors, the interests of the Ritter and Adonese began to conflict more and more, leading to the First Adon-Ritter war.

The Boreas Accord Wars (2110-2114)

Several systems centered on the star Boreas became a point of contention between the Ritter and Adonese as both governments made claims on the worlds located within. As diplomatic exchanges gave way to threats of war, both sides moved military forces into the area, with the eventual start of hostilities in the Hades system. The Ritter had begun to land ground forces on the airless world of Maibaum, leading to NADO attempting a blockade of any additional reinforcements. The Ritter 3rd Fleet moved in to break the blockade and all-out fighting began in earnest.

The Malvernians found itself drawn into the conflict after the Ritter attacked the Malvernian colony on Lir, fearing the Malvernians were attempting to ally themselves with the Adonese. After four years of intense fighting, all three star-nations set down at the peace table and ended the conflict with the signing of the Boreas Accords, reaching an ownership agreement in regards to the contested systems. Of note is the transfer of technology and equipment from the Adonese to the Malvernians that took place during and after the end of the war, allowing for a major step forward for the Malvernian military and the eventual deployment of their Cy-Bot designs.

The Imperial Wars (2145-2161)

As the Adonese and Ritter exploration ships moved coreward in the galaxy, contact was eventually made with the Greater Empire of the Rach. Somehow managing to avoid annihilating themselves on their own home world of Mohr, the Rach clans had pushed out into the galaxy in search of new worlds, fighting amongst themselves for ownership of any new system discovered.

The Adonese and Ritterlich, being "khresh" (translates in Rach as "prey" or "not-rach") in their way of thinking, the clans of the Rach spared no time in declaring war on both, attacking across a dozen worlds at once. Over the next decade millions died as the fighting scoured planet after planet, finally ending

TACTICAL BRIEFINGS

after all three sides had exhausted themselves. Meeting in the Rach system of Aeneas, the three star-nations set a treaty establishing the mutual borders each agreed to be bound to relative to each other.

First Spica War (2165-2168)

The Rach turned their sights towards the Malvernians, sending in a large invading force to strike the Spica system, overwhelming the small defense force on both worlds and clearing the colonists living there. Establishing a base to raid from, over the next four years the Rach seized six other Malvernian systems before the threat of a NADO intervention stopped any additional incursions with the signing of the Treaty of Regor.

Second Spica War (2170-2172)

Seemingly before the ink was even dry of the Treaty of Regor, the Rach claimed violations of the treaty by the Malvernians and attacked their colonies in the Ribor and Tarpur systems, claiming the need of a defensive zone. The Adonese, still weary over the devastating losses suffered during the Imperial Wars, begrudgingly moved forces to seize Spica, cutting off the Rach supply lines and prepared for the onslaught they knew would follow. Surprisingly the Rach agreed to a cease-fire and pulled back from their recent conquests. Malvernian forces moved in to re-occupy the majority of the worlds the Rach had taken, eventually taking over for NADO on Spica, allowing the Adonese to return to their own territory, breathing a sigh of relief that their decision to intervene had not launched a major interstellar war once again.

Vela War (2176-2183)

The Adonese had long been aware of the Terrans before the humans had taken their first small steps into space, keeping their existence a secret from the rest of the universe. After noting a decrease in activity along their own borders, the Adonese began sending out scout ships to see what the Rach might be up to. Unfortunately, by the time the Adonese pieced together what was going on; it was too late for majority of humans on Earth.

Peacekeepers (2184-2274)

After their intercession on behalf of the Malvernians and later the Terrans, the Confederation went into a period of isolationism, avoiding any external problems that did not directly affect them. In the last twenty years though, a new generation of Adonese has taken a stronger approach towards interceding in any conflicts it feels could disrupt the current status quo throughout the galaxy. A strong champion for free trade and a general desire for peaceful co-existence, the Adonese have used their military and economic might to follow a "carrot or stick" style of diplomacy when dealing with others. But not all within the AEC are content with their role as the self-

appointed "peacekeepers" of the galaxy. The recent "Adon First" movement, centered on its leader Dar Thal'Mon, a Hakirian merchant, has gained traction as it has attracted many new followers in recent years.

Geography

Adon is a temperate world located within the Avalorr binary star system and features two major continents that make up about fifty percent of the planet's surface. Jantilorr, the largest, sits in the northwestern hemisphere while Dantilorr is in the southeast. The planet has two small moons, Pendarri and Lonarri, that can cause severe tidal action at various times based on their location and proximity to the main world.

Arveni

A coastal nation on the east of Dantilorr, Arveni was a major naval power before the advent of space travel and this naval tradition has carried over to modern times with many Arvens serving in the Confederation space fleet as officers and engineers.

Breonne

The largest nation of Adon, Breonne occupies the majority of Dantilorr. The AEC and NADO headquarters are based in Breonne, as are many of the top universities and cultural centers.

Hakir

Long the hotbed of political rancor, Hakir sits in the far north of Dantilorr. Since the end of the Perrini wars, Hakir has had a constitution that limits its own internal military forces resulting in a disproportionate number of permanent brigades being supplied to NADO for a nation its size. Known for their tenacity in battle, Hakir infantry soldiers form the backbone of NADO assault divisions.

Haldor

Haldor, in the northeast corner of Jantilorr, is the least populated nation within the AEC and is mainly a fishing and farming country. With no large cities to speak of, Haldorians are simple folk known for their honesty and directness, making them superior diplomats and ambassadors. While the country maintains a small defense force, there are currently no Haldorian brigades serving in NADO. Haldorians wishing to serve in the military generally enlist in a neighboring nation or sign up directly with a NADO recruiter.

Heimdall

Set in the northern central plains of Jantilorr, Heimdall is the "breadbasket" of Adon, supplying the majority of grains to the rest of the planet year round due to their constant, mild climate. With their proximity to many of the other nations of Adon, Heimdall is also home to many large distribution and

TACTICAL BRIEFINGS

manufacturing centers.

The Highlands

The Highlands, located in the northwest section of Jantilorr, has always been a major shipbuilding nation and has carried over that tradition into modern spaceship construction. Adon's largest starport, Kras Morock, is located in the Highlands.

Kjord

Kjord sits on the north coast of Jantilorr, abundant in mineral resources among the mountainous region that covers of the majority of the small nation. Kjord is a harsh place to live, but is also home to some of the best alpine areas on the planet. NADO maintains is special operations training center in the city of Mormaar and Kjordish soldiers are some of the fiercest warriors Adon has ever produced.

Okura

An oceanic paradise, Okura occupies the lower coast of Dantilorr, along the warm waters of the Parmisno Ocean. Poor natural resources have made Okura dependent on other nations for materials to feed their large factory base and abundant population. Okura is home to NADO's jungle fighting school and a large underwater training facility located at the tip of the Jamal Peninsula in the southern tip.

The Principalities

Located along the south east coast of Jantilorr, the Principalities is a collection of small nations that were eventually joined together under one flag centuries ago. With their proximity to the planets equator, Adon's only space elevator is anchored here as well as hosting NADO's air and space college at Taravasco.

Racheau

The west coast of Jantilorr is dominated by the nation of Racheau. Racheau's access to the ocean and rivers that feed into it coupled with abundant mineral resources from the Spine Mountains has made this nation the manufacturing muscle of Adon. Three of Adon's largest cities are in Racheau and is home to NADO's infantry training school at Borleaud.

Government

With the establishment of the Adon Economic Confederation, set forth by the Breonne-Highlands Compact of 2085, each signatory, while remaining an independent democratic nation, agreed to cooperate and abide by a common framework for mutual aid and defense.

Equal in status, each member-nation elects a representative to the permanent Confederation Secretariat, one of which, every four years would be elected to the role of Secretary-General to lead the Secretariat in its responsibilities in dealing with any foreign affairs with other star-nations as well as any treaties or trade issues and the deployment and disposition of the forces currently assigned to NADO.

Military
New Adon Defense Organization

While each member-state maintains its own distinct military force, each nation also supplies a levy of troops and ships to the Confederation Army and Navy under the auspices of the New Adon Defense Organization (NADO). As the military arm of theAEC, NADO is directly responsible for the overall defense of the Confederation and reports directly to the Secretary-General, serving as the Commander-in-Chief.

Currently NADO is made up of two hundred and twenty-one standing divisions drawn from the militaries of all ten member-states who supply one or more brigades as part of a five-year deployment cycle. This rotation allows for more troops to become familiar with serving with other nationalities within a unified command structure in the event of a major conflict.

All NADO commanders of Colonel rank or higher are drawn from the High Intensity Conflict Training College located at NADO headquarters in Westinhall, Breonne and typically remain in NADO for their entire careers.

EMBLEM
Tactical
NADO Armed Forces

INFANTRY
Powered Armor
HK-14 Assault Rifle
Regiment 72 "Storm Wind"
The Adon Economic Confederation

New Adon Defense Organization Force Structure

The NADO Army is one of the largest standing militaries in the galaxy is and operationally formed around the division. These are grouped into corps which in turn makes up an army. There is no standard Table of Organization & Equipment (TO&E) from the corps level up as divisions are rotated in and out as needed (though typically a corps will consist of 2-5 divisions) while each army is responsible for a given area in the AEC.

Each division is made up of three regiments with each regiment containing four battalions. A typical division has over 5,000 soldiers plus support personnel.

NADO Force Ranks

Army (Enlisted)
- Trooper
- Senior Trooper
- Corporal
- Sergeant
- Warrant Sergeant
- Senior Warrant Sergeant
- Master Warrant Sergeant
- Senior Master Warrant Sergeant of the Confederation Army

Army (Officer)
- Lieutenant
- Senior Lieutenant
- Captain
- Major
- Colonel
- General
- Command General
- Marshal of Troops
- Senior Marshal of Troops
- Marshal of the Confederation Army

Force Structure *(all model types)*
- **Regiment** *(4 battalions, colonel)*
- **Division** *(3 regiments, general)*
- **Corps** *(2-5 divisions, marshal of troops)*
- **Army** *(2-5 corps, senior marshal of troops)*
- **NADO** *(marshal of the confederation army)*

Infantry
- **Fire Team** *(one model)*
  Infantry *(troopers x5, corporal, sergeant)*
  Powered *(troopers x3, corporal, sergeant)*
- **Platoon** *(one squad)*
  Fire Team x5 *(warrant sergeant, lieutenant)*
- **Company**
  Platoon x4 *(senior warrant sergeant, captain)*
- **Battalion**
  Company x4 *(master warrant sergeant, major)*

Combat Vehicle
- **Vehicle** *(one model)*
  Crew *(sergeant)*
- **Troop** *(one squad)*
  Vehicle x4 *(warrant sergeant, lieutenant)*
- **Company**
  Troop x4 *(senior warrant sergeant, captain)*
- **Battalion**
  Company x4 *(master warrant sergeant, major)*

Aircraft
- **Aircraft** *(one model)*
  Pilot/Crew *(sergeant)*
- **Flight** *(one squad)*
  Aircraft x2 *(warrant sergeant)*
- **Squadron**
  Flight x4 *(senior warrant sergeant, captain)*
- **Battalion**
  Squadron x4 *(master warrant sergeant, major)*

Combat Assault Vehicle (CAV)
- **CAV** *(one model)*
  Pilot/Crew *(sergeant)*
- **Troop** *(one squad)*
  Vehicle x4 *(warrant sergeant, lieutenant)*
- **Company**
  Troop x4 *(senior warrant sergeant, captain)*
- **Battalion**
  Company x4 *(master warrant sergeant, major)*

CAV
Extra-Large Chassis
Chancellor
Regiment 55 "Double Trouble"
The Adon Economic
Confederation

TACTICAL BRIEFINGS

Selected NADO Units

1 RADD (Rapid Deployment Division)
First to Fight
Commander: General Ern Jor'Dain
Division Headquarters: Breonne

Unlike most units in NADO, 1 RADD has a permanently assigned transportation group allowing it to respond and operate independently without the use of a forward base. 1 RADD has seen service in every major war that NADO has participated in as well as seeing deployment to Terra during 2183 as a peace-keeping force.

2 RADD (Rapid Deployment Division)
Red Spear
Commander: General Gor Yun'Nik
Division Headquarters: Heimdall

Another Rapid Deployment Division, 2 RADD is permanent unit within NADO since its inception during the Imperial Wars. In a baptism of fire, the 2 RADD's 1st and 2nd regiments were destroyed by the Rach on their first deployment to the Hades system in 2155.

Regiment 14
Iron Wood
Commander: Colonel Jon Ang'Ur
Regiment Headquarters: New Vesta

Regiment 14 is a Heimdall regiment and has been on New Vesta for the last year attempting to curtail recent pirate activity in the surrounding systems. The independent system of Pictor and the surrounding areas have always been a haven for pirates but as of late the brigands seem to be more organized and better equipped.

Regiment 55
Double Trouble
Commander: Colonel Oman Raz'Ul
Regiment Headquarters: Bounty

Regiment 55 is a Hakir regiment with a bit of a checkered past. While it did not actively support Thal'Mor during the Perrini Wars, the unit refused to take part in offensive operations against the disposed prince.

After several decades of less than ideal postings, one of the unit's CAV pilots Sergeant Avan Max'Gar was the focus of a recent reality sim-vid detailing his day to day experiences during his deployment. The show was a mega-hit and the unit's regimental patch has become a favorite among Adon's youth.

Regiment 72
Storm Wind
Commander: Colonel Oda Ham'Al
Regiment Headquarters: Fastanal

Regiment 72 is an Okura regiment and was recently moved to Fastanal as a deterrent to increased activity in the area by Principality forces.

The warriors of the "Storm Wind" have earned a reputation as dependable and ferocious under fire.

Adon Economic Confederation Faction Doctrines

Fire and Fury Warfare Doctrine
Aggressive Electronic Warfare
Much of the technology in use by the Adonese remains at least a generation ahead of that fielded by the other star nations. The use of electronics in warfare to help identify, target, and hinder an opponent remains a prime directive of NADO and its associated member-state militaries.

Game Rules: *All Adonese models with the SA: Active Phase Array or SA: ECM receive an additional 6" bonus to the base range of their area of effect.*

Hyrwyda Dyrnel Doctrine
Optical Camouflage
The Adonese have taken adaptive camouflage a step further with the use of retroreflective materials and nano-tech in the combat uniforms and armor of their infantry. Optical camouflage projects the scene directly behind a soldier onto their clothing, creating an illusion of "invisibility". This illusion though is only convincing when viewed from certain angles.

Game Rules: *All Adonese infantry models receive the SA: Rat at no extra cost.*

Martial Arts
Whereas most militaries reserve more advanced hand to hand combat techniques and training for their special forces, all Adonese military troops are taught "Hyrwyda Dyrnel" which basically translates to "battle by touch", earning additional mastery levels throughout their military careers.

Game Rules: *All Adonese infantry models receive a +1 close-combat assault bonus vs other infantry models. This bonus will stack with the SA: Grenadier.* ■

The Almirithil Principality

Background

A Quest for Power

The nations of Hakir and Racheau had been the driving force behind many of the regional conflicts that had plagued their respective continents long before the first Adonese ever took to space. With the advent of the first compression drive, the affect either nation had on the world economy lessened as new markets and resources opened up, reducing the dependence they had once counted on from the other nations of Adon. This resentment of the "new world order" led to both nations entering an alliance that would eventually lead to a level of destruction that no one could ever have imagined.

With the military prowess of the Hakir and the manufacturing might of Racheau, the crown princes of both countries, Prince Thal'Mor of Hakir and Prince Perr'Ini of Racheau, began their reign of terror with the formation of the first Star Chamber.

Each Star Chamber was made up of a specially trained cadre of agents that would eventually infiltrate each of Adon's other nations, recruiting malcontents and other subversives to carry out a series of brutal terrorist attacks. As these attacks swept across the world and into the new off-world colonies, fear and terror became riots as neighbor turned against neighbor. Into this chaos, the combined armies of Hakir and Racheau struck.

For the next twenty years the Perrini Wars dragged on, devastating Adon and its colonies. By 2065 Marshal Kidd'Wel, a Breonnian, led the allied armies of the other remaining Adonese nations to final victory over the despots, driving them and their most loyal followers to flee the planet and seek refuge far from those they had tried to conquer.

From the Ashes

The defeated princes found their way to the Mirith, a system many light years rimward of their formers realms. Unable to bring much of the technology they were accustomed to living with, the first few years were hard and many died. Back on Adon, the victors seemed content to focus on rebuilding, exhausted by the brutality of the war, hoping to just forget.

Regardless of the hardships they were faced with and endured, these new "Mirithians" maintained their lust for ultimate power, the need to control everything never seemed to wane, leading to both factions attempting to seize power once again. At the end, the Hakirians reigned supreme, killing all those who had opposed them. Millions of lives later, Crown Prince Thal'Mor had finally taken his place as the one true leader of all those who remained.

The Almirithil Principality was born.

A Taste for Revenge

In the last two hundred years, the Almirithil Principality has grown to encompass more than twenty other worlds within 16 star systems. Mirith remains the capital world, under the current Crown Prince, Jor'Hakir.

The only real contact the Mirithians have maintained outside their own realm is with the Ritter and the Templars, having purchased large amounts of military-related equipment from the Ritterlich, as well as frequently hosting "advisors" for training. Since 2265, several Templar "Free Companies" have served as garrisons on Principality worlds.

The Mirithians have avoided any of the wars or conflicts that have kept the rest of the galaxy on edge since their inception. While there is very little "official" contact between Almirithil and the AEC since the "purge", even after two centuries the old animosities remain from both sides. With the recent support by Jor'Hakir of several prominent Hakirians back on Adon, there seems very little chance of reconciliation any time soon. Rumors of the Mirithian intelligence personnel being involved with a series of terrorist attacks on military and civilian power centers throughout the AEC has also not helped with either side's willingness to let go of the past.

TACTICAL BRIEFINGS

Geography

Mirith is a single star system with two small planetoids, ice worlds in far outer orbits, and the planet Medea, a gas giant with eight moons. Three of these moons can support life, with the Principality capital based on the largest of these, Navat Hakir (New Hakir).

New Hakir has one continent that covers nearly ninety percent of the moon. Large forests of fungal organisms once dominated the moon's surface, their trunks full of water, that when dried becomes very tough and remains a common construction material. New Hakir suffers from an extremely slow axial rotation, providing for very long days and nights.

Government

The Crown Prince is the supreme leader of the Principality for life. The twelve-member Directorate reports directly to the prince, oversees the various councils of kommissars, ministers, and state executives responsible for the day to day operations of the realm.

Each Principality world is broken up into "states" under the direct control of an executive officer. Many of these executive officers are appointed for life, descendants of the original supporters of Thal'Mor.

The life of an average citizen is controlled in almost every aspect by the state. The state is responsible for the well-being of every citizen through economic and social programs, administrating all agriculture and industry workers as part of the collective.

Military

The Principality maintains a regular standing army and navy and a second "people's army" consisting of conscripts. These conscripts remain in their assigned unit for a period of two years, training and serving as a work force for any state projects that may be required. Every citizen must report upon reaching their majority for service unless receiving a waiver from a sponsor or other member of the ruling elite. At the end of this period, they will be assigned to their work station for the remainder of their lives but can be recalled should a state emergency arise.

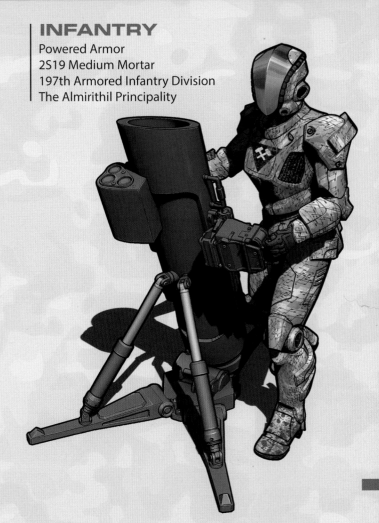

INFANTRY
Powered Armor
2S19 Medium Mortar
197th Armored Infantry Division
The Almirithil Principality

The regular army consists of twelve guard armies that rotate throughout the Principality. In recent years the Principality has used a number of mercenary units to provide "defense" on their own worlds but commonly use them to break up food riots or other displays of discontent.

The Almirithil Principality Force Ranks
Army (Conscript)
- Candidate
- Senior Candidate
- Dembel
- Senior Dembel (at demobilization)

Army (Enlisted)
- Soldier
- Efreiter
- Junior Sergeant
- Sergeant
- Senior Sergeant
- Starshina
- Praporshchik
- Senior Praporshchik

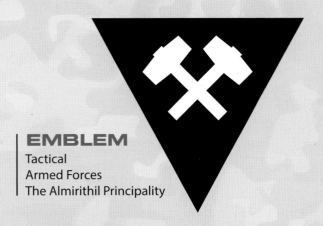

EMBLEM
Tactical
Armed Forces
The Almirithil Principality

TACTICAL BRIEFINGS

Army (Officer)
- Junior Lieutenant
- Lieutenant
- Senior Lieutenant
- Kaptain
- Kombat
- Kombrig
- Komdiv
- Komcor
- Komandarm, 2nd Rank
- Komandarm, 1st Rank

Force Structure (all model types)
- **Brigade** (3 battalions, kombrig)
- **Division** (2-3 brigades, komdiv)
- **Corps** (2-3 divisions, komcor)
- **Army** (2-3 corps, komandarm, 2nd rank)

Infantry
- **Section** (one model)
  Infantry (soldier x6, junior sergeant, sergeant)
  Powered (soldier x4, junior sergeant, sergeant)
- **Platoon** (one squad)
  Section x4 (senior sergeant, lieutenant)
- **Company**
  Platoon x4 (starshina, kaptain)
- **Battalion**
  Company x4 (praporshchik, kombat)

Combat Vehicle
- **Vehicle** (one model)
  Crew (sergeant)
- **Squad** (one squad)
  Vehicle x4 (senior sergeant, lieutenant)
- **Platoon**
  Squad x4 (starshina, senior lieutenant)
- **Company**
  Platoon x4 (praporshchik, kaptain)
- **Battalion**
  Company x4 (senior praporshchik, kombat)

Aircraft
- **Aircraft** (one model)
  Pilot/Crew (praporshchik)
- **Flight** (one squad)
  Aircraft x2 (senior praporshchik)
- **Air Squadron**
  Flight x4 (lieutenant, kaptain)
- **Air Regiment**
  Air Squadron x4 (senior lieutenant, kombat)

Combat Assault Vehicle (CAV)
- **CAV** (one model)
  Pilot/Crew (sergeant)
- **Squad** (one squad)
  CAV x4 (senior sergeant, lieutenant)
- **Platoon**
  Squad x4 (starshina, senior lieutenant)
- **Company**
  Platoon x4 (praporshchik, kaptain)
- **Battalion**
  Company x4 (senior praporshchik, kombat)

Selected Almirithil Principality Units

1st Guards CAV Division
Honor and Glory
Commander: Komdiv And Tre'Yak
Division Headquarters: Navat Hakir

Besides being the Principality's first CAV division, the 1st Guards is permanently assigned to the capital world. In recent years, with the help of Ritter advisors, the military base at Grozny has become the Principality's first war college. Several of the Guard's most senior officers spend time there as instructors and the 1st's 133rd Guards CAV Brigade is regularly used as an aggressor force during training.

CAV
Extra-Large Chassis
Striker (Concussion)
21st CAV Division
The Almirithil Principality

9th Heavy Tank Division

Arrow

Commander: Kondiv Bar Any'Uk

Division Headquarters: Kozel

Formed in 2210, the 9th is an all tank division currently stationed on the far coreward principality world of Kozel on garrison duty.

While many life forms have been found throughout the galaxy, none quite match the ferocity of Kozel's "Orochi". Measuring 10 feet tall at the front shoulder, this four-legged, eight-headed reptile dominates the planet's ecosystem. It will attack anything that enters its territory and is a favorite for off-world hunters who travel here. As a result the 9th is responsible for keeping poachers at bay and enforcing strict hunting regulations to help manage the Orochi population and protect the planet's population from any of the reptiles that encroach upon the various settlements scattered about the world.

12th Guards CAV Division

Deadeye

Commander: Kondiv Sek Und'A

Division Headquarters: Minska

A guards unit in the principality's military denotes their elite status, receiving this designation for distinguished service at some point during their existence.

The 12th received the honor for their assault on the Tao mines in 2255. Workers had seized the mines, executing several kommissars and other mine officials in the process, demanding changes to the working conditions. The 12th drove the defenders from the mines during a daring, night-time attack and capturing a communications center that the workers had been broadcasting from to neighboring systems.

17th Guards CAV Division

Never Forget

Commander: Kondiv Kuz Net'Sov

Division Headquarters: Kirovo

The 17th has been responsible for anti-pirate patrols in several of the principality's outer systems but for the last year their official whereabouts are unknown.

21st CAV Division

Hammer of Hakir

Commander: Kondiv Mik Ha'IL

Division Headquarters: Kurtz

Originally a tank division, the 21st has been undergoing a major refit in the last six months as they switch over to CAVs. Several Ritter ships have recently arrived in-system and have been unloading scores of brand new machines.

199th Motor Rifle Division

No Pain, No Gain

Commander: Kondiv Vla Dim'Ir

Division Headquarters: Pulaw

The 199th is a mechanized infantry division currently assigned to the Almirithil's Coreward Fleet. Second in size only to the Home Fleet, the Coreward Fleet has been on extended deployment in and about Sukhin, an independent system just rimward of the Adonese border at Fastanal. While not part of the Principality, Sukhin is home to a large mining consortium headquartered in Hakir back on Adon.

The Almirithil Principality Faction Doctrines

The Lend-Lease Doctrine

The Enemy of my Enemy is my Friend

By the time modern-era CAV designs began deploying in 2240, the manufacturing base of the Principality was not yet to a level to build these intricate machines from scratch. The First Chief Directorate of Foreign Intelligence Services was tasked with securing the technology needed. Since that time several Adonese-built CAVs have been "transferred" to the Principality and brought to the Topolov Defense Collective. Head engineer Mik Fra'Kov and his team then reverse-engineered the designs to develop their own prototypes.

In addition to their own strides in manufacturing, the Principality has established official diplomatic relations with the Ritterlich, allowing for trade and an influx of advisors to help with modernizing the Almirithil's armed forces.

Game Rules: *As part of a Almirithil force group, players may also select models from the Ritterlich force list (no SA: Unique) to include as part of their overall selection.*

The Dogs of War Doctrine

No Price too Big, No Job too Small

Over the last ten years the Principality has taken to hiring Templar "Free Companies" to supplement their own armed forces on several outer rim systems.

Game Rules: *An Almirithil force group may purchase, as a specialist squad, a Templar attack squad. Each Templar model will receive the Battlefield Upgrade: Veteran at no additional TVP cost.*

TACTICAL BRIEFINGS

The Ritterlich Republic

Background
Ritterlich is a People, Not a Place

To better understand the Republic, you must first understand the people. The Ritter seek to control every aspect of their lives and thrive on order. The Ritter have been a unified people for over one thousand years since the Treaty of Goetter established the "Great Peace", ending the war which saw the four great houses of Ritter combined under a single banner under the title of the Ritterlich (roughly translates as "the people of Ritter"). It is this need for order that has allowed the Republic to maintain control, slowly increasing their power over the everyday lives of its citizens ever since. Everything and everyone has a place and anything that disrupts the "status quo" or causes disorder is quickly dealt with.

This need for control also extends to their diet as the Ritter are true carnivores, preferring raw meat and fresh blood when they dine. They are also very empathic and relish in connecting with their "prey" while still alive, feeding on its emotions to the very end. It is this empathy that contributes to the perception by other races of a Ritter's aloofness. While the Ritter certainly hold a level of contempt for others outside their race, a Ritter must control their emotions in order to not overwhelm their fellow beings.

By the time the Ritter discovered the compression drive, they had already established a successful interplanetary space program within their own system, setting up a number of mining colonies on other nearby worlds. Their initial foray into interstellar space and the discovery of worlds capable of sustaining life allowed the Ritter to quickly expand even further, establishing over a dozen colonies and allowing an influx of new life forms for them to "sample".

First Contact

The Ritter's first interaction with another intelligent species came about in 2060 as they set about exploring the Syrma system. An initial survey of the four-planet system indicated that the second planet from the system's star was capable of supporting life but was for all purposes a rock. After landing and starting a series of seismic scans, the Ritter quickly discovered they were not alone. Under the surface was a maze of tunnels and vast caverns that spanned the entire world. Living in this underground system was a race of beings that called themselves the Malvernians.

While seemingly friendly, the alien appearance of the Malvernians and the inability of the Ritter to connect with their emotions in any way repelled the explorers. The Ritter set back to observe the planet, noting the frequent arrival of bulk ore carriers, landing and taking off, seemingly oblivious to the watching Ritter. Upon their return, the explorer crew reported their discovery, setting off a flurry of new ship construction as the Ritter sought to expand their inventory of combat-capable craft. The Malvernians, for their part, seemed content to carry on with their everyday lives, unfazed by the strange visitors and their even stranger "smell".

A Chance Encounter

By 2080 the Ritter had established a series of watch stations and forward military bases in a line along the systems on the trailing edge of their current holdings, facing the Malvernians. While no hostilities had been reported since first encountering the strange aliens, the Ritter were taking no chances. Several task forces had been built, based around one or more assault carriers which frequently rotated through the area, making sure there would be no unexpected incursions. So it was with some surprise when the first alien ships that showed up were "behind" them and unlike the strange aliens back on Syrma II, these new aliens had spaceships that could fight and showed much more interest in the Ritter, referring to themselves as the Adonese.

Geography

Ritter is a tropical world with four continents that comprise about sixty percent of the planet's surface, each named after the state located on it. There is a single moon, Neuritter and four other airless planets circling the single star system, Rigel.

Dornheim

Dornheim is the eastern continent-state and was the homeland of King Goetter, responsible for the conquest of the other three Ritter states and the establishment of the current governmental system. The capital city, Graustein, is located in Dornheim, and is a leading entrepreneurial center, providing much of the light industry and commerce that forms the backbone of the entire continent's economic structure. Surrounded by vast swatches of meadows and grassland cleared over the centuries, Dornheim is a major agricultural base for the planet as well.

Nebensee

Set to the far west, Nebensee extends across the equator of Ritter making much of the continent very hot year round. Deserts occupy over half the continent, with jungles covering the rest. As a result much of the population and industry remain along the coasts, boasting large commercial and fishing fleets. The state capital of Nebensee is Neu Osis and hosts the Space Academy for the Ritter Space Navy. With their location along the equator, Nebensee also maintains two large spaceports and the planet's busiest space elevator.

Schwarzenwald

Schwarzenwald, to the south, is the most temperate of the continents on Ritter as it sits far from the planets equator. Its large forests provide the majority of wood for the planet and are home too much of Ritter's heavy industry as well. Several large hunting preserves are maintained throughout the state and are favored vacation spots for many Ritter.

Weisburg

To the north, Weisburg is still covered by large primordial jungles and several active volcanoes throughout its massive mountain ranges. With very little industry to speak of, the people of Weisburg, mostly miners, have the highest military enrollment of any of the other Ritter states.

Government

In 2074 after years of heavy unemployment and recession, then President Pav Van Hidenbor appointed Ansel Kiefer Chancellor of Ritter in a bid to appease Kiefer's political party and avoid a potential uprising. Two years later, Hidenbor was dead and Kiefer combined the powers of the president and the chancellor, confirming his place as the sole leader of the Ritter. All power was centralized to Chancellor Kiefer, who set about restoring economic stability through heavy military spending and public infrastructure projects. With the discovery of the Adonese in 2080, Kiefer used their appearance to further push for the need of a massive arms build-up, eventually leading to the Boreas Accord Wars of 2110.

Since that time the position of Chancellor has remained a lifetime appointment, with each Chancellor selecting their own replacement. The current Chancellor of the republic is Ulan Albresch who has maintained the Ritter's penchant for military spending, citing the need to secure its borders with the Adonese, the Malvernians, and the Rach, all of whom have "attacked" the Ritter at one time or another.

Society

The Ritter are very fond of rank and titles and have maintained their lines of nobility and peerage over the centuries. While offering no real power in the modern government, being able to claim noble blood does provide privileges not available to the common Ritter.

While military service is not required, a person wishing to serve in public office must serve in the military for at least one term. Also, if not born of noble "blood", receiving a commission in the military grants an automatic "patent of nobility" along with the title of Esquire, resulting in the Ritter military academies being flooded with applications every year and to be chosen is an honor in itself.

Of note is the Law of Ascension, a leftover from the early days of the Ritter that still exists as part of the military's Code of Law. An ordinary citizen may, at their own expense, raise a levy of troops and assume the rank and title appropriate to the size of the force they command. Today, the cost to equip and maintain a modern unit is prohibitive for most, but several company-sized units do exist.

Military
The Army of the Republic of Ritterlich

The army of the republic is unique in the fact they have de-centralized the field-level command and control of their military forces, placing a greater emphasis on training at the brigade level and allowing these commanders to maneuver on their own when they see the opportunity to advance. While this can lead to a unit being cut off, it also allows for a hard-hitting unit to exploit a break through and ravage an enemy's rear area.

Larger operation requiring more than one brigade group are organized as a corps, with one leader being assigned to command all of the land and space assets being deployed. While the Ritter was one of the last to adopt the CAV into service, primarily relying on tanks and infantry fighting vehicles, their concept of "point of the spear" was a natural fit once they began fielding CAVs. Most modern armies tend to form a battle line, maximizing coverage and a layered defense. The Ritter, however concentrates their force into a column, putting pressure on a single point in the enemies line, providing for local superiority and the greatest opportunity for a potential break through.

Of course this style of combat has its drawbacks, notably in the ability of a brigade to operate effectively on defense and the lack of real combat experience for senior officers commanding larger forces.

A typical Ritterlich brigade consists of two infantry regiments, two armored/CAV regiments, and a support regiment consisting of an artillery and combat engineer battalion, a headquarters and medical company, two aviation squadrons, and a military police platoon.

The Grand Fleet

The Grand Fleet boasts the largest concentration of warships in the known galaxy. While centralized in the Ritter system, the Grand Fleet is made up of several task forces, containing a number of task groups built around an assault carrier. Each carrier provides support to an entire aerospace wing and two brigade groups, with the dropships needed to transport them. The Ritter have excelled in "carrier diplomacy" to express their displeasure at a perceived slight.

The Ritterlich Republic Force Ranks

Army (enlisted)
- Soldat
- Senior Soldat
- Exempted Soldat
- Senior Exempted Soldat
- Staff Exempted Soldat
- Subordinate
- Junior Field Guide
- Field Guide
- Staff Field Guide
- Senior Field Guide

Army (officer)
- Leutnant
- Senior Leutnant
- Hauptmann
- Major
- Colonel
- Brigadier
- Senior Brigadier

INFANTRY
Powered Armor (panzertruppen)
SG44 Assault Rifle
1st Nebensee Brigade
The Ritterlich Republic

Force Structure *(all model types)*
- **Brigade** *(5 regiments, brigadier)*
- **Korps** *(2+ brigades, senior brigadier)*
- **Army of the Ritterlich Republic** *(supreme commander)*

Infantry
- **Gruppe** *(one model)*
  Infantry *(soldat x4, exempted soldat subordinate)*
  Powered *(soldat x3, exempted soldat, subordinate)*
- **Zug** *(one squad)*
  Gruppe x6 *(junior field guide, leutnant)*
- **Kompanie**
  Zug x4 *(field guide, hauptmann)*
- **Bataillon**
  Kompanie x4 *(staff field guide, major)*
- **Regiment**
  Bataillon x4 *(senior field guide, colonel)*

Combat Vehicle
- **Panzer** *(one model)*
  Crew *(subordinate)*
- **Schutzenzug** *(one squad)*
  Panzer x4 *(junior field guide, leutnant)*
- **Schwadron**
  Schutzenzug x4 *(field guide. hauptmann)*
- **Abteilung**
  Schwadron x4 *(staff field guide, major)*
- **Regiment**
  Abteilung x4 *(senior field guide, colonel)*

Aircraft
- **Flugzeug** *(one model)*
  Pilot/Crew *(field guide)*
- **Schwarm** *(one squad)*
  Flugzeug x2 *(staff field guide, leutnant)*
- **Staffel**
  Schwarm x4 *(senior field guide, hauptmann)*

Combat Assault Vehicle (CAV)
- **Sturmpanzer** *(one model)*
  Crew *(subordinate)*
- **Schutzentrupp** *(one squad)*
  Sturmpanzer x4 *(junior field guide, leutnant)*
- **Schwadron**
  Schutzentrupp x4 *(field guide, hauptmann)*
- **Abteilung**
  Schwadron x4 *(staff field guide, major)*
- **Regiment**
  Abteilung x4 *(senior field guide, colonel)*

TACTICAL BRIEFINGS

Selected Ritterlich Units

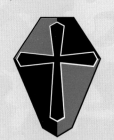

1st Schwarzenwald Brigade
Protectors of Honor
Commander: Brigadier Mataus Yamorino
Brigade Headquarters: Ritter

A core Ritterlich unit, the 1st Schwarzenwald has seen action in every conflict since the founding of the Republic. Their honorable treatment of prisoners of war is known galaxy wide and exemplifies their status as professional soldiers.

3rd Schwarzenwald Brigade
The Blood Eagles
Commander: Brigadier Tanz Wilbeck
Brigade Headquarters: Kruger

The 3rd dates back to the early days of the Republic and have a reputation for painting swatches of blood across their fighting machines before a battle. They are currently stationed on Kruger where they recently put down a rebellion by the local government and remain on alert to support Republic officials as they sort out the remaining troublemakers from the survivors.

1st Nebensee Brigade
The Huntsmen
Commander: Brigadier Kaavine Vilhelmz
Brigade Headquarters: Dekatoo

The 1st Nebensee was reactivated in 2260 as a deep strike force to drop behind enemy lines and destroy command and communication centers.

The unit is currently on Dekatoo for rest and refit but there are rumors they may soon be redeployed for a mission outside Ritterlich borders.

EMBLEM
Tactical
Armed Forces
The Ritterlich Republic

3rd Weisburg Brigade
The Hydra
Commander: Brigadier Janus Burnz
Brigade Headquarters: Barren

The 3rd Weisburg is a fast-attack unit made up of light CAVs and combat vehicles. They received their nickname due to their ability to quickly fill in their lines with another unit should one be destroyed. They are currently garrisoned on Barren to help keep a watchful eye on the Malvernians.

The Ritterlich Republic Faction Doctrines

Superior Tactics Doctrine
The Hunter's Edge

With their uncanny ability to anticipate the actions of an enemy commander, the Ritter always seem to be one step ahead.

Game Rules: *Once per turn, a Ritter force group commander may select the initiative card that was just turned over and send it to the bottom of the deck.*

Lightning Warfare Doctrine
Blitzkrieg

Ritter commanders spend their entire career training to fight while "on the move", exploiting any weakness the enemy may show.

Game Rules: *Every non-infantry model will receive the SA: Assault +1 at no additional TVP cost.*

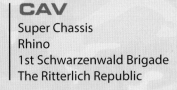

CAV
Super Chassis
Rhino
1st Schwarzenwald Brigade
The Ritterlich Republic

The Empire of Malvernis

Background
In the Beginning

Perhaps the "most alien" of any race in the galaxy, the majority of Malvernians are Khardullians, a religious sect that has become so interwoven with the government that today they are the one and the same. The church, along with its servants the Dark Brotherhood, sets forth the doctrines and decrees that control nearly every facet of the day to day lives of the average Malvernian, hoping to receive the holy blessing of Khardullis so they may one day take their rightful place in the afterlife at his side.

It is unknown when the prophet Khardullis first appeared before the Malvernians on their home world of Capella, bringing with him the teachings of "the creator", warning that those who did not accept the way of the Creator would be "lost", their souls condemned to eternal damnation. Khardullis and his most devout followers, referred to as the Brotherhood, spread out across Capella to preach "the way". One, young Malvernian Marston, a stone-shaper by trade, was particularly moved to take up the "crooked cross", joining the brotherhood and quickly became part of Khardullis's inner circle and his most trusted follower.

During his lifetime, Khardullis seemed content to take the long route, secure in the knowledge that any who heard his divine message would someday embrace "the way". As he lay on his death bed, surrounded by those closest to him, he spoke his final words: "I go now to take my place with the creator. I will wait there for all those that have heeded the word, to share the blessing and to introduce them to the almighty. I leave you to carry on that message, to find the souls of the lost and bring them to the light."

The Crusades

With the ascension of Khardullis, Marston, a gifted diplomat, convinced the others of the Brotherhood that in order to carry out the last wishes of the prophet, new methods would be required; setting forth a series of moves that would culminate with the First Crusade. For the next 400 years, Capella was plunged into a holy war as the first Inquistors, wearing their signature black robes and bearing the crooked Blade of Khardullis, set out to convert the rest of Capella to the "one way", by choice or by force, alive or dead.

Marston set forth to build the first Khardullian church, selecting the capital city of Alaghax for its location. Acting as chief architect, Marston oversaw the construction of the massive cathedral of Khardullis. With its completion, the Brotherhood named Marston Grand Inquisitor, carving the infamous Onyx Throne himself , a symbol of his exalted office and the power of the church, overseeing the start of a dynasty

that remains through today.

First Contact

As a race, the Malvernians are engineering masters, unmatched in their ability to work under the surface of a world, extracting the raw materials needed to keep up with a population base that far outpaces the rest of the galaxy. With Capella lacking many of the heavy metals needed for an advance technological base, their first forays into nearby space were simply to mine the resources they required. With the acquisition of interstellar travel, they quickly set to establishing large mining collectives in neighboring systems, stripping a world of its resources to be transported back to Capella Prime.

The system of Syrma was one such project; containing several uninhabited metal/silicate rocky planets, the Malvernians had built massive underground facilities on the worlds to house the thousands of miners working to extract the metals and minerals they had found there. It was here that the Ritter first encountered the Malvernians, who for the most part seemed uninterested in their arrival and unable to come to any type of understanding with these "aliens" the Ritter left. While the Malvernian miners paid little concern to these "creatures", intent on maintaining their high quotas, the arrival and subsequent departure by the Ritter certainly didn't go unnoticed. The High Inquisitor of Syrma set out on the next ore shipment to personally make his report to the Dark Brotherhood, as they were now known since the end of the crusades.

The discovery of another race of beings implied that the Malvernians might not be that "special" after all, possibly providing the impetus for their followers to question the church and those who represented it. The scholars of the church raced to explain how these new beings fit within the word of Khardullis and his teachings, leading to the Dark Brotherhood to impose an "interdiction" in an attempt to keep word from spreading to the masses. Any talk of these "aliens" was strictly forbidden and any further contact was to be avoided at all costs.

As it became more and more evident that other races, beside the Ritter, may also exist throughout the stars, the Grand Inquisitor at that time issued a "fatwa", detailing how Khardullis had spoken of "others".

"If parents have a child and later decide to have a second one, is that second child any less special? So too if the Creator decides to bring life to another world, and then another, and another. It doesn't make us less special."

The church explained that the Creator had revealed these other "children" as the time had come for them to learn of "the way" and it was the sacred duty of the church to show these "others" the path to their salvation.

The decision of the church to establish diplomatic relations with the Adonese in late 2110, led the Ritter, fearful of the two forming any sort of an alliance, to launch a preemptive attack on the Malvernian colony on Lir, bringing them into the Boreas Accord Wars in 2112. With the Rach invasion of Spica and its surrounding systems in 2165 and again in 2170, the Malvernian's introduction of Khardullis and "the way" to the rest of the galaxy was off to a rough start.

Geography

Capella is an ocean world with no moon, a single continent accounting for the planet's only land mass of note, covering approximately 10 percent of the planet's surface. Malvernix is a binary star system, with two yellow suns that keep the atmosphere super-heated, providing for violent storms throughout the year. Over the centuries the capital city of Alaghax has expanded to cover much of the continent, forming one continuous megalopolis from coast to coast. The rest of the planet's population lives in an immense network of connecting underground tunnels that sprawl throughout the planet's crust and the large, floating cities (the Aquapolis) that travel across Capella's black-watered oceans providing the majority of food for the planet's population.

Capella's only orbital lift elevator, the Black Needle, sits within the Tania District on the southern coast, near to the planet's equator.

Government

Malvernis is a theocracy, the church and the government having long since become one central body and is overseen by the Dark Brotherhood's High Inquisitors. Answering only to the Grand Inquisitor the Dark Brotherhood administers the day to day activities of the empire, setting its laws, collecting the tithes that support it, and maintaining the government bureaucracy through the legions of Prelates of the various holy orders that enforce their wishes.

The Grand Inquisitor, the living embodiment of Khardullis and the Creator here on Capella, holds his position for life and his true identity is known to only to a very few of his most trusted advisors. When seen in public, he wears a black armored suit and robe, covered from head to toe, surrounded by his military guard the Onyx Fist.

Society

The day to day life of the average Malvernian centers on their faith and making the Empire stronger. The Prelates make sure that the faithful adhere to the tenets of the church, making the tithes required by their social standing. Those not of the faith are typically treated as second-class citizens and closely watched for any signs of heresy.

The Khardullian church frowns on female Malvernians of age being seen outside the home. They are expected to marry, provide for their mate and produce as many offspring as possible. In recent years a group known as the Shining Sisterhood has worked to change this view, leading to the arrest of several of their leaders and being sent to reeducation camps for hypnotherapy to correct their apostasy.

As master engineers, the Malvernians have produced a system of surveying and mining second to none. Their experience with hostile environments and their own physiology have allowed them to inhabit systems that no one else would want, expanding at a rapid rate across the galaxy. The Cy-Bots, articulated work platforms built by the Malvernians to protect their workers from pirates and local fauna, are considered by many as the precursor to the modern CAV. Their ability to extract resources has carried over to their industry and manufacturing arms as well, fueling the meteoritic rise of Mark IV Industries and Grundor House Manufacturing, both companies having become major players in intergalactic trade.

Military

The Grand Army of the Empire of Malvernis is led by the Seraphim Council, an order within the Dark Brotherhood of High Inquisitors responsible for the military. Most Malvernian soldiers are conscripts inducted to the armed forces upon reaching their fourteenth life cycle, remaining in the military for the remainder of their lives. Death while serving Khardullis and the creator is said to guarantee entry to the blessed afterlife. Due to the Malvernian emphasis on child-bearing, the Malvernian army is the largest standing force in the galaxy, the majority of them light infantry.

The Blade of Khardullis, based upon the crooked walking stick the prophet used, is part of every Malvernian unit. Vicars, responsible for ensuring the loyalty of the troops, all carry the Blade of Khardullis as symbols of their authority.

Malvernis Force Ranks

Army (Enlisted)
- Apatis (private)
- Dathapatis (corporal)
- Satapatis (sergeant)
- Hazarapatis (pilot)

Army (Special)
- Vicar
- Master Vicar
- Supreme Vicar

Army (Officer)
- Sub-Commander (lieutenant)
- Commander (captain)
- Wing Commander (major)
- Force Commander (colonel)
- Genarix (general)
- High Genarix (general of the army)
- District Commander

Force Structure (all model types)
- **Army** (10 regiments, genarix, master vicar)
- **The Grand Army of Malvernis** (high genarix, supreme vicar)
- **Myriax** (district commander)
- **Seraphim Council** (high inquisitor)
- **Grand Inquisitor**

Infantry
- **Section** (one model)
  Infantry (apatis x8, datapatis, satapatis)
  Powered (apatis x3, datapatis, satapatis)
- **Platoon** (one squad)
  Infantry (Section x10, satapatis 1st, sub-commander)
  Powered (Section x6, satapatis 1st, sub-commander)
- **Company**
  Platoon x5 (satapatis 2nd, commander)
- **Regiment**
  Company x5 (satapatis 3rd, force commander, vicar)

Combat Vehicle
- **Vehicle** (one model)
  Crew (satapatis)
- **Platoon** (one squad)
  Vehicle x5 (satapatis 1st, sub-commander)
- **Company**
  Platoon x5 (satapatis 2nd, commander)
- **Regiment**
  Company x5 (satapatis 3rd, force commander, vicar)

Aircraft
- **Craft** (one model)
  Pilot/Crew (hazarapatis)
- **Section** (one squad)
  Craft x2 (hazarapatis 1st)
- **Wing**
  Section x5 (wing commander)
- **Squadron**
  Wing x5 (force commander, vicar)

Combat Vehicle
- **CAV** (one model)
  Pilot/Crew (hazarapatis)
- **Platoon** (one squad)
  CAV x5 (hazarapatis 1st, sub-commander)
- **Company**
  Platoon x5 (hazarapatis 2nd, commander)
- **Regiment**
  Company x5 (hazarapatis 3rd, force cmdr, vicar)

Selected Malvernis Units

1st Regiment
The High Guard
Commander:
Force Commander Mangu Timar
Regiment Headquarters: Capella

The High Guard is responsible for protecting the Grand Inquisitor and the Malvernis home world. Only the most experienced warriors are assigned to the 1st Regiment and many current High Inquisitors have served as the unit's commander through the years.

INFANTRY
Powered Armor
FA-45 Assault Rifle
165th Assault Regiment
"Heavy Mag"
The Empire of Malvernis

2nd Regiment
The Black Guard
Commander:
Supreme Vicar Ilkahn Daxon
Regiment Headquarters: Capella

The 2nd Regiment is a military force in name only, serving as the strong arm of the Malvernis Secret Police, the Brotherhood of Silence. Fear and intimidation are their weapons of choice as they seek out the enemies of the Khardullan Church.

77th Regiment
Black Lightning
Commander:
Force Commander Karaan Kothmore
Regiment Headquarters: Spica

Known for quick and decisive strikes against the enemies of Malvernis, the 77th is commonly found policing surrounding systems against pirates. The unit recently saw action on the independent world of Laredo to punish the local population for their treatment of Khardullan missionaries.

165th Assault Regiment
Heavy Mag
Commander:
Force Commander Lorac Geng
Regiment Headquarters: Tania

As planetary assaults became more common, the Seraphim Council developed the assault regiments to lead the attack and pave the way for follow-up troops. Primarily made up of heavy CAVs and powered armored infantry, the 165th is very effective in the use of sheer weight and brute force to break the will of enemy defenders.

The Empire of Malvernis Faction Doctrines

Fanaticism Doctrine
The Hammer of Khardullis
During battle, followers of Khardullis have been known to commit "martyrdom", sacrificing themselves in a last-ditch attack to cause as much damage as possible before dying.

Game Rules: *The Hammer of Khardullis allows any non-infantry model to "sacrifice" itself (removed from play), regardless of its current damage track, in an attempt to destroy an enemy model in one last desperate attack.*

A variant of salvo fire, a player using the Hammer of Khardullis attack may use any direct-fire weapon system (including guided missiles, provided an existing target-lock/TAG is available) as part of the ranged assault and will make a combat roll for EACH weapon system being used.

The player will designate one weapon system as the primary attack weapon, using its RAV and any SAs for the ranged assault, adding a +1 situation modifier for each additional weapon being used. When determining range, a Hammer of Khardullis attack uses the shortest range band from the weapon system's being fired.

Example: *An Assassin CAV firing both medium MACs and its light guided missile at a target as part of a Hammer of Khardullis attack would make three combat rolls, each receiving a +2 situation modifier (in addition to any others applicable ones) for the salvo fire bonus. Upon completion of the attack, the Assassin is removed from play.*

Conscription Doctrine
Defense Force Militia
A Malvernian male can be called up for military service at any time. As a result it is common for force commanders to activate additional troops from planetary militias to bolster their regular troop strength before a battle.

Game Rules: *Each Malvernian infantry or mechanized infantry squad will receive two additional infantry models (of the same type) for free (no additional TVP cost), regardless of normal squad limitations.*

Optional upgrades and transport must be purchased separately.

CAV
Super Chassis
Revenant
77th Regiment
"Black Lightning"
The Empire of Malvernis

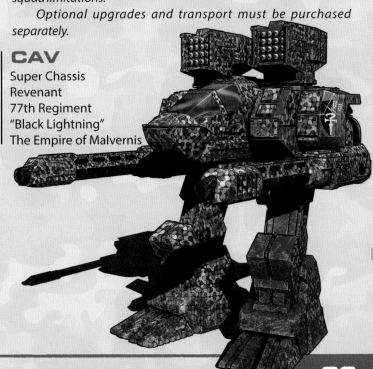

The Greater Empire of the Rach

Background
The Children of the Storm

In the Book of Omens, the Rach's primary religious text, it is said that that Tharett Ka, the god of lightning, created the first one-thousand souls from the great storm at the dawn of time, decreeing they would war until only 100 remained, purifying the bloodlines by sword and flame, establishing the 100 clans of the "Children of the Storm" that would one day rule the galaxy.

The Season of the Storms

Konta, leader of the Dakan tribe, was the first to seize power over all the clans, becoming Kaharach (emperor) and establishing the Gonsai Kahaban, (the center of the empire) in the new capital city of Mygar on the Rach's home world of Mohr. To ensure only the strongest would rule in the future, Konta established that upon his death, the clans would gather on the fields outside Mygar, sending forth their champions to battle for the right to be the next Kaharach, bringing glory and wealth to the winner's clan, a time that would become known as the season of the storms.

The Rach have never known peace, the only word in the Rach language for it is also the same word for "weak", fighting amongst themselves to settle any dispute. By the time of Kaharach Yonga and their first foray into space, the discovery of each new world would result in the Toza (the choosing), as clans would compete for the honor to rule the world in the name of the Kaharach, receiving a share of the taxes and tribute paid each year.

First Contact

With the discovery of the Adonese and Ritter in 2144, the Rach wasted no time in launching a series of attacks, hitting a dozen worlds at once, killing any non-Rach they encountered. Over the next sixteen years the Imperial Wars claimed the lives of millions from every side, eventually even causing the Rach to give pause at the casualties the fighting had inflicted upon the children of the storm. The current Kaharach, Gharl the Evenhanded, allowed the envoys of the Adonese and Ritter to travel to the Rach world of Aeneas in 2161, negotiating a truce that ended the current fighting. While the Rach were allowed to keep the worlds they had conquered, any surviving non-Rach were allowed to leave in peace.

The Spica and Vela Wars

To say the Rach came to "respect" the Adonese and Ritter would be a major over-statement, but they certainly learned the ritualized combat they had known for centuries did not translate to the unrestrained war they had experienced with the two alien races. The technology used by both were generations ahead of the Rach, who depended more on dependability and ease of repair, two characteristics that rarely go hand in hand with hi-tech. This realization forced the Rach to give these other races a wide berth, to at least tolerate those they saw not as equals but as "not-prey".

With the eventual discovery of the Malvernians and the Terrans though, the Rach found two races they could "bully" around and if not for the eventual intervention on behalf of both races by the Adonese, would no longer exist in any real fashion.

The "Modern" Rach

By 2274, while the Rach have matured as a race, learning to control the urge to attack at every instance, they have no allies and remain aggressive towards all of the other races of the galaxy. A state of war still exists between them and the Terrans, frequently marked by border clashes and incursions by both sides into each other's territory. Even the Adonese seem content to keep the status quo as is as it keeps the main focus of the Rach away from everyone else.

Rach technology and industry has raced to catch up, led by Koda Works, the empire's largest manufacturer. In a rather strange turn of events, Rach equipment is a favorite among mercenary companies and other independent worlds and organizations. Their lower cost and ease of use, with the dependability and reparability that Rach manufacturers have become famous for, along with a merchant caste all too eager to trade for other race's technology, has created a ready-market for their use.

Geography

Mohr, the second planet from the systems star, is the birthplace of the Rach. A planet with two moons, Vhas and Mydean, is a subtropical steppe world with major volcanic activity along the equator, a result of the planet's fast rotation, producing constant lightning storms throughout the year. Giving way to dense jungles, filled with deadly flora and fauna before opening up to the shortgrass plains that dominate the far northern and southern hemispheres. There are no oceans, but approximately 30% of the planet is covered by large, deep seas that rise and fall with the passing of Mohr's moons.

Government

The Kaharach rules supreme, overseeing the Ongban (chieftain) of each clan and the Imperial Council. Every clan must maintain a holding within the capital city, providing "hostages" to ensure their continued loyalty and discourage any thought of revolt, at least in practice.

The Imperial Council includes representatives from each of the one-hundred tribes, overseeing the bureaucracy and establishing the laws of the empire, with the Kaharach having final say over all matters.

The Rach enforce a three-tier caste system that defines all Rach by their occupation, maintained by a hereditary system that sees very little crossover. The first tier include those in the ruling or priestly classes, followed by the second tier with those connected with the military and war-related pursuits, with the third tier focused on production, agriculture, craft, and commerce. The crossing between castes is very, very rare

Society

Fortunately for the rest of the galaxy, only about 25 percent of the Rach population belongs to the warrior caste. While all Rach are aggressive by nature, physically imposing and possessing a morbid personality, the majority of those outside the warrior caste are more tolerant of other races. While as a race the Rach remain anti-social, they have begrudgingly come to acknowledge the right of existence by the other races. While it is uncommon to see a Rach outside their own holdings, more and more Rach have been leaving the empire, seeking to fight with one of the many mercenary companies in existence. They are favored by unit commanders because many seek no remuneration for their services, seeking only to fight.

Military

There is no organized military like those found in other star-nations. Each clan's warrior caste fights until they die. Older clan warriors eventually end up as Moguk Rann, berserkers in the infantry charging across the field, seeking honorable death in battle at last.

While each clan's Ongban can seek battle on their own accord, challenging other Rach or the other races of the galaxy as they see fit, it is the wise Ongban that first seeks the approval of the Kaharach before setting the empire on a path of galactic war.

Rach Force Ranks
Army (enlisted)
- Hun *(warrior)*
- Nurhun *(exalted warrior)*
- Tuhun *(first warrior)*
- Khun *(high warrior)*
- Nurkhun *(exalted high warrior)*
- Metkhun *(leader of warriors)*

Army (officer)
- Koan (leader of leaders)
- Saikoan (second leader of leaders)
- Tukoan (first leader of leaders)
- Nurkoan (exalted leader of leaders)
- Tchaikoan (superior leader of leaders)
- Metkoan (supreme leader of leaders)
- Ongban (clan chieftain)
- Kaharach (emperor)

Force Structure *(all model types)*
- **Regiment** (five battalions, nurkoan)
- **Division** (4-6 regiments, tchaikoan)
- **Corps** (2-8 divisions, metkoan)
- **Army** (ongban)

EMBLEM
Tactical
Armed Forces
The Greater Empire of the Rach

The Rach tactical emblem is a stylized rendition of the twin-bladed Scisk, an ancient weapon said to be used by the first Kaharach to kill his opponents in single combat.

Camouflage is rarely used by the Rach, favoring garish colors and designs when going into battle. ∎

Infantry

- **Ong** (one model)
  Infantry (hun x4, nurhun, tuhun)
  Powered (hun x4, nurhun, tuhun)
- **Platoon** (one squad)
  Ong x5 (khun, koan)
- **Company**
  Platoon x4 (nurkhun, saikoan)
- **Battalion**
  Company x4 (metkhun, tukoan)

Combat Vehicle

- **Vehicle** (one model)
  Crew (tuhun)
- **Troop** (one squad)
  Vehicle x4 (khun, koan)
- **Armored Squadron**
  Troop x5 (nurkhun, saikoan)
- **Battalion**
  Armored Squadron x5 (metkhun, tukoan)

Aircraft

- **Craft** (one model)
  Pilot/Crew (tuhun)
- **Flight** (one squad)
  Craft x2 (khun)
- **Wing**
  Flight x4 (nurkhun, saikoan)
- **Flight Squadron**
  Wing x6 (metkhun, tukoan)

Combat Assault Vehicle (CAV)

- **CAV** (one model)
  Pilot/Crew (tuhun)
- **Troop** (one squad)
  CAV x4 (khun, koan)
- **CAV Squadron**
  Troop x5 (nurkhun, saikoan)
- **Battalion**
  Squadron x5 (metkhun, tukoan)

Selected Rach Units

The Kharlong Division
Talons of the Kharl
Commander: Tchaikoan Korakh
Division Headquaters: Mohr

The Kharlong are the Kaharach's personal bodyguard as well as overseeing the security of the Imperial Palace. Many of its members are former Ongbak winners, gladiatorial games fought by the Rach each year, who have pledged their undying loyalty and service to the emperor.

While the majority of the division remains on Mohr with the Kaharach, one or more regiments are frequently dispatched to a current "hot spot" to help maintain their combat readiness.

The Detra Tr'Vast Regiment
The Destroyer of Worlds
Commander: Nurkoan Temur
Regiment Headquarters: Hellspire

Hellspire is a Terran desert planet attacked by the Rach nearly a decade ago and has become the focal point of fighting between the two star-nations as they both seek to oust the other from the planet.

The regiment is based on the world's southern hemisphere at an abandoned mining facility and are part of the Qarak clan.

The Army of Dakan Kharl
The Gatherer of Souls
Commander: Ongban Kagak
Army Headquarters: Dakan

As the current Kaharach Varaak is a Dakan, the clan is allowed to add "kharl" as an honorific to their units as the imperial bloodline clan. The clan has won the Ongbak 21 times, including the last three years.

Dakan infantry units have a reputation for brutality and a bloodlust that even other Rach fear in battle.

INFANTRY

Powered Armor
TX-4 Light Machine Gun
The Fakk Tr'Khul Regiment
"The Blood of Heros"
The Greater Empire
of the Rach

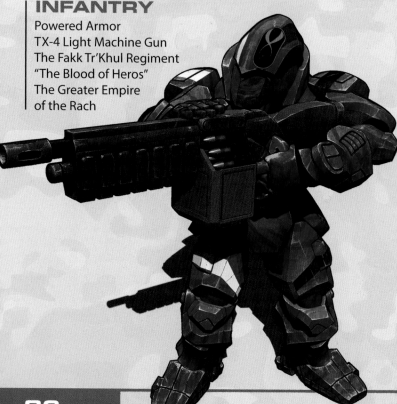

TACTICAL BRIEFINGS

The Army of Ong Moguk Rann
Talons of the Moguk Rann
Commander: Ongban Mongke
Army Headquarters: Moguk

The Moguk Rann clan is one of the strongest clans in the Rach empire with several holdings along the Terran-Rach border. Members of the clan have won the Ongbak 34 times since its inception.

The Fakk Tr'Khul Regiment
The Blood of Heros
Commander: Nurkoan Mok
Regiment Headquarters: Martuth

The Fakk Tr'Khul are part of the Grakan clan and have been on Martuth for the last year, undertaking several raids across the border against the Terran world of Vega.

The Greater Empire of the Rach Faction Doctrines

Children of the Storm Doctrine
Storm Strike

Rach warriors favor close-in fighting, sacrificing defense in an effort to overwhelm their opponent and take them out in one devastating blow.

Game Rules: *Non-infantry Rach models conducting a ranged assault at point-blank range receive a (+2) situation modifier to their attack instead of the normal (+1).*

Storm Winds

In an effort to get in close as fast as possible, the Rach will override the safeties on their machine's breeder in an effort to increase their maximum speed.

Game Rules: *In addition, all non-infantry Rach models will reduce their armor values by (-1) and increase their base movement value by (+2).*

No Mercy Doctrine
Berserker

Rach that have become too old to pilot a CAV or other combat craft typically finish their time as a warrior in the infantry. These veteran troops will close with an enemy, attacking with abandoned frenzy as they seek an honorable death in combat.

Game Rules: *Rach infantry models acting as the primary attacker in a close-combat assault will do one additional point of damage on any successful attack.*

CAV
Extra-Large Chassis
Dictator-B
The Dakan Kharl Army
"The Gatherer of Souls"
The Greater Empire of the Rach

BRIEFING

Date: November 14, 2274

To: Hellspire Operations Command

From: Office of Naval Intelligence (ONI)

Subject: Recent Rach Troop Movements

The recent events in Martuth and the surrounding systems indicate a build up of Rach military units with the intention of launching a major assault very soon.

It is imperative that we direct all available resources to the area to learn their final objectives at any cost. Any mission allows for acceptable collateral damage and personnel losses. ∎

The United Terran Federation

Background
Era of Strife

By 2034 the Earth nation of China, recently completing its reunification with the break-away province of Taiwan, turned their attention towards India, having recently become the world's most populous country. With a younger population and an even faster growing economy, the Indians had begun a massive program to modernize its armed forces, a move that China took as a serious threat to their domination of the region. Unwilling to allow the power gap to equalize, China launched a series of offensive strikes along their shared border areas, hitting Indian army and air bases while simultaneously striking their naval assets from submarines in the Bay of Bengal.

The surprise attack forced the Japanese to intervene, having signed a treaty of mutual defense with New Delhi in 2031. With their new treaty and having acquired a nuclear capability of their own earlier, the United States had felt Japan would be a sufficient deterrence to any Chinese aggression and had withdrawn all of their forces in Japan in 2032. The Chinese, for their part, had gambled the Americans would not intervene as they had become increasingly isolationist since their withdrawal from the Middle East and Afghanistan a decade earlier. Begrudgingly the United States finally entered the war against China, drawing in their Pacific allies, Australia and the Philippines, with the addition of Canada, Britain, and Poland, the only three who choose to honor their commitment to NATO.

Russia, long embroiled in a proxy war in Ukraine used the conflict and a seemingly broken NATO to broaden their efforts in Eastern Europe. Agreeing to secure China from the north, Russia increased the flow of materials and military hardware to the Chinese as well as providing a limited number of personnel to fly fighter jets and armed drones for them. While no formal war is declared in Europe, hostilities increase between Russia and several former NATO/EU countries.

Each combatant remains all too aware that the use of nuclear weapons would result in mutual destruction and refrain from their use, limiting the scope of the conflict and preventing a full mobilization of human and material resources.

Against this backdrop of conflict, social unrest in the United States had continued to escalate. By 2054 large riots had become common across the country, forcing the nation to attempt to confiscate privately owned weapons and nationalize the companies that manufactured them. This results in a full rebellion in several portions of the country and pulling back of American military forces fighting overseas to help stabilize the turmoil at home. Fearful of being cut off without the American's aid, other nations begin draw-downs as well, leading to the final collapse of India and a wind down of hostilities in the region.

The returning military units in the United States, disillusioned by their sudden withdrawal from the Asian campaign, disregarded orders by the central government to put down the rebellions of their fellow citizens. Entire divisions mutinied and within a few months of their return, the United States had ceased to exist as one nation.

With the loss of the United States as a stabilizing force in the world, the United Nations made a last ditch appeal to the world to end the strife but fell to the madness that had engulfed the world when unknown terrorists destroyed their New York City headquarters, killing the majority of the ambassadors that had remained at their posts. The last half of the 21st century saw a level of destruction never before seen as religious, cultural, and political groups across the world no longer feared the consequences of their actions and sought to right every perceived wrong from the last two hundred years.

Voyage into Space

With the beginning of a new century, the world had seen a

massive realignment of borders and power as many of Earth's old nations had ceased to exist. Russia and China were the only remaining superpowers on the planet and used their influence to help found the Terran Exploration and Research Administration (TERA). Along with France, the New Republic of Texas, the Southern Atlantic Cooperative, and several major corporations from other remaining nations, TERA set forth to build a new space station in orbit around Earth. This new station allowed for the establishment of permanent research stations on the Moon and Mars and the human discovery of the Compression Drive in 2140. Over the next decade, humans had built new colonies on worlds in the Alpha Centauri, JOC 45, and Dorado star systems followed by Cetus, JB89D, and Vela in 2153.

First Contact

The new colony of Vela was a joint venture between the Republic of Texas and Australia's Citapol Communications Corp, as they sought to build a series of radio telescopes to explore further into the space beyond. The Rach stumbled across the humans in 2174, razing the colony, killing every human on the world in the process before moving on to the nearby system, JB89D (known as "Jeb" by its inhabitants) and destroying the science outpost there.

The Vela Wars (2176-2189)

As word reached Earth of the destruction of the two outposts, TERA was tasked with building the planet's first purpose-built warships as troops were readied for transport to the front. The first human fleet entered the Vela system in 2179, destroying the Rach scout ships in the system and retaking the world. While victorious, casualties were high, the remaining ships fighting a delaying action in an effort to slow down the Rach, hoping to give Earth more time to prepare for the onslaught that would follow.

The first wave of Rach ships moved through Sol's heliosphere in 2181, unleashing a torrent of plasma fire as they bombarded Earth from afar, killing billions. Earth's newest warships, relying on technology they had salvaged from the Rach ships on Vela, and a handful of converted transports threw themselves at the attackers with a ferocity that surprised the Rach, forcing them to withdraw.

The Adonese had long been aware of the humans before their first steps into space, content to observe from afar, with several Adonese research teams secretly visiting the planet over the years to learn more about their history and civilization. Noting an increase of Rach activity and transmissions far from their own shared border, the Adonese had sent out their scout ships in an attempt to learn what they may be up too. Unfortunately for the humans, their discovery came too late to save the majority of Earth's population.

The destruction caused by the Rach forced the planet's

survivors to form a new single, unified government to organize a last ditch effort to stop the Rach's next attack. Meeting in an underground bunker, deep beneath the walls of the surviving fortress known as "Big D" in the Texas republic, representatives from across the world came together to form the United Terran Federation, selecting Sydney, Australia as the Federation's new capital and promoting General Curtis Ryan, a Texan, to lead the United Federal Forces. With the armed forces of every nation being transferred to the new Federal military command, General Ryan had to integrate a variety of military units into one cohesive force as quickly as possible. He chose the old Roman legion system to use as the basis for his new command, restructuring the troops according to the region they came from.

By late 2182 the Adonese had arrived on Terra and while they were unwilling to engage the Rach militarily, fearful of pushing the localized conflict into a much larger galactic war, they would provide the Terrans with advanced technology and advisors to train with. On June 8th, 2184 the Terrans met the Rach fleet at the Battle of Orion, surprising them en route to Terra. While suffering horrendous casualties of their own accord, the Terrans destroyed the majority of the fleet. With the war now on more even footing, technology wise, the fighting continued on but for the moment the human's home world was safe.

The Vela Accords (2189)

With the human victory in the Orion System, the Adonese reached out to the Rach to end the fighting, still fearful that the conflict could become a much larger, galaxy-wide event. With much of their own fleet destroyed and the war claiming more and more lives the Rach finally agreed to a cease-fire, provided the systems they had already conquered would remain theirs. The Vela Accords were signed on Adon in 2189, establishing a truce of sorts and setting the official border between Terran and Rach space.

To commemorate the millions of soldiers who had died during the fighting, the Federation reserved the First Legion "The Legion of the Lost", for their honored dead, their names added to the unit's roll-call list for perpetuity. As a monument to their memory, the Hall of the Lost was built in Rome, Italy.

The Templars

After the 1307 purge of the Knights Templar by the French King Philip IV, the surviving members of the order went into hiding, forming a secret society that focused on recruiting high-ranking government officials, leading scientists, and the heads of major financial and corporate institutions to their ranks over the next 900 years. This access and influence allowed the Templars to manipulate many of Earth's most important points in history to their benefit. With several of their own companies working as contractors for TERA as they developed the first human Compression Drive, the Templars were able to covertly

TACTICAL BRIEFINGS ////////////

build their own copy, using it to secretly send a ship to a system far rimward of Earth and establishing a colony they named Temple. Over the next forty years the Templars transferred a large number of their members to the new world while building the infrastructure that would be needed to support them as the established their own world order.

The arrival of the Rach set about a series of events that would reshape the Templar's core beliefs, creating a schism among the order as they debated on helping their former planet with these aliens. The largest of these factions, referring to themselves as Crusaders, were intent on leaving those on Earth to their own devices. It was only after the arrival of the Adonese that the Templar's revealed their existence to the rest of mankind, extending an offer to help in exchange for access to the new tech the Adonese had promised. With the signing of the Vela Accords the Templars provided much of the capital and resources needed by Terra to rebuild.

Terra Today

By 2274 the Terrans have remained in a state of war with the Rach for almost one hundred years. Constant border skirmishes and the occasional raid deeper into their own territory have required the humans to maintain a steady war footing. Weary from the constant fighting and rebuilding efforts, recruitment by the Terran Legions reached an all-time low by 2205. Then President Sabatini proposed the Marian Reforms of 2206, establishing a series of benefits that would elevate the soldiery in status and wealth above that of the average citizen. Seeing the reforms as a way to rise above the drudgery that had endured since the plasma bombardment the Terrans, many still living in refugee camps and bombed-out cities, signed up for the military in droves adding legion after legion to the Federal forces. This new class of citizen helped spur an economic boom that helped the planet as a whole rise from the ashes.

As the Terrans rebuilt, the focus on the new military organization by General Ryan provided inspiration for a new style of architecture that has been referred to as "Romanesque". Many buildings, especially those used by the government, have embraced this look with their many columns and white duracrete exteriors. A visitor to Terra today will find a world that has erased most of the scars left by the bombing and the environmental damage done long before the Rach ever arrived.

Government

With Australia escaping much of the destruction wrought by the Rach to the rest of the world, Sydney was selected to serve as the capital for the new central government. As part of this reorganization the planet was divided into dozens of self-governing districts that elected, by popular vote, their governing officials, including a senator for the People's Assembly. The People's Assembly is responsible for passing laws that affect the Federation as a whole as well as electing from their own ranks a new president every six years to lead in matters of state. Since other planets within the Federation are only allowed to send a single senator to the People's Assembly, Terra has maintained a strong voting bloc and considerable political power. This has led to resentment by several systems within the Federation who feel they are not receiving fair representation and a government body unresponsive to their problems.

Long before the arrival of the Rach, much of Terra had been moving towards a type of corporate capitalism as large hierarchical corporations had taken over much of the development of new technology and off-world expansion. Many corporations, in an attempt to acquire a cheap and willing labor force, sponsored the large-scale resettlement of populations, typically due to ethnic, political, or religious reasons, seeking the self-determination a new world offered, free from any outside interference.

As a result, after the bombing of Earth, many of these planets, especially those far away from the fighting, found themselves alone and cut off. By the time the new Federation reestablished contact with these systems, many of them had become self-sufficient enough that they chose not to join the new government. In fact, no other race has as many independent worlds within their borders as the humans.

An example of this arrangement is the desert world of Uakhet, the second planet in the Algoab star system. The VolenArc Mining Corp arranged for the transport of a large group of dissidents from Terra's middle-east region to Uakhet to mine super-silicates, a newly discovered compound used in the manufacture of duracrete. VolenArc abandoned the world after the first Rach attack on Vela, fearing an attack by the aliens there. Since that time the remaining miners have reimagined the world as a new "Egypt", complete with pyramids, temples, and obelisks right out of a holovid on ancient Egyptian culture. Under Pharoah Akhenka I and later his son, Atenmest, Uakhet has remained a sovereign world even as VolenArc has unsuccessfully tried to reclaim the planet, first through the Terran courts and later, a failed coup attempt by mercenaries in 2269.

Military

The legions of the United Federal Forces (UFF) are an all-volunteer force tasked with protecting the Federation and its members. Each district or planet (referred to as prefectures) is responsible for forming and maintaining at least one active legion at all times and keeping a ready reserve of ex-soldiers to form an additional legion in times of dire need. Unlike most militaries, the only soldiers to hold rank within the legions are those that do the actual fighting. Other support personnel (referred to as auxiliaries) are simply addressed by their job title, remaining in that position until they retire or join the fighting portion of the legion.

The UFF remains headquartered at the massive "Big D" fortress in the Texas Prefecture on Terra. Port Arthur, a planet within the York system serves as the UFF's main training and distribution center and is home of several corporations with long-standing contracts with the military. The planet Mars in the Sol system remains the Terran's primary shipyards.

While the 1st Legion remains a ceremonial unit, the 2nd through 10th Legions, known as the Praetorian Guards, are permanently stationed to Terra as a home defense force as well as the Fleet's Home Guard.

The Federation Fleet Marine Corps

The only other military force within the Federation is that of Fleet Command, operating outside the normal Legion structure and providing all air and space assets to the Federal forces.

The marine corps is assigned to defend the warships and installations of the fleet as well as serving as special forces for the entire military.

Federation Force Ranks

Army (enlisted)
- Legionnaire
- Second Legionnaire
- First Legionnaire
- Senior Legionnaire
- Centurion
- Second Centurion
- First Centurion
- Senior Centurion

Army (officer)
- Optus
- Primus
- Tribune
- Legate
- Prefect
- Legion Legate

Force Structure *(all model types)*
- **Legion** *(10 centuries, legate)*
- **Prefect** *(2+ legions, prefect)*
- **The United Federal Force Army** *(legion legate)*

Infantry
- **Hastati** *(one model)*
  Infantry *(legionnaire x6, senior legionnaire, centurion)*
  Powered *(legionnaire x4, senior legionnaire, centurion)*
- **Pilus** *(one squad)*
  Infantry *(Hastati x10, second centurion, optus)*
  Powered *(Hastati x5, second centurion, optus)*
- **Cohort**
  Pilus x10 *(first centurion, primus)*
- **Century**
  Cohort x10 *(senior centurion, tribune)*

Combat Vehicle
- **Vehicle** *(one model)*
  Crew *(centurion)*
- **Turma** *(one squad)*
  Vehicle x5 *(second centurion, optus)*
- **Cohort**
  Pilus x10 *(first centurion, primus)*
- **Century**
  Cohort x10 *(senior centurion, tribune)*

Aircraft *(fleet)*
- **Craft** *(one model)*
  Pilot/Crew *(ensign)*
- **Flight** *(one squad)*
  Craft x2 *(lieutenant)*
- **Wing**
  Flight x5 *(commander)*
- **Squadron**
  Wing x5 *(captain)*

Combat Assault Vehicle *(CAV)*
- **CAV** *(one model)*
  Pilot/Crew *(centurion)*
- **Turma** *(one squad)*
  CAV x5 *(second centurion, optus)*
- **Cohort**
  Turma x10 *(first centurion, primus)*
- **Century**
  Cohort x10 *(senior centurion, tribune)*

EMBLEM
Tactical
Federal Forces (Army)
The United Terran Federation

EMBLEM
Tactical
Federal Fleet Marine Corps
The United Terran Federation

TACTICAL BRIEFINGS

Selected Federation Units

The 10th Legion
The Grim Reapers
Commander: Legate Luke Walker
Legion Headquarters: Terra

The 10th Legion, as part of the Praetorian Guard, is permanently assigned to Terra as a home defense unit. Based at Fort Leavenworth in the Texas Prefecture, the 10th is detailed with protecting several planetary defense installations while also acting as a reserve to the 2nd Legion, stationed at the Federal Forces HQ "Big D".

The 17th Legion
The Iron Horse
Commander: Legate Alice Quigley
Legion Headquarters: Port Arthur

The 17th Legion is a heavy armor unit drawn from the Texas Republic military and was responsible for the first retaking of Vela from the Rach. The 17th is currently on Port Arthur for rest and refit before heading back out to the border.

INFANTRY
Powered Armor
M34 Light Mini Gun
The 101st Legion
The Silver Eagles
The United Terran Federation

The 42nd Legion
The Blackwatch
Commander: Legate Gordon Wallace
Legion Headquarters: Alpha Centauri

During the Vela Wars, the 42nd Legion was tasked with recapturing the planet of Hellspire from the Rach. Unknown to the Terran strategists was that the Rach had been using to world as a jump-off point for an attack further into Terran space.

As the 42nd began landing, three Rach Saikoan Clan regiments attacked, inflicting heavy losses on the legion. Fighting back, the 42nd managed to destroy two of the regiments before withdrawing.

The 42nd Legion remains one of the Terran's premiere heavy assault units.

The 43rd Legion
The White Knights
Commander: Legate Alek Fedorov
Legion Headquarters: Ford

The 43rd Legion, along with the 101st, was tasked with striking the Rach in their own territory, disrupting their supply and communication lines. The legions and the small task force of Fleet warships assigned to them drove deep into Rach space destroying several command and control centers and numerous supply depots.

There was much speculation that the two units might attempt a raid on Mohr itself. Ironically the UFFS Hornet, a light assault carrier, was part of the fleet accompanying them.

The 91st Legion
The Golden Dragons
Commander: Legate Yataro Kurasama
Legion Headquarters: Dracon Major

The 91st Legion is one of three legions from the Dracon Major Prefecture. Primarily of Chinese and Japanese descent, the officers of the 91st are allowed to carry a katana into battle and as part of their dress uniform for official occasions.

The 101st Legion
The Silver Eagles
Commander: Legate Gregor Mittman
Legion Headquarters: Vega

The 101st is one of the most active Terran legions, deploying to hot-spots along the Terran-Rach border as needed. Currently the unit is operating on Hellspire to help quell the recent surge of Rach activity on the planet.

TACTICAL BRIEFINGS

The 5th Fleet Marine Division

The Fighting 5th
Commander: Maj Gen Stephan Mann
Division Headquarters: Mars

The 5th provides the majority of Fleet Marines stationed aboard the Fleet's warships. The 2nd Force Recon Company is currently attached to the 5th and has been on extended deployment to an unspecified location.

Force Recon companies are typically used for deep reconnaissance, short duration strikes and other small-scale offensive operations deep in enemy territory.

The 11th Fleet Marine Division

The Silent Ones
Cmdr: Maj Gen Dexter Boyington
Division Headquarters: Sudenland

The 11th is assigned to the Federation's Rapid Deployment Force (RDF), requiring it to be ready to deploy at a moment's notice. The unit has recently been responding to a series of attacks in the systems near Sudenland thought to be the work of pirates, but General Boyington feels the raids are to organized for pirates looking to make a quick "buck".

Boyington has recently requested the deployment of additional Fleet destroyers to help locate these mysterious raiders and their base of operations.

The United Terran Federation Faction Doctrines

Air Superiority Doctrine

Dedicated Air Support
The Federation Fleet works closely with the legions to provide close-air ground support, attacking enemy targets in close proximity to friendly forces. To improve coordination, the Fleet provides Forward Air Controller specialists that deploy directly with the legions to which they are assigned.

Game Rules: *A Terran force group will receive a Forward Air Controller that may, once each turn, request a free Gunship Assault (see Battlefield Support Strike Packages, p. 141) during the activation of any friendly squad for immediate deployment anywhere on the game-board surface.*
An attack not used by the end of a turn is lost.

Air Power
In no military does air power play such an integral part as that of the Federation, assigning multiple assets to support the troops on the ground.

Game Rules: *A Terran force group may purchase an additional flight squad for each primary squad taken that does not count towards the normal primary/secondary squad ratio.*

Artillery Superiority Doctrine

Dedicated Artillery Support
The majority of Terran legions include a dedicated artillery force to directly provide fire support to the units they are assigned to.

Game Rules: *A Terran force group may, once each turn, request a free Artillery Strike (see Battlefield Support Strike Packages, p. 140) during the activation of any friendly squad for immediate deployment anywhere on the game-board surface.*
An attack not used by the end of a turn is lost.

Networked
Federation infantry receive extensive training as forward observers to improve the accuracy of artillery fire, especially when requesting a "danger close" fire mission over the BattleNet.

Game Rules: *All Terran infantry models receive the SA: FIST 1 at no extra cost.*

CAV
Extra-Large Chassis
Starhawk VI
The 101st Legion, *The Silver Eagles*
The United Terran Federation

TACTICAL BRIEFINGS ///////////

The Grand Order of the Temple

Background
Before the Legend

Originally known as the Poor Fellow-Soldiers of Christ and of the Temple of Solomon, the Templars were a wealthy and powerful military order beginning around 1119 on Terra. The height of their power came during a period the humans refer to as the Crusades and by their end, support from outside the Order began to fade. Looking to seize their wealth for himself, the French King Philip IV, set a series of events in motion that ultimately resulted in their demise and were officially disbanded by Pope Clement V in 1312.

The surviving members of the Order fled to the neighboring Swiss Confederacy, a fledgling country that was eager to accept the Templars, forming a secret society. Unknown to Philip was the fact the Templars had managed to flee with the majority of their wealth intact, hidden across Europe and the Middle East. The influx of the Templars led to Switzerland becoming one of the wealthiest countries in the world and renowned for their military prowess as mercenaries.

Over the next 900 years the Templars remained in hiding recruiting high-ranking government officials from other countries as well as leading scientists and the heads of major financial and corporate institutions to their ranks. This access and influence allowed the Templars to manipulate many of Earth's most important points in history to their benefit. With several of their own companies working as contractors for TERA as they developed the first human Compression Drive, the Templars were able to covertly build their own copy, using it to secretly send a ship to a system far rimward of Earth and establishing their own colony. Over the next forty years the Templars transferred a large number of their order to their new world, constructing the infrastructure that would be needed to support them in the establishment of their own galactic-state.

The arrival of the Rach set about a series of events that would reshape the Templar's core beliefs, both religiously and secularly, ultimately leading to a schism within the Order that for reshaped their future. The largest of these factions, the Crusaders and the Defenders, debated over helping their former planet (including thousands of members still on the planet) with these aliens. The Crusaders, intent on leaving those on Earth to their own fate, argued that the faith of the Order in a divine purpose had been misguided over the centuries and the arrival of the aliens was proof there was no supreme being. The Defenders countered that the protection of mankind in its darkest hour was the ultimate proof in a divine plan and that the existence of aliens were testament to the mission they had

been appointed to fulfill.

It was only with the arrival of the Adonese on Earth and their offer for assistance that the Crusaders finally relented in their opposition, aware of the new technology that it would bring. After revealing their existence to those back on Earth, Templar scientists and engineers rushed to help build the fleet that would eventually meet the Rach in the belts of Orion and bring about the end of the current hostilities. After the signing of the Vela Accords, the Templars provided much of the capital and resources needed by Terra to rebuild.

A New World Order

Since the end of the Vela Wars, the Templars have worked on expanding their emerging domain from the capital world of Temple. While maintaining much of the symbolism acquired after centuries of being a religious order, the influence of the Crusaders has shaped a realm intent of maintaining a cutting edge in advanced technology over the rest of the galaxy and the creation of a military infrastructure that would ensure the Order never having to worry about persecution again. Their location, far from the borders of the rest of the other galaxy-states, has allowed them to expand without the potential of interference or conflict with an alien government intent on the same system or resource. The Templars have also allowed the immigration of several human and alien groups looking for their own "new start", not suffering the xenophobia that plagues many of their brethren back in Terran space.

With their more "relaxed" view of the universe and their experience in banking and financial matters, the Templars have gained a reputation for remaining neutral with their dealings with the majority of other races and are a major player when it comes to interstellar commerce through their holdings in ThirdCorp. While a private corporation within Templar space, ThirdCorp maintains banks and communication networks throughout the galaxy. They are also the main force behind the Mercenary Bonding Authority (MBA). While many contracts and transactions exist outside the jurisdiction of the MBA, most mercenaries (including all of the "Free Companies") prefer to work under their auspices. After reaching an agreement, both parties submit to a bond based upon the overall value of the finalized contract. Typically the employer will submit cash or other item(s) of value while the mercenary will have a lien placed on their assets. Should either side have a grievance that is submitted to the MBA, the case will be investigated and a judgment rendered with damages paid from the losing side's bond.

ThirdCorp is also responsible for the Warmaster Tournament held each year on the Templar world of Pelles. The event is the premiere showcase for fighting forces throughout the galaxy to test their "mettle" against other opponents. The event is broadcast across the galaxy and even the Rach has attended the event, sending their first "team" in 2265.

The odds-on favorite to with this year is the Red Spades.

Geography

The capital world of the Templars, Temple is a temperate world with a single sun and one moon. Its five major continents cover approximately 40% of the surface area of a planet that is very similar in makeup to the Templars original home on Earth if somewhat cooler on a yearly average. The capital city of Solomon sits just north of the planet's equator along the coast of the largest continent Outremer.

Government

The Grand Master sits as head of the Templar government, a position they retain for life after being "elevated" by the other Masters of the Order. Each Templar system (referred to as provinces) is governed by a single Master, a post they hold at the pleasure of the Grand Master. The current Grand Master, Jacques de La Fère, has held his post since his elevation in 2253 and oversees a variety of Visitors-General who travels the different provinces correcting any malpractices they may find as well as introducing any new regulations and resolving disputes that may be present.

Military

Each Templar province is required to provide a set number of regiments for active service each year as proscribed by the Grand Master and the Visitor-General of the Army to the Commander of the Lands, a post responsible for the defense of each province. Service is by volunteer only; resulting in a well-trained, professional military with very high morale. Templar soldiers do not have a set period of time they must serve as the decision to join the armed forces is a life-long commitment. A soldier may choose to go "inactive" at any time after serving a minimum of two years, returning to civilian life or joining one of the Templar's Free Companies.

The Free Companies were established decades ago as a means for the Templars to stimulate their very young economy and to allow their soldiers a chance to train in real combat situations without the government's "official" participation.

Free Companies are used as mercenaries throughout the galaxy, the majority as garrison forces on worlds near the Terran-Rach border but have also served with the Adonese, the Ritterlich, the Almirithilians, and countless other independent systems.

The Grand Army of the Knights Templar Force Ranks
Army (enlisted)
- Recruit
- Private
- First Private
- Under Sergeant
- Sergeant
- First Sergeant
- Command Sergeant
- Master Sergeant
- Confanonier (standard bearer of the regiment)

Army (officer)
- Knight
- First Knight
- Knight Commander
- Under Marshal
- Marshal
- Turcopolier
- Seneschal
- Commander of the Lands

Force Structure *(all model types)*
- **Regiment** (4 battalions, confanonier, marshal)
- **Division** (2+ regiments, turcopolier)
- **Army** (2+ divisions, seneschal)
- **Province** (1 army, commander of the lands)
- **Visitor-General of the Army**
- **Master**
- **Grand Master**

INFANTRY
Powered Armor
FM-13 Lancer SAM
2nd Knights Guard Regiment
The Jaegers
The Grand Order of the Temple

Infantry
- **Section** *(one model)*
  Infantry *(private x5, under sergeant, sergeant)*
  Powered *(private x3, under sergeant, sergeant)*
- **Squad** *(one squad)*
  Section x5 *(first sergeant, knight)*
- **Company**
  Squad x5 *(command sergeant, knight commander)*
- **Battalion**
  Company x5 *(master sergeant, under marshal)*

Combat Vehicle
- **Vehicle** *(one model)*
  Crew *(sergeant)*
- **Conrois** *(one squad)*
  Vehicle x4 *(first sergeant, knight)*
- **Troop**
  Conrois x5 *(command sgt, knight commander)*
- **Battalion**
  Troop x5 *(master sergeant, under marshal)*

Aircraft
- **Craft** *(one model)*
  Pilot/Crew *(sergeant)*
- **Flight Section** *(one squad)*
  Craft x2 *(first sergeant, knight)*
- **Flight Squadron**
  Flight Section x5 *(command sgt, knight cmdr)*
- **Flight Echelon**
  Flight Squadron x5 *(master sgt, under marshal)*

Combat Assault Vehicle (*CAV*)
- **CAV** *(one model)*
  Pilot/Crew *(sergeant)*
- **Conrois** *(one squad)*
  CAV x4 *(first sergeant, knight)*
- **Troop**
  Conrois x5 *(command sgt, knight commander)*
- **Battalion**
  Troop x5 *(master sergeant, under marshal)*

Selected Templar Units

1st Knights Templar Regiment
Sword of the Temple
Commander: Marshal Andre de Laude
Regiment Headquarters: Temple

The 1st traces their origin back to the men and women of the original security detail that accompanied the first Templar ship from Earth to their new home on Temple. With the introduction of additional colonists, many of them with military experience, then Grand Master Marcian de Etter directed the formation of the Templar's first official military unit. Since that time the 1st Knights has been tasked with the protection of Temple and its highest-ranking officials.

2nd Knights Templar Regiment
Shield of the Temple
Commander: Marshal Godfrey de Clairvaux
Regiment Headquarters: Temple

As new worlds were added to the Templar domain, the need for a military unit that could move off-world, without weakening their home defense, required the formation on a second unit. After the formation of the first guard units, the 2nd Knights Templar returned to the capital world as a permanent garrison regiment.

1st Knights Guard Regiment
The Iron Regiment
Commander: Marshal Geoffroi de Molay
Regiment Headquarters: Acre

Guard and defender regiments serve mainly as a home defense force on the world's they are headquartered on. While the soldiers that serve in these units tend to be veterans, especially by troops that have served in one or more of the free companies, their are rarely staffed to their authorized strength levels and tend to be a "dumping ground" for second-line equipment.

TACTICAL BRIEFINGS

2nd Knights Defender Regiment
The Jaegers
Commander: Marshal Adelaide de Saint-Omer
Regiment Headquarters: Tortosa

While similar to the guards function as a home-defense force, a defender regiment will move from world to world to act as a reserve in times of crisis. Recently a large number of Ritterlich warships have been seen operating in the next system over under the pretext of anti-piracy patrols. While they have stayed out of Templar space so far, they have made a point to shadow Templar merchant fleets moving out of Tortosa, a major shipping nexus for the Order, in that direction.

1st Knights Protector Regiment
The Guardians of Order
Commander: Marshal Bernard de Payens
Regiment Headquarters: Hattin

Protector regiments serve as the special force units of the Templars as well as providing defense for Templar embassies, important military and industrial installations, and navy warships.

4th Knights Assault Regiment
The Black Horse
Commander: Marshal Nathaniel Walker
Regiment Headquarters: Mound

The assault regiments are the heavy hitters of the Templar forces, responsible for landing on a contested world under fire and taking the fight directly to the enemy.

The 4th has seen major action along the Terran-Rach border, recently participating in a series of attacks against the Rach forces on the Terran world of Hellspire as part of a joint-defense agreement between the two star nations.

The Grand Order of the Temple Faction Doctrines

Elite Training Doctrine
Bonds of Brotherhood
Many Templar soldiers spend their entire active careers in a single unit, resulting in a fanatic-like devotion to the men and women they serve with. This has led to an unwillingness by the Templar high command to move troops from one unit to another, resulting in many units fighting below their authorized force levels.

CAV
Super Chassis
Centurion
2nd Knights Templar Regiment, *The Shield of the Temple*
The Grand Order of the Temple

Game Rules: *The following squad types, as part of a Templar force group, have their minimum model requirement reduced by one: Attack, Fire Support, Flight, and Recon.*

Superior Equipment Doctrine
Cutting Edge
The Templars have always been on the cutting edge of new tech development, devoting a large portion of their annual budget to state-run research facilities and the engineers and scientists required to man them. Much effort is also spent by the Order of Scientific Intelligence in the gathering of "competitive intelligence" across the galaxy in the form of economic and industrial espionage.

Game Rules: *A Templar force group will receive additional specialization points, equal to 10% of their starting threat value pool, to use on any non-infantry models for the purchase of battlefield upgrades only.*

Mercenaries

Background

While often referred to as mercenaries in popular culture, the majority of the organizations fighting outside the confines of an "official" military structure are more akin to private military companies (PMC). The services and expertise offered by these PMCs are similar to those of a recognized government, including security, military, and/or police forces, but typically on a smaller scale.

Mercenaries are used to train or supplement the armed forces of a government, providing body guards for high-ranking officials or key corporate staff as well as the protection of important installations, especially in hostile environments. Mercenaries are also commonly used by factions looking to break away from a recognized government entity. It is for this reason, even though almost every galactic nation has used mercenaries at one point or another, do not recognize mercenaries as lawful combatants. This can lead to the confiscation of any equipment belonging to a mercenary company caught operating illegally within the borders of a star-nation as well as possible confinement and even death (see Article 47, the Laws of War).

Selected Mercenary Companies

The Black Cobras
Commander: Colonel Rik Ma'tern

The Black Cobras is an all-Adonese unit that has recently been used by NADO for a series of covert operations against the Principality in retaliation for a series of terrorist attacks on the Adonese home-world thought to be sponsored by their secret police.

The Blade
Commander: Unknown

The Blade is one of the galaxies oldest mercenary companies, fighting for the Ritter against the Malvernians during the Boreas Accord Wars. Since that time they have become more multi-national, taking on several contracts within the Ursae Protectorate Zone, a zone established by the Templars in an effort to stop the proliferation of advanced weapon systems to the emerging systems in that area of space. So far the embargo has had little influence over the warlords there as they fight amongst themselves over the rights to valuable resources on several uninhabited planets.

The Order has filed numerous complaints against The Blade's activities in the zone with the Ritter government but so far has had little success in getting a response.

General Drake
Commander: Artemis Drake

The Drake, as he is often referred to as, seems to have a knack for coming out on top, regardless of his current situation. Specializing in small, one of a kind type contracts, Drake has made a name for himself as the go-to guy. With friends and contacts across the galaxy, the self-proclaimed general, is relatively easy to reach but is rarely seen in person.

Should the mission be one outside his normal range of operations, Drake will get you in contact with someone who can handle a client's needs, taking a small 10% brokerage fee of the final contract price for arranging the meeting. Several corporations work exclusively with the General due to his reputation for quality.

Needless to say, through the years General Drake has made several enemies, many of which have offered a reward for his capture. In defiance, Drake will typically offer a discount for his services when acting in opposition to those that have done so.

BACKGROUND

The Laws of War
As the use of paid "military contractors" became more prevalent in conflicts, both internal and external, the Terrans recognized the need to define the role of "mercenaries" and establish a system for those caught acting against their interests.

In 2245 representatives of the Federation, the Templar Order, and the Adonese met, resulting in the document now referred to as the Laws of War. Of particular note is Article 47 which defines what a mercenary is. The following is an excerpt from that document:

Art 47. Mercenaries
1. A mercenary shall not have the right to be a combatant or a prisoner of war.
2. A mercenary is any person who:
(a) is especially recruited locally or abroad in order to fight in an armed conflict;
(b) does, in fact, take a direct part in the hostilities;
(c) is motivated to take part in the hostilities essentially by the desire for private gain and, in fact, is promised, by or on behalf of a Party to the conflict, material compensation substantially in excess of that promised or paid to combatants of similar ranks and functions in the armed forces of that Party;
(d) is neither a national of a Party to the conflict nor a resident of territory controlled by a Party to the conflict;
(e) is not a member of the armed forces of a Party to the conflict; and
(f) has not been sent by a State which is not a Party to the conflict on official duty as a member of its armed forces. ∎

TACTICAL BRIEFINGS

Kolditz
Commander: Colonel Hans Tolbers

Another mercenary company with ties to Ritter, Kolditz maintains a base of operations on Ritter and is one of the largest groups in the galaxy.

Their motto "Hire us or fight us, either way you pay!" sums up the general attitude of the unit. Boasting modern equipment and a reputation for paying it's employees well, Kolditz is as much known for the rates they charge as for the results they achieve.

The Red Spades
Commander: Colonel Andrea de Beers

The Red Spades are a Templar Free Company with headquarters on the Templar world of Acre.

A favorite to win this year's Warmaster Tournament, the Red Spades are coming off a recent fight with the Blades on the independent world of Viper that killed that unit's current commander. This is sure to increase the bitter rivalry that already exists between these two units in the future.

The Slayers
Commander: Captain Jack Ryan

A mostly human unit, the Slayers are frequently used by several of the larger Terran corporations as security forces. Known for their aggressive tactics in battle, the Slayers are a highly respected unit and should never be underestimated during a fight.

MercNet, a division of ThirdCorp, recently upgraded the unit's bond rating to AAA, allowing them to purchase several new CAVs for the formation of a second company.

The Yellow Jackets
Commander: The Bossman

A multi-national mercenary unit based on the free world of Cetus, the Yellow Jackets are extremely selective when it comes to picking new team members. Over the last eleven years, their prowess for combat has built them a strong reputation for winning. The are frequently a favorite of General Drake as they specialize in heavy assault contracts.

The Yellow Jackets are currently banned from the Warmaster tournament due to an seemingly unprovoked attack on the Red Spades compound in 2267. Little is known about their current commander, a human that simply goes by the moniker Bossman.

The Polar Bears
Commander: Captain Jax Morrow

A relative new comer to the mercenary field, the Polar Bears are one of the few units with their own capital warship. The North Star is a Terran battle-cruiser purchased by the unit after it had received major damage from an asteroid strike while parked in orbit around an uninhabited world far enough from any repair facilities that the Federation decided to sell the ship to breakers for salvage. A group of investors purchased those rights and moved the ship to a private shipyard for refitting, eventually selling the warship to the Bears.

The Steel Dragons
Commander: Colonel Tiberius Gates

The Steel Dragons are known more for they didn't do as opposed to what the have accomplished since. Once the Terran's 86th Legion, the Steel Dragons were ordered to drop on the heavily populated Rach world of Trakka. Heavily outnumbered, the unit chose to disobey the deployment order and mutiny, fleeing into uncharted space away from Terra. For a time the unit took to piracy in an effort to survive, raiding several backwater planets for supplies. Since that time they have taken to being mercenaries but their tainted reputation has prevented any major contracts from coming their way as of yet.

CAV
Large Chassis
Gnomic
The Steel Dragons
Mercenary

The Furies
Commander: Colonel Jeremy Mueller

The Furies are a multi-national unit under long term contract with the Malvernians, operating along their shared border with the Rach. Tasked with acting as a deterrent to the Rach from crossing the border, their deployment has actually caused an increase in raids as the Rach in the area have grown weary of the ease in which they defeat Malvernian home guard units and seek a more competent adversary.

The First Cimarron Rangers
Commander: Captain Jarrod Logan

The Rangers are a human mercenary company from the once free world of Cimarron, a system located coreward of Terra. The planet's population was "cleansed" by the Rach in 2269, the only survivors a number of ranchers and their families and a small contingent of the local defense force that managed to fight their way to the planet's space port and escape.

Fleeing to the Terran planet of El Dorado, the refugees have established a small enclave there, ensuring the safety of their non-combatants and forming the Rangers to take the fight back to the Rach.

The unit is currently on contract to the free world of Vagabond training the local defense force in the use of four ancient CAVs the planet's president managed to purchase at auction. The arrival of the Rangers has caused some controversy with several of the local miner's union, who see the mercs presence as an attempt to strong-arm them into signing a new contract.

INFANTRY
Light
HK-5 SMG
The First Cimarron Rangers
Mercenary

Pirates

Background

While a variety of run of the mill pirates are scattered across the galaxy, three groups are renowned for their brazen raiding-style, unafraid of going after the "mother lode" when selecting their next target.

While lacking any formal structure, these bands have multiple secret bases to operate from across the galaxy and are aggressively increasing their membership as they look to expand and go after even larger prizes.

Large bounties have been placed on all of their leaders but beware, many have tried to collect and so far have been unsuccessful.

Sir Hawkins Social Society
Commander: Stede Bonnet

This group of pirates take their name from an early Terran pirate, Sir John Hawkins, plowing the space lanes in their ship, the *Jolly Roger*.

Once a centurion in the Federation's 98th Legion, Bonnet was on his way to a court-martial when several of his men broke him out and fled in a captured civilian yacht.

The Society tends to go after non-human ships and worlds, fielding a large lift and transport capacity to haul the labors of their work. They are rumored to be currently in the Thrane sector of space, an Adonese system rimward of the Adon capital.

The Black Rose
Commander: Richard Worley

Worley commands his merry pirate band from the bridge of a captured Rach battlecarrier, the *Cadogan*. Along with his half-human, half-adonese daughter Rebecca, the Black Rose pirates frequently attack KDM facilities within Ritter space, having been known to attack even the most heavily-guarded installations.

The Rock Rovers
Commander: Tarpur Kinta

The Rock Rovers are a band of Malvernians that have rejected the teachings of their religion and seem to delight in attacking their race.

Their most famous attack came in the seizing of the Malvernian spaceyard in the Bor system and the theft of an entire division of space destroyers that had just finished construction.

The Malvernians have made their capture a priority.

CONSTRUCTION

CAV
Medium Chassis
Kestral
The Black Rose
Pirate

APPENDIX A: Construction System

The Basics

The CAV: SO construction system allows a player to design their own CAV, vehicle, aircraft, and infantry models or modify an existing design. While models designed using this system are considered legal for non-tournament play, each player should agree to the use of custom or modified designs before the start of a game.

To design a new model in CAV: SO, a player will need a piece of scratch paper for taking notes and making calculations (a calculator would also be very helpful), a writing tool, this construction system, and at least one blank record sheet (download at: www.cavhq.com/downloads).

The CAV: SO construction system allows a player to make many choices to the model they are designing, and—as is human nature—some players may be tempted to select the maximum amount allowed for the various options available. Players are cautioned from building the "uber" war machine in deference to the spirit of the game as well as remembering that a model's threat value (TV) is based upon the options and equipment selected for it. A model with a high TV will limit the number of models in a force group and may unbalance the overall force if the model is destroyed early in battle.

Step One: Model Type

The player must first decide what type of model they wish to design, choosing from four model types: aircraft, CAVs, combat vehicles, or infantry.

Aircraft

Most aircraft found over the modern battlefield are single-piloted craft providing close-air support for the troops below. Advances in ducted fans and other vertical maneuvering technologies allow aircraft to remain close at hand while retaining the ability to quickly move around the battle area.

All to aware of their average life expectancy, combat pilots tend to be a cocky lot. A combat pilot with at least five air-to-air kills (dogfighting) is considered an "Ace".

Combat Assault Vehicle (CAV)

The typical CAV is twenty-five to thirty-five feet in height, weighing from 25 to 150 tons, generally humanoid in shape, and tower over other model types. With their tremendous armor, firepower, and agility, they are the ultimate projection of power in the 23rd century and are in use by every major faction in the galaxy.

Each CAV will have a pilot, trained to control a multitude of systems and weapons while coordinating with other allied troops on the battlefield. Most unit commanders will be found behind the "stick" of a CAV.

A CAV may also have one or more additional crew-members assigned to help the pilot operate the auxiliary systems of the machine. Weapon systems operators, known as "wizzos", are tasked with tracking enemy targets and firing the weapon systems of the machine as the pilot maneuvers into position. Many pilots begin their career as a weapon systems operator before being promoted to command their own CAV.

Combat Vehicles

Cheaper to build and maintain than CAVs, combat vehicles serve a multitude of roles in every military force. Generally protected by strong armor and armed with a variety of weapon systems, tanks, armored fighting vehicles (AFV), and armored personnel carriers (APC) are just some of the combat vehicles that can be found on the battlefield using tracks, wheels, hover jets or anti-grav drives for propulsion.

Most combat vehicles will typically have a crew of three: a driver, a gunner, and a commander.

Infantry

Fighting on foot, infantry tend to fight the enemy up-close and suffer the greatest number of casualties. Infantry are relatively inexpensive to field and can be extremely effective when deployed correctly, especially when used to defend a fixed position.

Infantry can also enter and maneuver in terrain that is inaccessible to CAVs and other combat vehicle types. Urban warfare, with its many places to hide in, can often negate the advantage of heavy armor, allowing infantry a chance to destroy an exposed enemy with a well-executed ambush.

In CAV: SO an infantry model refers to a single base of three or more infantry figures mounted to it.

CONSTRUCTION

Step Two: Select Model Task Type

Every model is required to have a model task. A model's task type is used to determine what it's primary role is as part of a squad and what type of squad it may belong too. A model may have more than one task in certain circumstances, such as an aircraft (flight/attack).

Model Task Type

- **Attack**
- **Fire-Support**
- **Recon**
- **Flight**
- **Transport**
- **Specialist**

Step Three: Select Chassis Size (non-infantry models only)

The chassis is the internal framework of every aircraft, CAV, and combat vehicle and includes a variety of complex equipment a machine needs to operate. Breeders, fuel cells, power inverters, silicone-fiber actuators, wiring, computer systems, ferro-steel framework, shock absorbers, cooling and heating systems, monitoring sensors, and the vast array of nuts, bolts, and micro-welds all combine to make-up the chassis of a modern fighting machine.

Chassis Size: Quad CAVs

Most CAVs are bipedal (two legs and two arms) but four-legged models (no arms), known as quads, do exist. Quad-CAVs have a better weight distribution level, providing greater stability when not moving, improved handling, and a greater level of armor protection but do require dynamic walking controls to coordinate the movement between all four legs, reducing the machine's overall movement speed.

Their larger overall size allow quad-CAVs to be fitted with a turret and can also be designed with internal cargo space for the transfer of equipment and personnel.

Chassis Size: Damage Tracks and Hard-Points

Besides determining the type of model being built, the size of a model's chassis is used to set the amount of damage a model can take before it is removed from play in the form of damage tracks (DT). The loss of one or more damage tracks will also affect the ability of a model to move and fight, degrading with each additional point of damage.

Each damage track provides a model one hard-point (HP). Hard-points are used when assigning the weapon systems and special abilities or attributes a model may use during play.

Some chassis sizes allow for more than one damage track choice, leading a player to ask why they would choose to take a lower value and the answer to that would be threat value. No factor influences a model's final threat value more than the number of damage tracks it possesses. The more damage tracks a model has, the more threat value points it is worth.

In addition, some weapon systems require a minimum number of damage tracks to mount, preventing smaller machines from mounting larger weapon systems to large their chassis type. All quad-CAVs receive a +1 hard-point bonus.

Chassis Size: Automatic Special Abilities & Attributes

A model's chassis size may also provide one or more special abilities and attributes that do not count towards a model's hard-point total.

Chassis Size: Aircraft

- **Ultra-Light Chassis (2 DT/HP):** Ultra-Light chassis aircraft models tend to be very specialized in design, commonly used for reconnaissance and are typically drones.
  SA: *Improved Handling, Pop-Up, Soft*

- **Light Chassis (3 DT/HP):** Light chassis aircraft models are typically used for supply and transport in low-threat areas.
  SA: *Improved Handling, Pop-Up, Soft*

- **Medium Chassis (4 DT/HP):** Medium chassis aircraft models are used for a variety missions including close-air support, transport, and fighters.
  SA: *Improved Handling, Pop-Up, Soft*

- **Heavy Chassis (5 DT/HP):** Heavy chassis aircraft models typically carry more armor, allowing them to better engage ground-based targets under fire.
  SA: *Improved Handling, Pop-Up, Soft*

- **Ultra-Heavy Chassis (6 DT/HP):** Ultra-heavy chassis aircraft are typically are used as transports and specialized gun-ships.
  SA: *Improved Handling, Pop-Up, Soft*

Chassis Size: Combat Assault Vehicles (CAV)

- **Small Chassis (3 or 4 DT/HP):** Most small chassis CAVs are designed for speed, allowing them to act as scouts and forward observers for indirect-fire. Small chassis CAVS are not built to withstand a lot of punishment and should avoid engaging in a stand-up fight, especially with larger chassis types.   SA: *Hard*

- **Medium Chassis (5 or 6 DT/HP):** A good mix of armor and speed allow medium chassis CAVs to function in a variety of roles. Medium chassis CAVs are typically used for advanced targeting and ECM platforms, typically acting as "wild weasels" in an effort to take out enemy defense systems.
  SA: *Hard*

- **Large Chassis (7 or 8 DT/HP):** Large chassis CAVs form the "backbone" of every major military force, their size

allowing for a good mix of armor and weapon systems without sacrificing overall speed.
SA: *Hard*

- **Extra-Large Chassis (9 or 10 DT/HP):** Extra-large chassis CAVs are the heavy-hitters of a strike force, their speed sufficient enough to allow them to spread out and carry the fight to the enemy.
SA: *Hard*

- **Super Chassis (11 or 12 DT/HP):** Super chassis CAVs mount the most armor and weapon systems of any ground-based mobile platform. While slow, super chassis models provide a force group with its biggest "punch".
SA: *Bulky, Hard*

Chassis Size: Combat Vehicles

- **Light Chassis (1 or 2 DT/HP):** Light chassis vehicles tend to be reconnaissance models, unarmored personnel carriers, and other specialized utility vehicles.
SA: *Soft*

- **Medium Chassis (3 or 4 DT/HP):** Medium chassis vehicles allow for more armor and equipment without sacrificing too much top speed. Armored personnel carriers, artillery models, light tanks, and anti-personnel vehicles tend to fall in this class of vehicles.
SA: *Soft or Hard*

- **Heavy Chassis (5 to 6 DT/HP):** Heavy chassis vehicles carry the punch to knock out a CAV and enough armor to survive on the modern battlefield. Heavy chassis vehicles are mainly encountered as main battle tanks and other forward combat type roles.
SA: *Hard*

- **Extra-Heavy Chassis (7 to 8 DT/HP):** Extra Heavy chassis vehicles are similar in role to the ultra large chassis CAVs in providing a strong defensive model to secure and hold a static location. Slow and lumbering, extra heavy vehicles can bear massive weapon arrays and armor.
SA: *Bulky, Hard*

Chassis Size: Infantry

Infantry models do not have a "chassis", automatically receiving three damage tracks/hard-points. Infantry models are designated by the type of armor they are equipped with.

- **Light Armor (3 DT/HP):** Conventional infantry wearing standard battle dress uniforms armed with a variety of small arm weapon systems.
SA: *Pop-Up, Soft*

- **Heavy Armor (3 DT/HP):** Heavy infantry wear non-powered armor for increased protection at the expense of their overall speed.
SA: *Pop-Up, Soft*

- **Powered Armor (3 DT/HP):** Powered armor infantry wear fully-enclosed armor suits that increase their protection and assist with movement. They will also typically carry heavier weapons when fighting.
SA: *Bulky, Pop-Up, Soft*

Step Four: Movement Class (combat vehicles only)

The movement class of a model determines the affect various terrain types will have on it's move value. While aircraft, CAVs, and infantry are pre-set, combat vehicles require a player to decide the movement class for their design.

- **Wheeled:** Wheeled combat vehicles with their lighter weight and suspension, are more restricted when moving through some types of terrain, preferring wide-open spaces for maximum maneuverability.
SA: *Improved Handling.*

- **Hover:** Hover combat vehicles are valued for their speed and their ability to travel over many terrain types, especially water, unhindered. Hover-craft have the lightest armor of any combat vehicle design.
SA: *Improved Handling.*

- **Tracked:** With their continuous treads, tracked combat vehicles can grind their way through almost any type of terrain and mount the heaviest armor of any combat vehicle design.

- **Anti-Grav:** Anti-grav combat vehicles use the gravity of a planet to "push" off from it's surface, allowing it to "skim" over many terrain types.
SA: *Improved Handling, Pop-Up*

Step Five: Select Move and Armor Values

With the selection of a model's chassis type (or armor) and their movement class, a player will need to select the base move and armor values of the model.

The move value (MV) sets the number of inches a model can move in a straight line over open terrain with a single move action.

The armor value (AV) represents the overall "toughness" of a model.

See p. 106 for the **Move and Armor Value Selection Table**.

Step Six: Select Weapon Systems and Special Attributes/Abilities

A player will next select a model's weapon systems and any

special abilities or attributes that may be assigned to it. Each of these has a set hard-point cost that must be paid from a chassis type's base hard-point allotment. These descriptions can be found in Appendix B: Weapon Systems (p. 111) and Appendix C: Special Abilities & Attributes (p. 118).

Matched Weapons

Matched weapons allow a model to mount two weapon systems of the same type in one location, decreasing the number of hard points required by half. Up to two weapon systems may use this option.

Matched weapons may be mounted in the same model location or parallel to each other in the left and right mounting location.

Example: *The Dictator-B's two medium MACs, mounted in the left and right arm, are matched weapons, requiring only 2.5 hard-points to equip instead of the usual 5.*

Select Weapon Systems and Special Abilities & Attributes

Some weapon systems and special abilities & attributes can only be equipped by specific chassis sizes and/or model and task types as detailed by their description.

Fractional Hard Points

Many weapon systems and special abilities & attributes do not require a full hard-point to equip as detailed by their description.

Step Seven: Determine Close-Combat Value

A model's close-combat value (CCV) is a reflection of it's overall "toughness" and ability to inflict damage in a close-assault attack. Each model will have a Hard and Soft CV which will be added to the model's opposed roll when participating in a close-assault attack.

When determining the CCV of a model, weapon systems with the SA: *Indirect-Fire* and/or SA: *Minimum Range* are not used. Aircraft models cannot engage in a close-combat attack and have no close-combat value.

Calculate Base Hard CCV

Add together the starting hard RAV of each eligible weapon system and multiple the result by .10.

Example: *The Dictator-B CAV has two medium MACs (RAV 6/2), one light GM (4/4), and one light R10 (3/3). All three weapon systems have the SA: Indirect-Fire or SA: Minimum Range and are not used when calculating the model's base hard CV. With no eligible weapon systems, the model's base hard CV is "0".*

The Halberd CAV has four light LBGs (RAV 3/3), two medium LBG (4/4), and one heavy RAC (4/8). As none of these weapon systems have the SA: Indirect-Fire or SA: Minimum Range they are used when calculating the model's base hard CCV. The total value

of their hard RAV is "24", multiplying by .10 provides a base hard CCV of "2.4".

Calculate Base Soft CCV

Add together the starting soft RAV of each eligible weapon system and multiple the result by .10.

Example: *Using the same two model's again we get an base soft CCV of "0" for the Dictator-B and a base soft CCV of "2.8" for the Halberd.*

Calculate CCV Armor Bonus

Multiple a model's armor value by .2 and add this value to both base CCV amounts.

Example: *The Dictator-B has a AV of 8 (1.6) and the Halberd has a AV of 7 (1.4). Added to the base CCV numbers for both models brings their totals to 1.6/1.6 for the Dictator-B and 3.8/4.2 for the Halberd.*

Calculate Model Type's CCV Bonus

Some models may receive a CCV bonus based upon their chassis type. Add this value (if any) to both base CCV amounts.

Aircraft
- All Chassis Types   NA

Combat Assault Vehicle (CAV)
- Small Chassis   +1 CV
- Medium Chassis   +2 CV
- Large Chassis   +2 CV
- Extra-Large Chassis   +3 CV
- Super Chassis   +4 CV

Combat Vehicles
- All Chassis Types   +0 CV

Infantry
- Light Armor   +1 CV
- Heavy Armor   +1 CV
- Powered Armor   +2 CV

Example: *Both the Dictator-B and the Halberd are extra-large chassis CAVs, receiving a model type CCV bonus of +3. Added to the base CCV numbers for both models brings their totals to 4.6/4.6 for the Dictator-B and 6.8/7.2 for the Halberd.*

Calculate Model's Final Close-Assault Attack Values

After adding the CCV bonus for armor and model type to both base CVs, round any fractions. This is the model's final close-assault attack values.

Example: *After rounding the Dictator-B's final close-combat assault values are 5/5 and the Halberd's are 7/7.*

Step Eight: Calculate Threat Value Total

The threat value of a model is used to when building a force group for play and counts against the overall threat value point total for the entire force.

Calculate Threat Value Total: Move and Armor Values

Multiple a model's final move value by five (x5) and armor value by twenty-five (x25), adding the two value together.

Example: The Dictator-B CAV has a MV of 5 and a AV of 8 providing a total threat value cost of "225".

Calculate Threat Value Total: Weapon Systems and Special Abilities & Attribute Values

Add together the threat value cost of each weapon system and special ability or attribute a model is equipped with.

Example: The Dictator-B has the following weapon systems and SAs to use for determining its threat value cost

• Medium MAC (97 x2)	194
• Light GM	113
• Light R10	105
• SA: Advanced Targeting Computer 1	25
• SA: Ammo Bin 1	5
• SA: Hard	0
• SA: Improved Armor	0
• SA: Piercing (25x2 weapons)	50
• SA: Reinforced 1	25
• SA: Wizzo	25
• **TOTAL**	**542**

Calculate Threat Value Total: Final Calculation

Add the move and armor value threat point totals to the weapon systems/SA total. Next, divide the model's damage track value by "12" and multiply the threat point total by this number, rounding any fractions. This is the model's final threat value point cost.

Example: The Dictator-B has a total of 767 threat value points. Dividing its nine damage tracks by "12" results in a value of .75. Multiplying 762 x .75 we get "575.25", rounding down for a final threat value cost of "575".

Step Nine: The Data Card

As already noted, if a model takes damage during a game, some of it's functions will degrade. After designing a new model a player will need to place its final base number for move, armor, and close-assault values on the data card under the "0" damage column.

Using each base value's reduction chart (pp. 107-109), multiply the base value by the listed value for each column the model may possess, rounding up or down.

DICTATOR-B	CAV										
[DAMAGE TRACK]		0	1	2	3	4	5	6	7	8	9
MOVE (WALKER)		5	5	5	4	4	4	4	3	3	3
ARMOR		8	8	7	7	6	6	5	5	4	3
CLOSE-COMBAT		5/5	5/5	4/4	4/4	3/3	3/3	3/2	2/2	2/2	1/1
DAMAGE CONTROL		-	-	4	4	3	2	1	0	-1	-2

[WEAPONS]

MEDIUM MAC 6/2 6/2 5/2 5/2 5/2 4/1 4/1 4/1 3/1 3/1
x2 (L/R), RNG (12), AMMO, BLASTER 1, MIN RNG (1), STRIKE, PIERCING

LIGHT GM 4/4 4/4 4/4 3/3 3/3 3/3 3/3 2/2 2/2 2/2
x1 (L), RNG (16), IMPROVED RANGE, LIMITED AMMO, MIN RNG (14), SHOCK (4)

LIGHT R10 3/3 3/3 3/3 3/3 2/2 2/2 2/2 2/2 2/2 2/2
x1 (R), RNG (14), AOE 1, INDIRECT-FIRE, LIMITED AMMO, MIN RNG (12), RAVAGE, SMART

[SPECIAL ABILITIES & ATTRIBUTES]
ADVANCED TARGETING COMPUTER 1, AMMO BIN 1, HARD, REINFORCED 1, WIZZO, IMPROVED ARMOR

CLASSIFIED

COPYRIGHT 2015 TALON GAMES

TV: 575

Next, using the damage control table for the appropriate chassis type, mark the correct number for each column as indicated.

Next, use the weapon system reduction charts to multiply each weapon's hard and soft RAV by the listed value for each column the model may possess, rounding up or down to the closest whole number.

Finally, mark down any special abilities or attributes a model may have along with it's final threat value on the data card and your all done, ready to play!

Design Note: This construction system has been provided to allow a player the ability to design custom models for non-tournament play or to make alterations on an existing design. A player may find a model deemed "official" that does not necessary conform to this system as presented. Typically this is a result of a decision made by the designer(s) to provide a model that is required for a specific reason and was determined to not affect game balance or play.

BONUS

Model Tonnage

While not required for play, a player may wish to designate the actual "tonnage" of a non-infantry design using the following chart:

Base Value (tons)

Aircraft (empty)	CAV	Combat Vehicle
Ultra-Light 5	Small 25	Light 5
Light 10	Medium 50	Medium 20
Medium 15	Large 75	Heavy 40
Heavy 30	Extra-Large 100	Extra-Heavy 60
Ultra-Heavy 50	Super 125	

Add +2 tons for EACH weapon system and +1 for each special ability or attribute.

Example: The Dictator-B's loaded tonnage is 100 (chassis size) + 8 (four weapons) + 7 (seven SAs) for a total tonnage of 115. ■

CONSTRUCTION

BASE MOVE & ARMOR VALUE TABLE

Aircraft

Chassis Type:	Ultra-Light			Light			Medium			Heavy			Ultra-Heavy		
Move Value	20	18	16	19	17	15	18	16	14	17	15	13	16	14	12
Armor Value	1	2	3	2	3	4	3	4	5	4	5	6	5	6	7

CAV (Non-Quad)

Chassis Type:	Small			Medium			Large			Extra-Large			Super		
Move Value	12	10	8	11	9	7	10	8	6	9	7	5	8	6	4
Armor Value	3	4	5	4	5	6	5	6	7	6	7	8	7	8	9

CAV (Quad)

Chassis Type:	Small			Medium			Large			Extra-Large			Super		
Move Value	10	8	6	9	7	5	8	6	4	7	5	3	6	4	2
Armor Value	4	5	6	5	6	7	6	7	8	7	8	9	8	9	10

Combat Vehicle (Hover)

Chassis Type:	Light			Medium			Heavy			Extra-Heavy		
Move Value	15	14	13	14	13	12	13	12	11	12	11	10
Armor Value	1	2	3	2	3	4	3	4	5	4	5	6

Combat Vehicle (Wheeled & Anti-Grav)

Chassis Type:	Light			Medium			Heavy			Extra-Heavy		
Move Value	13	12	11	12	11	10	11	10	9	10	9	8
Armor Value	2	3	4	3	4	5	4	5	6	5	6	7

Combat Vehicle (Tracked)

Chassis Type:	Light			Medium			Heavy			Extra-Heavy		
Move Value	11	10	9	10	9	8	9	8	7	8	7	6
Armor Value	3	4	5	4	5	6	5	6	7	6	7	8

Infantry

Armor Type:	Light	Heavy	Powered
Move Value	3	2	4
Armor Value	1	2	3

The Base Move & Armor Table

During design a player will need to choose the base move and armor value of the non-infantry model being built. The center value of each chassis type is a "balance" between movement and defense, while the other two values (left or right) are weighted towards a higher move value, decreasing the model's base armor value or a lower move value, increasing the model's base armor value.

Which value set to use is up to the player and can be further modified by the addition of some special abilities and attributes later in the design process or battlefield upgrades before play.

Infantry models have no variable values to choose from but their move and armor vale do not degrade during play. The value stated is used for each infantry model's damage track and is used until the model is removed from play.

MOVE VALUE REDUCTION TABLE

Aircraft, CAV (Non-Quad), Combat Vehicle

DT	0	1	2	3	4	5	6	7	8	9	10	11	12
12	1	.97	.93	.90	.87	.83	.80	.77	.73	.70	.67	.63	.60
11	1	.96	.93	.89	.85	.82	.78	.75	.71	.67	.64	.60	
10	1	.96	.92	.88	.84	.80	.76	.72	.68	.64	.60		
9	1	.96	.91	.87	.82	.78	.73	.69	.64	.60			
8	1	.95	.90	.85	.80	.75	.70	.65	.60				
7	1	.94	.89	.83	.77	.71	.66	.60					
6	1	.93	.87	.80	.73	.67	.60						
5	1	.92	.84	.76	.68	.60							
4	1	.90	.80	.70	.60								
3	1	.87	.73	.60									
2	1	.80	.60										
1	1	.60											

Note: The "0" column represents a model's base move value (no SAs) with no damage. For each additional damage track a model possesses, move one column to the right and multiply the base value by the listed amount, rounding any fractions to the closest whole number (.01-.49 down and .50 to .99 up).

Quad-CAVs receive a +.10 to each listed move reduction value. No value is increased higher than 1.0.

Infantry model's move (and armor) value is never reduced. Place their full move value in each column. A model's move value can never be reduced below 1 unless disabled or destroyed.

ARMOR VALUE REDUCTION TABLE

Aircraft, CAV (Non-Quad), Combat Vehicle

DT	0	1	2	3	4	5	6	7	8	9	10	11	12
12	1	.96	.92	.88	.83	.79	.75	.71	.67	.63	.58	.54	.50
11	1	.95	.91	.86	.82	.77	.73	.68	.64	.59	.55	.50	
10	1	.95	.90	.85	.80	.75	.70	.65	.60	.55	.50		
9	1	.94	.89	.83	.78	.72	.67	.61	.56	.50			
8	1	.94	.88	.81	.75	.69	.63	.56	.50				
7	1	.93	.86	.79	.71	.64	.57	.50					
6	1	.92	.83	.75	.67	.58	.50						
5	1	.90	.80	.70	.60	.50							
4	1	.88	.75	.63	.50								
3	1	.83	.67	.50									
2	1	.75	.50										
1	1	.50											

CONSTRUCTION

● CLOSE-COMBAT ASSAULT VALUE REDUCTION TABLE

All Model Types

DT	0	1	2	3	4	5	6	7	8	9	10	11	12
12	1	.94	.88	.81	.75	.69	.63	.56	.50	.44	.38	.31	.25
11	1	.93	.86	.80	.73	.66	.59	.52	.45	.39	.32	.25	
10	1	.93	.85	.78	.70	.63	.55	.48	.40	.33	.25		
9	1	.92	.83	.75	.67	.58	.50	.42	.33	.25			
8	1	.91	.81	.72	.63	.53	.44	.34	.25				
7	1	.89	.79	.68	.57	.46	.36	.25					
6	1	.88	.75	.63	.50	.38	.25						
5	1	.85	.70	.55	.40	.25							
4	1	.81	.63	.44	.25								
3	1	.75	.50	.25									
2	1	.63	.25										
1	1	.25											

Note: *Repeat the steps for each additional reduction table required. Any bonus (or negative) values as the result of special abilities or attributes are added or subtracted to the modified base value as a whole number directly to the final data card.*

● RANGED ASSAULT VALUE REDUCTION TABLE

AC, AT, B, FAS, FT, G, GL, MG, MT, RKT Weapon Systems

DT	0	1	2	3	4	5	6	7	8	9	10	11	12
12	1	.97	.93	.90	.87	.83	.80	.77	.73	.70	.67	.63	.60
11	1	.96	.93	.89	.85	.82	.78	.75	.71	.67	.64	.60	
10	1	.96	.92	.88	.84	.80	.76	.72	.68	.64	.60		
9	1	.96	.91	.87	.82	.78	.73	.69	.64	.60			
8	1	.95	.90	.85	.80	.75	.70	.65	.60				
7	1	.94	.89	.83	.77	.71	.66	.60					
6	1	.93	.87	.80	.73	.67	.60						
5	1	.92	.84	.76	.68	.60							
4	1	.90	.80	.70	.60								
3	1	.87	.73	.60									
2	1	.80	.60										
1	1	.60											

RANGED ASSAULT VALUE REDUCTION TABLE

AR, GM, MAC, MAR, MRAC, SAM Weapon Systems

DT	0	1	2	3	4	5	6	7	8	9	10	11	12
12	1	.96	.92	.88	.83	.79	.75	.71	.67	.63	.58	.54	.50
11	1	.95	.91	.86	.82	.77	.73	.68	.64	.59	.55	.50	
10	1	.95	.90	.85	.80	.75	.70	.65	.60	.55	.50		
9	1	.94	.89	.83	.78	.72	.67	.61	.56	.50			
8	1	.94	.88	.81	.75	.69	.63	.56	.50				
7	1	.93	.86	.79	.71	.64	.57	.50					
6	1	.92	.83	.75	.67	.58	.50						
5	1	.90	.80	.70	.60	.50							
4	1	.88	.75	.63	.50								
3	1	.83	.67	.50									
2	1	.75	.50										
1	1	.50											

Note: *Repeat the steps for each additional reduction table required. Any bonus (or negative) values as the result of special abilities or attributes are added or subtracted to the modified base value as a whole number directly to the final data card.*

RANGED ASSAULT VALUE REDUCTION TABLE

IDC, LBG, LBR, PBG Weapon Systems

DT	0	1	2	3	4	5	6	7	8	9	10	11	12
12	1	.95	.89	.84	.78	.73	.68	.62	.57	.51	.46	.40	.35
11	1	.94	.88	.82	.76	.70	.65	.59	.53	.47	.41	.35	
10	1	.94	.87	.81	.74	.68	.61	.55	.48	.42	.35		
9	1	.93	.86	.78	.71	.64	.57	.49	.42	.35			
8	1	.92	.84	.76	.68	.59	.51	.43	.35				
7	1	.91	.81	.72	.63	.54	.44	.35					
6	1	.89	.78	.68	.57	.46	.35						
5	1	.87	.74	.61	.48	.35							
4	1	.84	.68	.51	.35								
3	1	.78	.57	.35									
2	1	.68	.35										
1	1	.35											

CONSTRUCTION

● DAMAGE CONTROL VALUE ALLOCATION TABLE

CAV

DT	0	1	2	3	4	5	6	7	8	9	10	11	12
12	-	-	6	6	5	5	4	3	3	2	2	1	0
11	-	-	6	6	5	5	4	3	3	2	1	0	
10	-	-	6	6	5	5	4	3	2	1	0		
9	-	-	6	6	5	4	3	2	1	0			
8	-	-	6	5	4	3	2	1	0				
7	-	-	6	5	3	2	1	0					
6	-	-	6	4	2	1	0						
5	-	-	6	4	2	0							
4	-	-	6	3	0								
3	-	-	3	0									
2	-	-	-										
1	-	-											

Combat Vehicles

DT	0	1	2	3	4	5	6	7	8	9	10	11	12
12	-	-	-	-	-	-	-	-	-	-	-	-	-
11	-	-	-	-	-	-	-	-	-	-	-	-	
10	-	-	-	-	-	-	-	-	-	-	-		
9	-	-	-	-	-	-	-	-	-	-			
8	-	-	5	5	4	3	2	1	0				
7	-	-	5	4	3	2	1	0					
6	-	-	5	3	2	1	0						
5	-	-	5	2	1	0							
4	-	-	5	1	0								
3	-	-	5	0									
2	-	-	3										
1	-	-											

Aircraft

DT	0	1	2	3	4	5	6	7	8	9	10	11	12
12	-	-	-	-	-	-	-	-	-	-	-	-	-
11	-	-	-	-	-	-	-	-	-	-	-	-	
10	-	-	-	-	-	-	-	-	-	-	-		
9	-	-	-	-	-	-	-	-	-	-			
8	-	-	-	-	-	-	-	-	-				
7	-	-	-	-	-	-	-	-					
6	-	-	4	3	2	1	0						
5	-	-	4	2	1	0							
4	-	-	4	1	0								
3	-	-	4	0									
2	-	-	2										
1	-	-											

Infantry

DT	0	1	2	3	4	5	6	7	8	9	10	11	12
3	-	-	3	2	-	-	-	-	-	-	-	-	-

WEAPON SYSTEMS

Appendix B: Weapon Systems

About this Appendix

The weapon systems appendix contains detailed descriptions of each weapon system found in CAV: SO. Following each description is the information required for adding these systems to a custom design and any game rules specific (if any) to their use during play.

Weapon Systems (non-infantry)

Autocannon (AC)

An autocannon is a large-caliber projectile weapon that fire rapid bursts of high-explosive, armor-piercing ammunition (HEAP) toward an enemy target. The shells of an autocannon are filled with a high-velocity producing hypergel propellant that requires no outside power source to fire, decreasing the space needed to equip.

- **Light Autocannon**
  Range: *8"*
  RAV: *1/2*
  Special Attributes: *Ammo, Full Auto*
  Hard-Point Cost: *.5 HP*
  Model Restrictions: *Available to aircraft, CAV, and vehicle models only.*
  Threat Point Cost: *49 TVP*

- **Medium Autocannon**
  Range: *8"*
  RAV: *2/4*
  Special Attributes: *Ammo, Full Auto*
  Hard-Point Cost: *1 HP*
  Model Restrictions: *Available to 5+ DT aircraft, CAV, and vehicle models only.*
  Threat Point Cost: *69 TVP*

- **Heavy Autocannon**
  Range: *8"*
  RAV: *3/6*
  Special Attributes: *Ammo, Full Auto*
  Hard-Point Cost: *2 HP*
  Model Restrictions: *Available to 7+ DT aircraft, CAV, and vehicle models only.*
  Threat Point Cost: *89 TVP*

Field Artillery System (FAS)

While normally seen only on vehicles or larger CAVs, a field artillery system fires a large caliber that is capable of hitting a target several kilometers away. Modern self-propelled artillery uses inertial navigation systems and satellites (if available) to provide constant positioning data to the onboard fire control and ballistic computers, allowing for constant movement to avoid counter-battery fire and still deliver accurate and timely fire on-target.

WEAPON SYSTEMS

The standard "dumb" round used by most military forces is a high-explosive projectile (HE) and is a bursting round, primarily used against infantry, light armor, and non-hardened structures, with fragmentation and blast effects.

Guided "smart" munitions are also available for field artillery systems as well (see Appendix C: Battlefield Upgrades, p. 134).

While many versions and variants of field artillery systems exist, they typically fall in one of the following types:

- **Light Howitzer**
  Range: *24"*
  RAV: *1/3 (HE)*
  Special Attributes: *AoE 1, Indirect-Fire, Limited Ammo, Minimum Range (12), Ravage, Shock (6)*
  Hard-Point Cost: *2 HP*
  Model Restrictions: *Available to 5+ DT CAV and vehicle models only. A model may equip up to two light howitzers.*
  Threat Point Cost: *92 TVP*

This smaller version of the field artillery system has a faster firing sequence than its larger brothers and is ideally suited for a more direct-fire role if needed. It is more limited in the ammo types available to it, using bulk-loaded hypergel liquid as a propellant to fire a shell. This allows for a greater number of rounds to be carried during an extended deployment in the field.

- **Heavy Howitzer**
  Range: *36"*
  RAV: *3/5 (HE)*
  Special Attributes: *AoE 3, Indirect-Fire, Limited Ammo, Minimum Range (18), Ravage, Shock (8)*
  Hard-Point Cost: *4 HP*
  Model Restrictions: *Available to 7+ DT CAV and vehicle models only. A model may only equip one heavy howitzer.*
  Threat Point Cost: *157 TVP*

The "big daddy" of modern artillery, the heavy howitzer can deliver a massive shell on-target, causing substantial damage. These large caliber rounds are sometimes referred to as "flying pigs" (a reference to their size; artillery is referred to as "hogs" by their crews) and while reducing the overall number of rounds carried, a wider variety of payload types are available.

- **Rocket Artillery Launcher**
  Range: *48"*
  RAV: *2/4 (HE)*
  Special Attributes: *AoE 2, Indirect-Fire, Limited Ammo, Minimum Range (24), Ravage, Shock (7), Slow-Fire*

Hard-Point Cost: *3 HP*
Model Restrictions: *Available to 7+ DT CAV and vehicles models only. A model may equip up to four rocket artillery launchers.*
Threat Point Cost: *160 TVP*

Typically used for a saturation attack on a fixed position, and have a self-contained rocket motor. They are slow-firing and have a more difficult time adapting to a fast moving front. A wide variety of payloads are available for use by rocket artillery launchers.

Flamethrower (FT)

Generally considered an anti-infantry weapon, the flamethrower sprays an area with a burning liquid gel designed to "stick" and burn at very high temperatures. Only total immersion under water (or anything that will cut off the oxygen supply), specialized fire-fighting foam, or time will put out the flames.

- **Flamethrower**
  Range: *2"*
  RAV: *NA*
  Special Attributes: *Limited Ammo, Minimum Range (1)*
  Hard-Point Cost: *.5 HP*
  Model Restrictions: *Available to CAV and vehicle models only.*
  Threat Point Cost: *25 TVP*

Game Rules: *Flamethrowers or "flamers" are very hard to control, making it nearly impossible to target a specific model. Instead, a flamethrower will generate a 1" wide corridor, extending in a straight line from the base of the attacking model to the end of the weapon system's extreme range band. Any model(s) caught in this area will receive the state: burning.*

Note: *Flamers will automatically set residential and commercial structures on fire, as detailed in the* **Structure Critical Event Table** *(see Structures p. 66).*

Unless extinguished by an external source, a model will remain "burning" for an additional three turns following an attack.

Guided Missile (GM)

A guided missile is a powered munition fired from a launch tube that has been targeted at a single enemy. Multiple guided missiles may be fired but each requires a separate launcher. Unlike rockets, which are mass-fired at an area in an attempt to hit any enemy machines that might be there, guided missiles require a laser or radar lock-on before firing to have any chance of striking the desired target.

Most guided missiles use a ramjet engine for propulsion to

quickly accelerate it from the launcher, away from the attacker to avoid any collateral damage, and results in a minimum travel distance the missile must go before it can arm and damage the intended target. The larger size of a single guided missile also allows for a much larger warhead than what a rocket would carry, greatly improving the damage potential of a successful strike.

● Light Guided Missile
Range: *16"*
RAV: *4/4*
Special Attributes: *Improved Range, Limited Ammo, Minimum Range (14), Shock (4)*
Hard-Point Cost: *1 HP*
Model Restrictions: *Available to aircraft, CAV, and vehicle models only.*
Threat Point Cost: *113 TVP*

● Medium Guided Missile
Range: *16"*
RAV: *5/5*
Special Attributes: *Blaster 1, Improved Range, Limited Ammo, Minimum Range (14), Shock (6)*
Hard-Point Cost: *2 HP*
Model Restrictions: *Available to 5+ DT aircraft, CAV, and vehicle models only.*
Threat Point Cost: *144 TVP*

● Heavy Guided Missile
Range: *16"*
RAV: *6/6*
Special Attributes: *Blaster 2, Improved Range, Limited Ammo, Minimum Range (14), Shock (8)*
Hard-Point Cost: *3 HP*
Model Restrictions: *Available to 7+ DT aircraft, CAV, and vehicle models only.*
Threat Point Cost: *172 TVP*

Game Rules: Guided missiles can be used for both direct or indirect-fire ranged assaults but require an existing target-lock or TAG on the enemy model before firing.

Infantry models cannot be targeted by a guided missile attack.

Heavy Machine Gun (HMG)
Heavy machine guns are large, fully automatic weapon systems that fire large-caliber, non-explosive ammunition at a very high rate—typically several hundred rounds a minute—from a large-capacity magazine. The amount of ammunition a HMG requires, as well as its size, generally restricts its use to being mounted on self-propelled combatants (or fixed positions) as an anti-infantry weapon or against soft vehicles and structures.

● Heavy Machine Gun
Range: *4"*
RAV: *0/2*
Special Attributes: *Ammo, Blitz 1, Ravage*
Hard-Point Cost: *.5 HP*
Model Restrictions: *Available to aircraft, CAV, and vehicle models only.*
Threat Point Cost: *26 TVP*

Ion Disruptor Cannon (IDC)
The ion disruptor cannon is designed to damage or destroy onboard electronic systems on a targeted model. The IDC ionizes hydrogen gas atoms within an acceleration chamber, releasing this stored energy when fired. The effect appears as a "ball" of glowing energy racing through the air, impacting on the intended target and generating a "lightning storm" of released energy along the surface of the target.

● Light Ion Disruptor Cannon
Range: *8"*
RAV: *4/4*
Special Attributes: *NA*
Hard-Point Cost: *1 HP*
Model Restrictions: *Available to 5+ DT aircraft, CAV, and vehicle models only.*
Threat Point Cost: *50 TVP*

● Heavy Ion Disruptor Cannon
Range: *8"*
RAV: *6/6*
Special Attributes: *NA*
Hard-Point Cost: *2 HP*
Model Restrictions: *Available to 7+ DT aircraft, CAV, and vehicle models only.*
Threat Point Cost: *75 TVP*

Game Rules: Unlike other weapon system types, an ion disruptor directly targets the onboard electronic systems of a model but instead of doing any "damage", the defending model will receive the State: Disrupted for a number of turns equal to the amount of "damage" called for (if any).

Infantry or non-infantry models with the SA: Shielding are not affected by an ion disruptor attack.

Laser Bolt Gun (LBG)
A laser bolt gun is an energy weapon powered directly from a machine's onboard breeder unit, requiring no expendables, and is favored when stationed in a remote area or during operations with a limited supply train.

Unlike industrial-grade lasers that are designed to focus a constant "stream" and cut, a laser bolt gun uses a condenser to collect charged particles. These particles compress into a "bolt" that releases a tremendous amount of energy when triggered, energy that is transferred to a target, increasing the damage potential of the weapon exponentially.

- **Light Laser Bolt Gun**
  Range: *10"*
  RAV: *3/3*
  Special Attributes: *Improved Range, Overdrive*
  Hard-Point Cost: *.5 HP*
  Model Restrictions: *Available to aircraft, CAV, and vehicle models only.*
  Threat Point Cost: *90 TVP*

- **Medium Laser Bolt Gun**
  Range: *10"*
  RAV: *4/4*
  Special Attributes: *Improved Range, Overdrive*
  Hard-Point Cost: *1.5 HP*
  Model Restrictions: *Available to 5+ DT aircraft, CAV, and vehicle models only.*
  Threat Point Cost: *105 TVP*

- **Heavy Laser Bolt Gun**
  Range: *10"*
  RAV: *5/5*
  Special Attributes: *Improved Range, Overdrive*
  Hard-Point Cost: *2.5 HP*
  Model Restrictions: *Available to 7+ DT aircraft, CAV, and vehicle models only.*
  Threat Point Cost: *120 TVP*

Magnetic Accelerator Cannon (MAC)

The magnetic accelerator cannon is the workhorse of every major modernized fighting force in the 23rd century. The weapon uses a system of alternating negative- and positive-charged "rings" to fire an anti-armor penetrator "rod" at the desired target.

A MAC's penetrator rod is made of a hardened metal alloy (the exact composition depends on the manufacturer) encased in a super-conducting casing (known as a SABOT) that allows it to travel down the barrel of the weapon at hyper-velocity speeds. Once the rod has cleared the barrel, the SABOT falls away, allowing the round to continue on.

- **Light Magnetic Accelerator Cannon**
  Range: *12"*
  RAV: *3/1*
  Special Attributes: *Ammo, Blaster 1, Minimum Range (1), Strike*
  Hard-Point Cost: *1.5 HP*
  Model Restrictions: *Available to aircraft, CAV, and vehicle models only.*
  Threat Point Cost: *72 TVP*

- **Medium Magnetic Accelerator Cannon**
  Range: *12"*
  RAV: *5/2*
  Special Attributes: *Ammo, Blaster 1, Minimum Range (1), Strike*
  Hard-Point Cost: *2.5 HP*
  Model Restrictions: *Available to 5+ DT aircraft, CAV, and vehicle models only.*
  Threat Point Cost: *97 TVP*

- **Heavy Magnetic Accelerator Cannon**
  Range: *12"*
  RAV: *7/3*
  Special Attributes: *Ammo, Blaster 2, Minimum Range (1), Strike*
  Hard-Point Cost: *3.5 HP*
  Model Restrictions: *Available to 7+ DT aircraft, CAV, and vehicle models only.*
  Threat Point Cost: *134 TVP*

Magnetic Rotary Accelerator Cannon (MRAC)

The rotary accelerator cannon multiples the penetration of a MAC by adding additional barrels, allowing it a much higher rate of fire. While sacrificing the overall initial impact of the larger-caliber MAC, a MRAC will literally "melt" its way through an armored target as it hammers away with a steady stream of rounds.

The placement of the accelerator rings around the barrels generates the alternating magnetic pulses needed to propel each round as a barrel rotates into firing position, locking the next barrel in. This set-up places a large power demand on the model's breeder unit, as well as requiring massive ammo bins to feed the destruction being unleashed at the target.

- **Light Magnetic Rotary Accelerator Cannon**
  Range: *12"*
  RAV: *4/2*
  Special Attributes: *Anti-Aircraft, Limited Ammo, Minimum Range (1)*
  Hard-Point Cost: *2 HP*
  Model Restrictions: *Available to 3+ DT aircraft, CAV, and vehicle models only.*
  Threat Point Cost: *79 TVP*

- **Medium Magnetic Rotary Accelerator Cannon**
  Range: *12"*
  RAV: *6/3*
  Special Attributes: *Anti-Aircraft, Limited Ammo, Minimum Range (1)*
  Hard-Point Cost: *3 HP*
  Model Restrictions: *Available to 5+ DT aircraft, CAV, and vehicle models only.*
  Threat Point Cost: *104 TVP*

- **Heavy Magnetic Rotary Accelerator Cannon**
  Range: *12"*
  RAV: *8/4*
  Special Attributes: *Anti-Aircraft, Limited Ammo, Minimum Range (1)*
  Hard-Point Cost: *4 HP*
  Model Restrictions: *Available to 7+ DT aircraft, CAV, and vehicle models only.*
  Threat Point Cost: *129 TVP*

Particle Bolt Gun (PBG)

The particle bolt gun was developed to provide a heavier energy-based weapon for the battlefield that could be used in extended campaigns without the need for constant ammo re-supply.

The weapon works by "ripping" atomic particles apart in the main condensing chamber. This reaction is focused into a bolt of electrically charged, high-energy, neutral hydrogen atoms that move in a straight line at near the velocity of light to its target.

The beam will burn through most power armor with little or no resistance, reducing the person inside to blackened husk. A person killed by a particle bolt is commonly referred to as a "briquette." Even the thick armor plating of a vehicle or CAV can be burned through with a strong enough beam.

The main drawbacks to the weapon system are its short range and power requirements. The atmosphere of a planet quickly degrades a bolt as it travels to the target. Naval versions of this weapon system in space do not suffer from this degradation and are very effective weapons for ship-to-ship combat.

- **Light Particle Bolt Gun**
  Range: *6"*
  RAV: *4/4*
  Special Attributes: *Blitz 2, Overdrive, Ravage*
  Hard-Point Cost: *1 HP*
  Model Restrictions: *Available to CAV and vehicle models only.*
  Threat Point Cost: *100 TVP*

- **Medium Particle Bolt Gun**
  Range: *6"*
  RAV: *6/6*
  Special Attributes: *Blitz 2, Overdrive, Ravage*
  Hard-Point Cost: *2 HP*
  Model Restrictions: *Available to 5+ DT CAV and vehicle models only.*
  Threat Point Cost: *130 TVP*

- **Heavy Particle Bolt Gun**
  Range: *6"*
  RAV: *8/8*
  Special Attributes: *Blaster 1, Blitz 2, Overdrive, Ravage*
  Hard-Point Cost: *3 HP*
  Model Restrictions: *Available to 7+ DT CAV and vehicle models only.*
  Threat Point Cost: *177 TVP*

Pylon (P)

A pylon serves as an adapter to connect the frame of an aircraft to an external device (typically a bomb rack).

- **Pylon**
  Range: *NA*
  RAV: *NA*
  Special Attributes: *NA*
  Hard-Point Cost: *.5 HP*
  Model Restrictions: *Available to aircraft models only.*
  Threat Point Cost: *37 TVP*

Game Rules: *Each pylon allows an aircraft model to mount a single bomb or bomb rack (see Upgrades, p. 136) to conduct an indirect-fire ranged assault on a designated strike-point on the ground below its movement path while in flight.*

Each pylon is equipped with a single Mk I general purpose bomb by default that may be used at no extra cost during a game.

- **Mk I GP Bomb**
  Range: *NA*
  RAV: *1/2*
  Special Attributes: *AoE 1, Limited Ammo, Ravage, Shock (6)*
  Hard-Point Cost: *NA*
  Model Restrictions: *NA*
  Threat Point Cost: *NA*

Rocket (R)

Unlike missiles, rockets do not require any additional targeting assistance before being fired, relying on multiple warheads to saturate an area around a target(s) in an attempt for a successful strike. Rockets use a solid fuel propellant for acceleration, producing a winding smoke-trail behind them as they arc into the air, and burn out quicker than a missile, decreasing their overall range.

Semi-guided rockets are available (See Upgrades, p. 136) that can be used in conjunction with a TAG system to increase the chance of successfully striking the desired target area. The addition of a TAG sensor and thrusters to make slight in-flight corrections decreases the size of warhead that can be used (-1 RAV).

Rockets can also be fitted out with cluster munitions (See Upgrades, p. 136) to drop mines over an area and prevent an enemy from moving through it.

W E A P O N   S Y S T E M S

- **Light Rocket 5/10/15/20**
  Range: *14"*
  RAV: *2/2, 3/3, 4/4, 5/5*
  Special Attributes: *AoE 1,1,2,3, Indirect-Fire, Limited Ammo, Minimum Range (12), Ravage, SMART*
  Hard-Point Cost: *.5/1/2/3 HP*
  Model Restrictions: *Available to 1/3/5/7+ DT aircraft, CAV, and vehicle models only.*
  Threat Point Cost: *88/105/123/142 TVP*

- **Heavy Rocket 5/10/15/20**
  Range: *14"*
  RAV: *4/4, 5/5, 6/6, 7/7*
  Special Attributes: *AoE 1,1,2,3, Indirect-Fire, Limited Ammo, Minimum Range (12), Ravage, SMART*
  Hard-Point Cost: *1/2/3/4 HP*
  Model Restrictions: *Available to 3/5/7/9+ DT aircraft, CAV, and vehicle models only.*
  Threat Point Cost: *121/137/156/175 TVP*

Game Rules: *Rockets are used with the combat action to target the area occupied by an enemy model(s) and cannot be used to attack an aircraft model in-flight.*

Rotary Autocannon (RAC)

A variant of the standard autocannon, the rotary autocannon uses multiple rotating barrels (generally 3 to 6) to dramatically increase the rate of fire. As a result of the increase in fire, the rotary autocannon will "spray" a larger area, increasing the number of target that may be hit.

- **Light Rotary Autocannon**
  Range: *8"*
  RAV: *2/4*
  Special Attributes: *Anti-Aircraft, AoE 1, Full Auto, Limited Ammo*
  Hard-Point Cost: *1 HP*
  Model Restrictions: *Available to aircraft, CAV, and vehicle models only.*
  Threat Point Cost: *76 TVP*

- **Medium Rotary Autocannon**
  Range: *8"*
  RAV: *3/6*
  Special Attributes: *Anti-Aircraft, AoE 1, Full Auto, Limited Ammo*
  Hard-Point Cost: *2 HP*
  Model Restrictions: *Available to 5+ DT aircraft, CAV, and vehicle models only.*
  Threat Point Cost: *96 TVP*

- **Heavy Rotary Autocannon**
  Range: *8"*

RAV: *4/8*
Special Attributes: *Anti-Aircraft, AoE 1, Full Auto, Limited Ammo*
Hard-Point Cost: *3 HP*
Model Restrictions: *Available to 7+ DT aircraft, CAV, and vehicle models only.*
Threat Point Cost: *116 TVP*

Weapon Systems (Infantry)

Assault Rifle (AR)

The assault rifle is the standard-issue infantry weapon of most light and heavy infantry and is in use by every military force in the galaxy.

- **Assault Rifle**
  Range: *2"*
  RAV: *NA/1*
  Special Attributes: *NA*
  Hard-Point Cost: *1 HP*
  Model Restrictions: *Available to infantry models only.*
  Threat Point Cost: *10 TVP*

Laser Bolt Rifle (LBR)

Powered by an HCC battery pack worn as a backpack and cabled to the weapon. Extremely accurate, a laser bolt rifle can cause considerable damage to the desired target.

- **Laser Bolt Rifle**
  Range: *4"*
  RAV: *0/1*
  Special Attributes: *Improved Range*
  Hard-Point Cost: *1 HP*
  Model Restrictions: *Available to infantry models only.*
  Threat Point Cost: *28 TVP*

Magnetic Accelerator Rifle (MAR)

A magnetic accelerator rifle is the standard-issue weapon system of most powered armor infantry. As the heavy magnetic accelerator rifle is mounted on a tripod, it can be used by all infantry types.

- **Magnetic Accelerator Rifle**
  Range: *6"*
  RAV: *1/0*
  Special Attributes: *Full Auto*
  Hard-Point Cost: *1 HP*
  Model Restrictions: *Available to powered infantry models only.*
  Threat Point Cost: *35 TVP*

- **Heavy Magnetic Accelerator Rifle**
  Range: *6"*

WEAPON SYSTEMS

RAV: *2/0*
Special Attributes: *Full Auto, Minimum Range (1)*
Hard-Point Cost: *2 HP*
Model Restrictions: *Available to infantry models only.*
Threat Point Cost: *45 TVP*

Mortar (M)

To counter the large number of armored combat machines on the modern battlefield, most militaries equip their infantry with mortars.

The mortar tubes of the 23rd century are quite different from their earlier predecessors, launching special terrain-hugging, active-homing, anti-armor rounds nicknamed "hummers" (due to the sound they make as they skim across the landscape) and are typically manned by a three-soldier crew.

● Light Mortar
Range: *16"*
RAV: *3/3*
Special Attributes: *Improved Range, Indirect-Fire, Limited Ammo, Minimum Range (14), Strike*
Hard-Point Cost: *2 HP*
Model Restrictions: *Available to infantry models only.*
Threat Point Cost: *90 TVP*

● Medium Mortar
Range: *16"*
RAV: *5/5*
Special Attributes: *Blaster 1, Improved Range, Indirect-Fire, Limited Ammo, Minimum Range (14), Strike*
Hard-Point Cost: *2 HP*
Model Restrictions: *Available to infantry models only.*
Threat Point Cost: *132 TVP*

Submachine Gun (SMG)

The submachine gun is an automatic weapon using pistol-caliber ammo at a very high rate of fire.

● Submachine Gun
Range: *1"*
RAV: *NA/1*
Special Attributes: *AoE 1, Blitz 1*
Hard-Point Cost: *1 HP*
Model Restrictions: *Available to infantry models only.*
Threat Point Cost: *15 TVP*

Grenade Launcher (GL)

A grenade launcher is used to fire a "grenade" with more accuracy at greater distances (as compared to a hand-tossed grenade). Grenade launchers can be used as a standalone weapon (either single-shot or repeating) or mounted under the barrel of an assault rifle.

● Grenade Launcher
Range: *3"*
RAV: *NA/2*
Special Attributes: *AoE 1, Indirect-Fire, Minimum Range (1), Ravage*
Hard-Point Cost: *1 HP*
Model Restrictions: *Available to infantry models only.*
Threat Point Cost: *21 TVP*

Grenade (G)

A grenade is a "small bomb" that can be thrown by hand and are especially useful during close-up assaults and clearing out structures.

● Grenade
Range: *1"*
RAV: *NA/1*
Special Attributes: *AoE 1, Blitz 1, Indirect-Fire, Minimum Range (1)*
Hard-Point Cost: *.5 HP*
Model Restrictions: *Available to infantry models only.*
Threat Point Cost: *15 TVP*

Panzerfaust (AT)

The Panzerfaust is representative of the many man-portable, shoulder-launched anti-armor weapons in use throughout the galaxy.

● Panzerfaust
Range: *4"*
RAV: *2/2*
Special Attributes: *Minimum Range (1), Strike*
Hard-Point Cost: *1 HP*
Model Restrictions: *Available to infantry models only.*
Threat Point Cost: *38 TVP*

Stinger (SAM)

The Stinger is representative of the many shoulder-fired, anti-aircraft, surface-to-air missile systems in use throughout the galaxy. SAMs may only be fired at aircraft models.

● Stinger
Range: *8"*
RAV: *NA/2*
Special Attributes: *Anti-Aircraft*
Hard-Point Cost: *1 HP*
Model Restrictions: *Available to infantry models only.*
Threat Point Cost: *25 TVP*

Minigun

The minigun is a multi-barrel machine gun that uses smaller, rifle-sized calibers at a high rate of fire, using an electric motor to rotate the barrels. As the heavy minigun is mounted

SPECIAL ABILITIES

on a tripod, it can be used by all infantry types.

- **Minigun**
  Range: *4"*
  RAV: *NA/2*
  Special Attributes: *Anti-Aircraft, AoE 1, Ravage*
  Hard-Point Cost: *1 HP*
  Model Restrictions: *Available to powered infantry models only.*
  Threat Point Cost: *28 TVP*

- **Heavy Minigun**
  Range: *4"*
  RAV: *NA/3*
  Special Attributes: *Anti-Aircraft, AoE 1, Minimum Range (1), Ravage*
  Hard-Point Cost: *2 HP*
  Model Restrictions: *Available to infantry models only.*
  Threat Point Cost: *35 TVP*

Light Machine Gun (LMG)

Light machine guns use standard rifle ammunition at an increased rate of fire and are typically used as a squad support weapon during a fire fight.

- **Light Machine Gun**
  Range: *3"*
  RAV: *NA/1*
  Special Attributes: *Anti-Aircraft, Blaster 1, Ravage*
  Hard-Point Cost: *1 HP*
  Model Restrictions: *Available to infantry models only.*
  Threat Point Cost: *30 TVP*

Appendix C: Special Abilities & Attributes (SA)

About this Appendix

The special abilities & attributes appendix contains detailed descriptions of each SA found in CAV: SO. Following each description is the information required for adding these systems to a custom design and any game rules specific (if any) to their use during play.

Special abilities & attributes are used in CAV: SO to help make a model more "unique" and provide a means to highlight different capabilities or equipment a specific model-type may have. A special ability or attribute will generally improve a model's performance but may also provide for a limitation or specific rule that may affect the model during play. Should the use of a SA conflict with an existing rule, use the SA description for determining the result of its use.

Equipping SAs

General special abilities & attributes may be added to a model using the construction system just like a weapon system. A restricted SA cannot be added during design and are specifically assigned to specific chassis-types or weapon systems only.

Some SAs may have more than one rating level as well, allowing for a more advanced version of the SA to be equipped.

Special Abilities & Attributes (General)

Ablative Armor

A model with the SA: *Ablative Armor* is equipped with a specialized armor that is more resistant to energy-based weapons. Unfortunately over time, this type of armor will "crystalize", making it brittle and susceptible to cracking when impacted, preventing its general use throughout the galaxy.

The SA: *Ablative Armor* provides a (+2) to a models base AV when it has been hit by a weapon system without the SA: *Ammo/Limited Ammo* but a (-1) when hit by a weapon system with this SA.

Only one armor-based SA is allowed per model.

- **Ablative Armor**
  Range: *NA*
  Hard-Point Cost: *1 HP*
  Model Restrictions: *Available to aircraft, CAV, and vehicle models only.*
  Threat Point Cost: *35 TVP*

Note: *The SA: Ablative Armor may not be combined with the SA: Improved Armor or Reactive Armor.*

Active Phase Array

The SA: *Active Phase Array* attempts to improve the targeting of enemy models by emitting various "beams" across

SPECIAL ABILITIES

multiple angles and frequencies. Friendly targeting systems can use this information to increase the chance of a successful hit.

A model with the SA: *Active Phase Array* may use a special action to perform one of the following functions each turn:

1. Provide a (+1) for each rating level to any friendly model's primary combat or strike-point roll if the targeted enemy model is currently located within its area of effect.

2. Attempt to "jam" (see Special Actions, p.64) any enemy model using the SA: *Active Phase Array* or SA: *ECM* on the game-board.

3. Receive an automatic target-lock on any model using the SA: *ECM* (within GM range) and fire one or more anti-radiation guided missiles at the enemy model, provided it has not already used a combat or target-lock action during the current turn.

Note: *Multiple SA: Active Phase Array bonuses do not stack.*

- **Active Phase Array 1**
  Range: *24"*
  Hard-Point Cost: *1 HP*
  Model Restrictions: *Available to aircraft, CAV, and vehicle models only.*
  Threat Point Cost: *50 TVP*

- **Active Phase Array 2**
  Range: *30"*
  Hard-Point Cost: *2 HP*
  Model Restrictions: *Available to aircraft, CAV, and vehicle models only.*
  Threat Point Cost: *100 TVP*

Advanced Targeting Computer

The SA: *Advanced Targeting Computer* provides for more advanced targeting systems beyond the rudimentary computers provided with most non-infantry models. By using the Target-Lock Action, a model may add (+) the rating level of the SA: *Advanced Targeting Computer* to a primary combat or strike-point roll.

- **Advanced Targeting Computer 1**
  Range: *NA*
  Hard-Point Cost: *.5 HP*
  Model Restrictions: *Available to aircraft, CAV, and vehicle models only.*
  Threat Point Cost: *25 TVP*

- **Advanced Targeting Computer 2**
  Range: *NA*
  Hard-Point Cost: *1.5 HP*
  Model Restrictions: *Available to aircraft, CAV, and vehicle models only.*
  Threat Point Cost: *50 TVP*

AEGIS

A defending model in a close-combat assault with the SA: *AEGIS* receives a (+1) to its final combat roll value.

- **AEGIS**
  Range: *B2B*
  Hard-Point Cost: *1 HP*
  Model Restrictions: *Available to CAV and vehicle models only.*
  Threat Point Cost: *15 TVP*

Airborne

Infantry models with the SA: *Airborne* may dismount a transporting aircraft at any point along its declared flight path during the activation of either the infantry or aircraft model as a free action.

- **Airborne**
  Range: *B2B*
  Hard-Point Cost: *1 HP*
  Model Restrictions: *Available to infantry models only.*
  Threat Point Cost: *5 TVP*

Ammo Bin

The SA: *Ammo Bin* provides for one or more internal ammo storage bins. Each ammo bin level allows a model to ignore one "out of ammo" critical fumble result as detailed by the SA: *Ammo/Limited Ammo.*

- **Ammo Bin**
  Range: *NA*
  Hard-Point Cost: *.5 HP per level*
  Model Restrictions: *Available to aircraft, CAV, and vehicle models only.*
  Threat Point Cost: *5 TVP per level*

Amphibious

A model with the SA: *Amphibious* has been equipped to travel underwater, allowing for complete submersion for an extended period, allowing it to move "through" water terrain that would normally be impassable to it. An additional 1 MV is required for each one inch traveled underwater and any attack actions are prohibited.

- **Amphibious**
  Range: *NA*
  Hard-Point Cost: *1 HP*
  Model Restrictions: *Available to CAV and vehicle models only.*
  Threat Point Cost: *5 TVP*

Anti-Infantry

A model with the SA: *Anti-Infantry* is equipped with a series

SPECIAL ABILITIES

of explosive "strips" around its lower sections that will detonate when attacked by one or more infantry models in a close-assault attack, firing a hail of deadly shrapnel right above the ground.

The SA: *Anti-Infantry* provides a (+1) to the models combat roll value when the equipping model is the primary attacker against a defending infantry model or, the model is the defender in a close-combat assault and any attacker is an infantry model.

A model with the SA: *Anti-Infantry* will not receive this bonus if it is a supporting attacker or there are no infantry models attacking it.

- **Anti-Infantry**
  Range: *B2B*
  Hard-Point Cost: *.5 HP*
  Model Restrictions: *Available to CAV and vehicle models only.*
  Threat Point Cost: *15 TVP*

Assault

The SA: *Assault* reduces the combat roll penalty for a model using a combat action to conduct a Run 'N Gun by (-1) for each rating level indicated.

The SA: *Assault* applies to the penalty only and cannot be used to provide a bonus to the combat roll.

- **Assault**
  Range: *NA*
  Hard-Point Cost: *.5 HP per level*
  Model Restrictions: *None*
  Threat Point Cost: *20 TVP per level*

Chain-Fire Pod

A model with the SA: *Chain-Fire Pod* allows other models in the same squad to use it's final strike-point location, provided they have not already attempted a strike-point attempt of their own during the current turn.

The model with the SA: *Chain-Fire Pod* must use the target-lock action before attempting the strike-point roll and each attacking model is still required to make a successful combat roll to damage any defending models.

A model is not required to have the SA: *Chain-Fire Pod* in order to "chain-in" and use the designated strike-point.

- **Chain-Fire Pod**
  Range: *NA*
  Hard-Point Cost: *1 HP*
  Model Restrictions: *Available to aircraft, CAV, and vehicle models only.*
  Threat Point Cost: *50 TVP*

CHAMELEON

The SA: *CHAMELEON* provides a model with an adaptive camouflage system that attempts to duplicate reflected light from the surrounding area and make a model "blend" in with the terrain around it (making it ineffective at night).

A model attempting a direct-fire ranged assault on a defending model at medium or greater range with the SA: *CHAMELEON* will add a (+1) to their target-point value.

- **CHAMELEON**
  Range: *NA*
  Hard-Point Cost: *1 HP*
  Model Restrictions: *Available to CAV, powered infantry, and vehicle models only.*
  Threat Point Cost: *25 TVP*

Counter-Battery

A model with the SA: *Counter-Battery* may use the defensive fire option to fire one or more weapon systems with the SA: *Indirect-Fire* at an enemy model that has targeted it with an indirect-fire ranged assault or a final strike point located within 12" of it (regardless of target).

Note: *Minimum range limitations still apply when using the SA: Counter-Battery to make the attack.*

- **Counter-Battery**
  Range: *12"*
  Hard-Point Cost: *1 HP*
  Model Restrictions: *Available to CAV and vehicle models only.*
  Threat Point Cost: *15 TVP*

Counter-Measures

A model with the SA: *Counter-Measures* is equipped with additional systems that can be used to block or deflect a target-lock or TAG attempt once per turn as a free action with a successful 10+ roll.

Each SA: *Counter-Measures* rating level will add a (+1) to the final roll value.

- **Counter-Measures**
  Range: *NA*
  Hard-Point Cost: *.5 HP per level*
  Model Restrictions: *Available to aircraft, CAV, and vehicle models only.*
  Threat Point Cost: *10 TVP per level*

Dropship

The SA: *Dropship* allows larger aircraft the ability to transport a greater number of personnel directly to the battlefield. These type of aircraft can also be used to transport one or more CAV and combat vehicles as well.

Each rating level allows for one CAV and/or combat vehicle model to be transported or one to four infantry models. Models with the SA: *Bulky* count as two models for this purpose.

- **Dropship**
  Range: *NA*
  Hard-Point Cost: *1 HP per level*
  Model Restrictions: *Available to 5+ DT aircraft models only.*
  Threat Point Cost: *0 TVP per level*

ECM

The SA: *ECM* provides for an improved electronic system array to "spoof" or block the detection and targeting systems of enemy models located within a model's area of effect. A model with the SA: *ECM* may use a special action to perform one of the following functions each turn:

1. Block any target-lock attempt by an enemy model currently located within its area of effect.

2. Attempt to "jam" (see Special Actions, p.64) any enemy model using the SA: *Active Phase Array* or SA: *ECM* on the game-board.

3. Receive an automatic target-lock on any model using the SA: *Active Phase Array* (within GM range) and fire one or more anti-radiation guided missiles at the enemy model, provided it has not already used a combat or target-lock action during the current turn.

- **ECM 1**
  Range: *24"*
  Hard-Point Cost: *1 HP*
  Model Restrictions: *Available to aircraft, CAV, and vehicle models only.*
  Threat Point Cost: *50 TVP*

- **ECM 2**
  Range: *30"*
  Hard-Point Cost: *1.5 HP*
  Model Restrictions: *Available to aircraft, CAV, and vehicle models only.*
  Threat Point Cost: *75 TVP*

EST

A model with the SA: *EST* (Electronic Source Targeting) will automatically share a target-lock on an enemy model currently located within its area of effect with any other model from its squad.

- **EST**
  Range: *36"*
  Hard-Point Cost: *1 HP*
  Model Restrictions: *Available to aircraft, CAV, and vehicle models only.*

Threat Point Cost: *50 TVP*

Expanded Chassis

The SA: *Expanded Chassis* allows for more internal space, adding an extra hard-point by reducing a model's base armor value by (-2).

- **Expanded Chassis**
  Range: *NA*
  Hard-Point Cost: *0 HP*
  Model Restrictions: *Available to aircraft, CAV, and vehicle models only.*
  Threat Point Cost: *0 TVP*

FCS

The SA: *FCS* (Fire Control System) allows two or more models in the same squad to link together (Free Action) and increase their chance for a successful strike-point roll.

For each additional model with the SA: *FCS* in a squad, a (+1) is added to each model's strike-point roll.

- **FCS**
  Range: *NA*
  Hard-Point Cost: *.5 HP*
  Model Restrictions: *Available to aircraft, CAV, and vehicle models only.*
  Threat Point Cost: *50 TVP*

Example: *If there is only one model in the squad with the SA: FCS, there is no bonus. If there is two models in the squad with the SA: FCS, both models would receive a (+1) to any strike-point rolls made by either. Any additional models in the same squad with the SA: FCS would each add another (+1).*

Fire-Proof

A model with the SA: *Fire-Proof* is equipped with a fire-suppression system designed to cover itself with a chemical agent and extinguish any fire (Free Action), making it immune to the State: *Burning*.

- **Fire-Proof 1**
  Range: *NA*
  Hard-Point Cost: *.5 HP*
  Model Restrictions: *Available to CAV and vehicle models only.*
  Threat Point Cost: *5 TVP*

- **Fire-Proof 2**
  Range: *3"*
  Hard-Point Cost: *1 HP*
  Model Restrictions: *Available to CAV and vehicle models only.*
  Threat Point Cost: *15 TVP*

SPECIAL ABILITIES

Note: *A model with SA: Fire-Proof 2 may also extinguish any fire within 3" of it's base by using a special action to activate.*

Grenadier

An infantry model with the SA: *Grenadier* has received additional training when engaging the enemy in a close-combat assault as a primary attacker or defender and will receive a (+1) to their final combat roll value.

- **Grenadier**
  Range: *NA*
  Hard-Point Cost: *1 HP*
  Model Restrictions: *Available to infantry models only.*
  Threat Point Cost: *15 TVP*

Gun Port

The SA: *Gun Port* can be added to a model with the Task: Transport, allowing a single infantry model inside to conduct a direct-fire, ranged assault during its activation. Multiple gun ports may be added to the model.

- **Gun Port**
  Range: *NA*
  Hard-Point Cost: *.5 HP per level*
  Model Restrictions: *Available to aircraft, CAV (quads), and vehicle models (with the Task: Transport) only.*
  Threat Point Cost: *5 TVP per level*

Improved Armor

The SA: *Improved Armor* sacrifices some speed and repair capability for increased protection. A model with the SA: *Improved Armor* will increase their armor value by (+1) and reduce their movement and damage control value by (-2).

- **Improved Armor**
  Range: *NA*
  Hard-Point Cost: *1 HP*
  Model Restrictions: *Available to aircraft, CAV, and vehicle models only.*
  Threat Point Cost: *0 TVP*

Note: *The SA: Improved Armor may not be combined with the SA: Ablative Armor or Reactive Armor.*

Improved Breeder

The SA: *Improved Breeder* replaces a model's main power source with a larger unit, providing more power and increasing a model's base MV by (+2).

- **Improved Breeder**
  Range: *NA*
  Hard-Point Cost: *1 HP*

Model Restrictions: *Available to aircraft, CAV, and vehicle models only.*
Threat Point Cost: *0 TVP*

Improved Chassis

The SA: *Improved Chassis* allows a model to mount a weapon system up to two damage tracks heavier than it would normally be allowed to use, decreasing it's base armor value by (-1).

- **Improved Chassis**
  Range: *NA*
  Hard-Point Cost: *0 HP*
  Model Restrictions: *Available to aircraft, CAV, and vehicle models only.*
  Threat Point Cost: *0 TVP*

Example: *A CAV model with only five damage tracks could use SA: Improved Chassis to mount a Heavy MAC, a weapon system normally restricted to 7+ DT models only.*

Improved Damage Control

The SA: *Improved Damage Control* increases redundancy among a model's onboard systems as well as adding additional nano-dispensers for emergency repairs during combat.

With the addition of the SA: *Improved Damage Control* a model may increase each damage control value by (+1).

- **Improved Damage Control**
  Range: *NA*
  Hard-Point Cost: *1 HP*
  Model Restrictions: *Available to aircraft, CAV, and vehicle models only.*
  Threat Point Cost: *25 TVP*

Large Sensor Profile

A model with the SA: *Large Sensor Profile* provides a (+1) to the primary combat or strike-point roll of any enemy model attacking the model with a ranged assault.

- **Large Sensor Profile**
  Range: *NA*
  Hard-Point Cost: *0 HP*
  Model Restrictions: *Available to aircraft, CAV, and vehicle models only.*
  Threat Point Cost: *-50 TVP*

Launcher

A model with the SA: *Launcher* is used to transport and launch one or more cruise missiles (one for each rating level) purchased as part of a Battlefield Support Strike (p. 141). The model with the SA: *Launcher* serves as the point of deployment for a cruise missile attack.

SPECIAL ABILITIES

- **Launcher**
  Range: *NA*
  Hard-Point Cost: *1 HP per level*
  Model Restrictions: *Available to aircraft, CAV, and vehicle models only.*
  Threat Point Cost: *0 TVP*

Piercing

The SA: *Piercing* will add a (+1) to any single weapon system type a model has equipped with a Hard RAV of "0+".

- **Piercing**
  Range: *NA*
  Hard-Point Cost: *1 HP*
  Model Restrictions: *None.*
  Threat Point Cost: *25 TVP per weapon system*

Example: *The Dictator-B has two medium MACs that have been modified by SA: Piercing, increasing their hard RAV by +1. This uses only 1 HP as the SA applies to all weapon systems of the same type but adds an additional +50 to the model's threat value total (+25 for each weapon system).*

Point Defense

A model with the SA: *Point Defense* can attempt to "intercept" and shoot-down an incoming guided missile, mortar, or rocket attack (any one combat roll) within it's range with a 10+ roll, each rating level providing a (+1) to the attempt.

A defending player must declare their intent to do so before any strike-point or combat rolls are made by the attacker.

The SA: *Point Defense* may be used once per each enemy model's attack.

- **Point Defense**
  Range: *2"*
  Hard-Point Cost: *1 HP per level*
  Model Restrictions: *Available to aircraft, CAV, and vehicle models only.*
  Threat Point Cost: *25 TVP per level*

Note: *A critical fumble while attempting a point defense 10+ roll will result in the disablement of the system for the remainder of the game.*

Rat

Infantry models with the SA: *Rat* are adept in using the surrounding terrain to mask their position and receive a light cover bonus, regardless of the terrain type they are in, when targeted by a ranged assault.

The SA: *Rat* also negates the SA: *Ravage,* removing any weapon system damage bonuses.

- **Rat**
  Range: *NA*
  Hard-Point Cost: *1 HP*
  Model Restrictions: *Available to infantry models only.*
  Threat Point Cost: *20 TVP*

Reactive Armor

A model with the SA: *Reactive Armor* is equipped with a specialized armor that uses an electromagnetic reaction to "deflect" the impact of kinetic-based weapons. Energy weapons typically will not trigger this reaction, reducing its effectiveness against these weapon types, preventing its general use.

The SA: *Reactive Armor* provides a (+2) to a models base AV when it has been hit by a weapon system with the SA: *Ammo/Limited Ammo* but a (-1) when hit by any other weapon system.

- **Reactive Armor**
  Range: *NA*
  Hard-Point Cost: *1 HP*
  Model Restrictions: *Available to aircraft, CAV, and vehicle models only.*
  Threat Point Cost: *35 TVP*

Note: *The SA: Reactive Armor may not be combined with the SA: Ablative Armor or Improved Armor.*

Reduced Turn

The SA: *Reduced Turn* removes the free facing change a non-infantry model receives when using the move action. Any facing change requires the model to spend 1 MV to perform.

- **Reduced Turn**
  Range: *NA*
  Hard-Point Cost: *0 HP*
  Model Restrictions: *Available to aircraft, CAV, and vehicle models only.*
  Threat Point Cost: *-50 TVP*

Reinforced

A model with the SA: *Reinforced* is less susceptible to a damaging hit and will reduce any margin of success value by the rating level of the SA.

- **Reinforced**
  Range: *NA*
  Hard-Point Cost: *.5 HP per level*
  Model Restrictions: *Available to aircraft, CAV, and vehicle models only.*
  Threat Point Cost: *25 TVP per level*

SPECIAL ABILITIES

Note: The SA: Reinforced cannot reduce a margin of success below "0".

Relentless

A model with the SA: Relentless ignores any MV critical damage results.

- **Relentless**
  Range: NA
  Hard-Point Cost: .5 HP
  Model Restrictions: Available to aircraft, CAV, and vehicle models only.
  Threat Point Cost: 15 TVP

Re-Supply

A model with the SA: Re-Supply may use a special action to reload the "ammo" of any model that it is currently in B2B contact with once per turn.

- **Re-Supply**
  Range: B2B
  Hard-Point Cost: 1 HP
  Model Restrictions: Available to aircraft, CAV, and vehicle models only.
  Threat Point Cost: 10 TVP

Rugged

A model with the SA: Rugged will always receive a critical success when successfully rolling for the repair action, repairing two points of damage (non-lingering only).

- **Rugged**
  Range: NA
  Hard-Point Cost: 1 HP
  Model Restrictions: Available to aircraft, CAV, and vehicle models only.
  Threat Point Cost: 50 TVP

Shielded

A model with the SA: Shielded has additional systems in place allowing it to ignore the effects of nano-disassemblers and ion disruptor cannons.

- **Shielded**
  Range: NA
  Hard-Point Cost: .5 HP
  Model Restrictions: Available to aircraft, CAV, and vehicle models only.
  Threat Point Cost: 15 TVP

Shredder

The SA: Shredder will add a (+1) to any single weapon system type a model has equipped with a Soft RAV of "0+".

- **Shredder**
  Range: NA
  Hard-Point Cost: 1 HP
  Model Restrictions: None.
  Threat Point Cost: 25 TVP per weapon system

Smoke

A model with the SA: Smoke is equipped with a smoke generator that can be used to disrupt targeting systems and block a TAG attempt.

Using a special action to activate, a model with the SA: Smoke can be used to create a smoke field in place (2" radius) or a "line" of smoke as the model moves (1" wide x 1" long) for each 1" spent moving in a straight line (any facing change ends the smoke line).

The smoke will provide a light cover bonus to any model that an attacker's line of sight passes through for a direct-fired, ranged attack. The smoke will also block any TAG attempt that traces a line through it.

- **Smoke**
  Range: Special
  Hard-Point Cost: 1 HP
  Model Restrictions: Available to CAV and vehicle models only.
  Threat Point Cost: 25 TVP

Storm

Infantry models with the SA: Storm use the mount or dismount action as a free action when disembarking from a ground-based transport.

- **Storm**
  Range: NA
  Hard-Point Cost: 1 HP
  Model Restrictions: Available to infantry models only.
  Threat Point Cost: 10 TVP

Superior Mobility

A model with the SA: Superior Mobility reduces the MV cost by (-1) when moving through the following terrain types: rough/broken, rubble, light woods, and elevation.

- **Superior Mobility**
  Range: NA
  Hard-Point Cost: 1 HP
  Model Restrictions: Available to CAV and vehicle models only.
  Threat Point Cost: 20 TVP

TAG

The SA: TAG is a low-energy laser designator used to "paint" a target for laser-guided weapon systems. While the laser is of a wavelength invisible to the human eye, most combatants can detect when they are the target of a TAG, allowing them to attempt any counter-measures if available.

The use of the SA: *TAG* requires a model to use the Special Action and have a valid LoS to the target model.

- **TAG**
  Range: *36"*
  Hard-Point Cost: *.5 HP (1 HP for infantry)*
  Model Restrictions: *None.*
  Threat Point Cost: *10 TVP*

Transport

Models with the SA: *Transport* are tasked with moving infantry models quickly and safely around a battlefield. Each rating level is the amount of transport space a model has to carry infantry models only. An infantry model with SA: *Bulky* counts as two models when determining transport space availability.

- **Transport**
  Range: *NA*
  Hard-Point Cost: *1 HP per level*
  Model Restrictions: *Available to aircraft, CAV (Quad), and vehicle models only.*
  Threat Point Cost: *0 TVP per level*

Turret

The SA: *Turret* provides for an armored enclosure on a model that can be used to house one or more weapon systems and allows for a 360-degree arc of fire.

A vehicle model with the SA: *Turret* adjacent (within 1") to an elevation level 1 hill is considered to be "hull-down", allowing it to receive a heavy cover bonus (-2) to any direct-fire ranged assaults with a LoS that crosses the elevation level being used.

- **Turret**
  Range: *NA*
  Hard-Point Cost: *.5 HP (per two weapons)*
  Model Restrictions: *Available to aircraft, CAV (Quad), and vehicle models only.*
  Threat Point Cost: *10 TVP*

Wizzo

A model with the SA: *Wizzo* is equipped with a two-seat cockpit providing additional space for a weapon systems officer (WSO or "wizzo"), allowing the pilot to concentrate on driving/flying the machine and the WSO to control the weapon systems.

The SA: *Wizzo* provides for a (+1) to any primary combat or strike-point roll made by the model.

- **Wizzo**
  Range: *NA*
  Hard-Point Cost: *1 HP*
  Model Restrictions: *Available to aircraft, CAV, and vehicle models only.*
  Threat Point Cost: *25 TVP*

Special Abilities and Attributes (Restricted)
Ammo/Limited Ammo

A player making a primary combat or strike-point roll with a weapon system with the SA: *Ammo/Limited Ammo* that rolls for a critical fumble will make an additional 1d6 roll. If the result of the roll is a 1 (for ammo) or a 1-2 (for limited ammo), that weapon system has exhausted its ammo stores for the remainder of the game.

- **Ammo/Limited Ammo**
  Range: *NA*
  Hard-Point Cost: *NA*
  Model Restrictions: *Weapon systems only.*
  Threat Point Cost: *0 TVP*

Anti-Aircraft

A weapon system with the SA: *Anti-Aircraft* can be used by a model currently in over-watch to make a direct-fired ranged assault on any air-based model currently flying nap of earth within it's LoS and weapon range.

- **Anti-Aircraft**
  Range: *NA*
  Hard-Point Cost: *NA*
  Model Restrictions: *Weapon systems only.*
  Threat Point Cost: *10 TVP*

AoE

A weapon system with the SA: *AoE* (Area of Effect) has the potential to damage any model caught within the radius of its attack. The level of the AoE determines the number of inches the radius is measured out from the final strike-point. Any model (friend or enemy) caught within this area is subject to a secondary combat roll with a **target-point roll (6+)**.

- **AoE**
  Range: *Special*
  Hard-Point Cost: *NA*
  Model Restrictions: *Weapon systems only.*
  Threat Point Cost: *5 TVP per level*

Blaster

A weapon system with the SA: *Blaster* has an increased chance to roll a critical success during a primary combat roll. SA: *Blaster 1* provides a critical success on a natural roll of "11+" and SA: *Blaster 2* provides a critical success on a natural roll of "10+".

SPECIAL ABILITIES

- **Blaster**
    Range: *NA*
    Hard-Point Cost: *NA*
    Model Restrictions: *Weapon systems only.*
    Threat Point Cost: *25 TVP per level*

Blitz

A weapon system with the SA: *Blitz* is better suited for the close-in fighting found during a close-combat assault. Multiple weapon systems with the SA: *Blitz* do not stack.

SA: *Blitz 1* provides for a (+1) to a model's combat roll when they are the primary attacker or defender in a close assault with an infantry model.

SA: *Blitz 2* provides for a (+1) to a model's combat roll when they are the primary attacker or defender in a close assault with any model type.

- **Blitz**
    Range: *Close Assault*
    Hard-Point Cost: *NA*
    Model Restrictions: *Weapon systems only.*
    Threat Point Cost: *10 TVP per level*

Bulky

A model with the SA: *Bulky* counts as two models for the purpose of transport and squad selection.

- **Bulky**
    Range: *NA*
    Hard-Point Cost: *NA*
    Model Restrictions: *None.*
    Threat Point Cost: *0 TVP*

C3

A model with the SA: *C3* is equipped with superior command, control, and communication abilities. For each SA: *C3* level, one C3 point is added to a force group's C3 point pool at the start of the game.

- **C3**
    Range: *NA*
    Hard-Point Cost: *NA*
    Model Restrictions: *None.*
    Threat Point Cost: *20 TVP per level*

Double-Time

The SA: *Double-Time* provides a model a heavy cover bonus (-2) to any attacker's combat roll provided it's current MV is 11+ and it used the move action twice during it's last activation.

The SA: *Double-Time* may not be used in conjunction with the Run N' Gun.

- **Double-Time**
    Range: *NA*

    Hard-Point Cost: *NA*
    Model Restrictions: *None.*
    Threat Point Cost: *0 TVP*

Full-Auto

A weapon system with the SA: *Full-Auto* fires a large number of rounds when conducting an attack, striking a target in multiple areas, increasing the chance of damaging a vital component.

As a result, a player may choose to re-roll one of the die on any combat roll, keeping the new result (even if lower).

- **Full-Auto**
    Range: *NA*
    Hard-Point Cost: *NA*
    Model Restrictions: *Weapon systems only.*
    Threat Point Cost: *25 TVP*

Hard

A model with the SA: *Hard* is considered a hard target and is subject to any game rules that may apply to a model with this SA.

- **Hard**
    Range: *NA*
    Hard-Point Cost: *NA*
    Model Restrictions: *Available to CAV and vehicle models only.*
    Threat Point Cost: *0 TVP*

Improved Handling

The SA: *Improved Handling* provides some models enhanced movement options based on their chassis type. These include:

Drift: *Wheeled combat vehicles and quad-CAVs can "drift", moving 1" forward and up to 1" left or right at the same time, using only 1 MV (plus any additional terrain-type costs) for the maneuver.*

Lateral Shift/Roll: *Aircraft, quad-CAVs, hover and anti-grav combat vehicles can use a lateral shift (a roll for aircraft) to move sideways up to 1" without changing their facing, using only 1 MV (plus any additional terrain-type costs) for the maneuver. Multiple lateral shifts/rolls can be used by the model during the same move action.*

- **Improved Handling**
    Range: *NA*
    Hard-Point Cost: *NA*
    Model Restrictions: *Available to aircraft, quad-CAV, hover and anti-grav vehicle models only.*
    Threat Point Cost: *0 TVP*

Improved Range

Weapon systems with the SA: *Improved Range* maintain their accuracy over longer ranges, reducing the target point value by (-1) on a primary combat roll when attacking a model in the long or extreme range bands.

- **Improved Range**
  Range: *NA*
  Hard-Point Cost: *NA*
  Model Restrictions: *Weapon systems only.*
  Threat Point Cost: *25 TVP*

Indirect-Fire

A weapon system with the SA: *Indirect-Fire* does not require a valid LoS to a target in order to be used as part of a ranged assault during the combat action.

- **Indirect-Fire**
  Range: *NA*
  Hard-Point Cost: *NA*
  Model Restrictions: *Weapon systems only.*
  Threat Point Cost: *0 TVP*

Locked-On

The SA: *Locked-On* allows a model to use the target-lock action as a free action during it's activation.

- **Locked-On**
  Range: *NA*
  Hard-Point Cost: *NA*
  Model Restrictions: *None.*
  Threat Point Cost: *25 TVP*

Minimum Range

A weapon system with the SA: *Minimum Range* cannot be used as part of a combat action to attack a target within the stated range (in inches).

- **Minimum Range**
  Range: *1"+*
  Hard-Point Cost: *NA*
  Model Restrictions: *Weapon systems only.*
  Threat Point Cost: *0 TVP*

Overdrive

A weapon system with the SA: *Overdrive* will double any damage done as part of a ranged assault, provided the attacker declares their intent to use the SA before making any combat rolls.

The use of the SA: *Overdrive* places an immense amount of stress of a weapon system and as a result requires an additional 1d6 roll after conducting the attack. If a "1" is rolled, the weapon(s) has over-heated and cannot be used the following turn. Any other result has no effect and play continues.

A critical fumble on the combat roll automatically results in a weapon failure, rendering it useless for the remainder of the game.

- **Overdrive**
  Range: *NA*
  Hard-Point Cost: *NA*
  Model Restrictions: *Weapon systems only.*
  Threat Point Cost: *25 TVP*

Pop-Up

A model with the SA: *Pop-Up* may rise above any blocking cover that is up to one elevation level higher than the model and conduct a ranged-assault, dropping back behind cover before an enemy model without a valid LoS to the model's location can make a direct-fire ranged assault in return (no defensive fire or over-watch).

- **Pop-Up**
  Range: *NA*
  Hard-Point Cost: *NA*
  Model Restrictions: *Available to aircraft, anti-grav vehicles, and infantry models only.*
  Threat Point Cost: *15 TVP*

Ravage

A weapon systems with the SA: *Ravage* will automatically double any damage done to an infantry model located in clear/open or paved terrain types.

- **Ravage**
  Range: *NA*
  Hard-Point Cost: *NA*
  Model Restrictions: *Weapon systems only.*
  Threat Point Cost: *2.5 TVP per Soft RAV*

Satellite Uplink

The SA: *Satellite Uplink* allows a model to use a free action once per turn during its activation for priority access to the *BattleNet* and request an attack from an orbiting space-based asset. The player will roll 1d6 and if a "6" is rolled, may choose any one attack from the Strike Package: *Space* for immediate deployment anywhere on the game-board surface.

- **Satellite Uplink**
  Range: *NA*
  Hard-Point Cost: *NA*
  Model Restrictions: *None.*
  Threat Point Cost: *50 TVP*

Shock

A weapon system with the SA: *Shock* can hit a target with so

SPECIAL ABILITIES

much force that they may become disorientated and confused temporarily.

Any model targeted by a weapon system with the SA: *Shock* must immediately make a **target-point roll**, using the level of the SA as its target number. A failed roll will result in the Model State: *Suppressed* being applied to the effected model.

If the weapon system also has the SA: *AoE*, any model caught within the attack's radius will be required to make the **target-point roll** as well.

- ● **Shock**
  Range: *AoE*
  Hard-Point Cost: *NA*
  Model Restrictions: *Weapon systems only.*
  Threat Point Cost: *4 TVP per level*

Slow-Fire

A weapon system with the SA: *Slow-Fire* cannot be used to make a ranged assault in any two consecutive turns.

- ● **Slow-Fire**
  Range: *NA*
  Hard-Point Cost: *NA*
  Model Restrictions: *Weapon systems only.*
  Threat Point Cost: *0 TVP*

SMART

A model with one or more weapon systems with the SA: *SMART* have the ability to adjust the RAV or AoE of the weapon system's munitions through micro-sensors integrated within the round and controlled by the model's onboard CPU.

Option A: *A player may choose to increase the AoE of a ranged attack up to 1" by subtracting from the RAV of the weapon system an equal amount. The RAV of a weapon system cannot be lowered below "0".*

Option B: *A player may choose to increase the RAV of a ranged attack up to (+1) by subtracting from the AoE of the weapon system an equal amount. The AoE of a weapon system cannot be lowered below "0".*

- ● **SMART**
  Range: *NA*
  Hard-Point Cost: *NA*
  Model Restrictions: *Weapon systems only.*
  Threat Point Cost: *50 TVP*

Soft

A model with the SA: *Soft* is considered a "soft" target and is subject to any game rules that may apply to a model with this SA.

- ● **Soft**
  Range: *NA*
  Hard-Point Cost: *NA*
  Model Restrictions: *Available to aircraft, infantry, and vehicle models only.*
  Threat Point Cost: *0 TVP*

Specialist

A model with the SA: *Specialist* may only be assigned to a specialist squad during force group construction.

- ● **Specialist**
  Range: *NA*
  Hard-Point Cost: *NA*
  Model Restrictions: *None.*
  Threat Point Cost: *0 TVP*

Strike

A weapon system with the SA: *Strike* is specifically designed to destroy an armored target with pin-point accuracy, making it virtually useless against dispersed infantry or fast-moving aircraft.

As a result, a weapon system with the SA: *Strike* cannot be used as part of an ranged assault against these two model types.

- ● **Strike**
  Range: *NA*
  Hard-Point Cost: *NA*
  Model Restrictions: *Weapon systems only.*
  Threat Point Cost: *0 TVP*

Unique

A model with the SA: *Unique* may only be selected once as part of a force group and/or by a specific faction (if any) as detailed by the model's description or data card.

- ● **Unique**
  Range: *NA*
  Hard-Point Cost: *NA*
  Model Restrictions: *None.*
  Threat Point Cost: *0 TVP*

Appendix D: Battlefield Upgrades

Soldiers in the field are experts at modifying weapons and gear to meet a specific need during wartime. This tradition is no stranger to the battlefield in the 23rd century and is referred to in CAV: SO as Battlefield Upgrades.

Before the start of any game, a force group commander may choose to use some of their Specialization or Threat Value Pool to purchase Battlefield Upgrades to increase the capabilities of one or more models under their command.

To determine the cost of any Battlefield Upgrade, multiply the upgrade's TV cost by the number of damage tracks a model being upgraded has.

Example: To add the Battlefield Upgrade: Turbocharger (TV 15) to a 9 DT Dictator-B would require spending 135 Specialization or Threat Value Pool points.

A model with more than one weapon system of the same type must purchase an upgrade for each weapon system on that model.

Example: To add the Battlefield Upgrade: Amped (TVP 10) to a Dictator-B's (9 DT) medium MACs, the upgrade must be applied to both weapons at the cost of 180 points (90 each).

Battlefield Upgrades cannot be used to modify Battlefield Assets or Support Strikes and do not stack. If two or more Battlefield Upgrades grant the same bonus to the same model, use the higher of the bonuses instead of adding them together.

Battlefield Upgrades (Non-Ammo)

Ablative Armor

Ablative Armor is designed to dissipate the focus of an energy-based weapon system across a wider surface area, reducing its damage potential. Over time this effect can cause Ablative Armor to "crystalize", making it brittle and susceptible to cracking when impacted from kinetic rounds, discouraging its use by engineers and designers across the galaxy.

- **Ablative Armor**
  Special Attributes: *NA*
  Model Restrictions: *Available to aircraft, CAV, and vehicle models only.*
  Upgrade Cost: *15 TVP*

Game Rules: A model with the Upgrade: Ablative Armor receives a (+2) AV bonus when hit by any ion, laser, or particle beam weapons. The model will also receive a (-1) to its AV when hit by any other weapon system type. This upgrade cannot be used in conjunction with any other armor upgrade.

Ace Pilot

Some pilots are more than just the sum of their training, seemingly invincible as their natural aptitude at being a warrior allows them to dominate their enemies.

- **Ace Pilot**
  Special Attributes: *NA*
  Model Restrictions: *Available to aircraft, CAV, and vehicle models only.*
  Upgrade Cost: *25 TVP*

Game Rules: An Ace Pilot will add a (+2) to any non-secondary combat die roll made by the model they have been assigned to.

Airborne Training

When the mission calls for you to jump out of a perfectly good aircraft, you had better hope the quick lesson you just got from that sergeant covered everything.

- **Airborne Training**
  Special Attributes: *Airborne*
  Model Restrictions: *Available to infantry models only.*
  Upgrade Cost: *10 TVP*

Game Rules: The Airborne Training Upgrade provides any infantry model the SA: Airborne.

Amped Weapons

A weapon system can be modified to be more effective in damaging a particular model type.

- **Amped Weapons**
  Special Attributes: *Piercing or Shredder*
  Model Restrictions: *Available to weapon systems only.*
  Upgrade Cost: *10 TVP*

Game Rules: The Amped Weapon Upgrade can be used to increase the Soft or Hard RAV of a single weapon type on a model by (+1). This upgrade may only be used once per model but must be applied to every weapon system of the same type.

Claymore Anti-Personnel Mine

Claymore AP mines can be mounted around the hull of a combat vehicle or the legs of a CAV to help ward off a close-combat infantry assault.

- **Claymore Anti-Personnel Mine**
  Special Attributes: *Anti-Infantry*
  Model Restrictions: *Available to CAV and vehicle models only.*
  Upgrade Cost: *5 TVP*

UPGRADES

Game Rules: *This upgrade is a single-use item only but provides for a (+2) bonus (see SA: Anti-Infantry) when making a close-combat assault combat roll vs infantry.*

External Anti-Nano Dispersion Pod

A series of pods, containing an anti-nano "powder", that can be mounted to the external surface of a machine to counter a nano-disassembler attack. When activated, the pod will explode, creating a cloud that will render any nanos it comes in contact with inert.

- **External Anti-Nano Dispersion Pod**
    Special Attributes: *NA*
    Model Restrictions: *Available to CAV and vehicle models only.*
    Upgrade Cost: *2.5 TVP*

Game Rules: *This upgrade is a single-use item only but may used (Free Action) to dissipate any nano clouds that it is currently in contact with. Multiple pods can be purchased and mounted to the model.*

External Chain-Fire Pod

A chain-fire pod that can be mounted to the external surface of a machine, allowing it upload a data-link through the BattleNet to another model in the same squad and upload accurate strike-point information.

- **External Chain-Fire Pod**
    Special Attributes: *Chain-Fire Pod*
    Model Restrictions: *Available to aircraft, CAV, and vehicle models only.*
    Upgrade Cost: *10 TVP*

Game Rules: *An external chain-fire pod provides a model the SA: Chain-Fire Pod but only allows one other model in the same squad to use the strike-point location.*

Close-Quarters Battle

Many military academies offer improved training for CAV pilots when engaging other CAVs in a close-combat assault.

- **Close-Quarters Battle**
    Special Attributes: *NA*
    Model Restrictions: *Available to CAV models only.*
    Upgrade Cost: *15 TVP*

Game Rules: *A CAV pilot will receive a (+1) to their CCV value as a primary attacker or defender in a close-combat assault with another CAV model.*

Combat Engineer

A combat engineer is responsible for a variety of tasks that

may be needed in the field by a combat unit. From clearing mines to blowing up bridges, a combat engineer must be ready for anything.

- **Combat Engineer**
    Special Attributes: *NA*
    Model Restrictions: *Available to CAV, infantry, and vehicle models only.*
    Upgrade Cost:

Combat Engineer 1	5 TVP
Combat Engineer 2	10 TVP
Combat Engineer 3	20 TVP

Game Rules: *This upgrade is required to allow a model to deploy one or more Battlefield Assets (p. 137). A scenario may also call for the use of a combat engineer for a specific mission.*

A combat engineer will typically require the use of a Special Action and a target-point or 10+ roll, using the rating level as a (+) situation modifier to any roll.

External ECM Pod

An ECM pod can be mounted to the external surface of a machine, allowing it provide some of the functionality found in a more dedicated array system.

- **External ECM Pod**
    Special Attributes: *ECM*
    Model Restrictions: *Available to aircraft, CAV, and vehicle models only.*
    Upgrade Cost: *15 TVP*

Game Rules: *An external ECM pod is provides for the SA: ECM, but is limited in range and capabilities due to power and software requirements. As a result, an ECM pod may only be used to block the use of the target-lock action by an enemy model(s) located within its active range (range: 18").*

External Ammo Bin

Modern weapon systems use an incredible amount of ammo during a battle and the ability to re-supply while fighting may be very limited. External ammo bins allow for additional ammo to be stored on a machine and "jury-rigged" into the feed mechanism of a weapon for a quick reload.

- **External Ammo Bin**
    Special Attributes: *Ammo Bin*
    Model Restrictions: *Available to aircraft, CAV, and vehicle models only.*
    Upgrade Cost: *5 TVP*

Game Rules: *This upgrade is a single-use item that allows for additional reloads to be equipped for weapon systems with the SA: Ammo/Limited Ammo, allowing them to ignore one critical*

additional reloads to be equipped for weapon systems with the *SA: Ammo/Limited Ammo*, allowing them to ignore one critical failure roll for each bin equipped.

Multiple bins can be purchased and mounted to the model.

External Fire Control Pod

A fire control pod can be mounted to the external surface of a machine, allowing it to integrate their fire control through the BattleNet with other FCS-equipped models in the same squad.

- **External Fire Control Pod**
  Special Attributes: *FCS*
  Model Restrictions: *Available to aircraft, CAV, and vehicle models only.*
  Upgrade Cost: *10 TVP*

Fire-Suppression System

Many pilots and drivers choose to add an after-market fire-suppression system to their "ride" to avoid ending up a "charcoal briquette".

- **Fire-Suppression System**
  Special Attributes: *Fire-Proof 1*
  Model Restrictions: *Available to aircraft, CAV, and vehicle models only.*
  Upgrade Cost: *5 TVP*

FIST (Fire Support Team)

Specialized training is required to improve the chance of artillery, air, or space-based fire-support hitting the right spot on the first shot!

- **FIST (Fire Support Team)**
  Special Attributes: *NA*
  Model Restrictions: *None.*
  Upgrade Cost:
FIST 1	5 TVP
FIST 2	10 TVP
FIST 3	20 TVP

Game Rules: *This upgrade is required to allow a model to deploy one or more Battlefield Support Strikes (p. 140).*

A FIST member will typically require the use of a special action to request immediate fire-support, using the rating level of the upgrade as a (+) situation modifier to the strike-point roll of an attack.

JDAM Kit

The JDAM program was developed for the Terran military by Integrated Defense Systems in 2220 as a "bolt-on" package to convert "dumb" weapons into "smart" munitions. Since their deployment, many other star-nations have followed their lead and developed similar add-ons.

- **JDAM Kit**
  Special Attributes: *SMART*
  Model Restrictions: *Available to weapon systems only.*
  Upgrade Cost: *10 TVP*

Game Rules: *This upgrade provides for the addition of the SA: SMART to any weapon system with the SA: AoE.*

Buffering

Another popular after-market upgrade, buffering provides redundancy and better shielding from an ion blast to important data and energy nexus points on a combat machine.

- **Buffering**
  Special Attributes: *NA*
  Model Restrictions: *Available to aircraft, CAV, and vehicle models only.*
  Upgrade Cost: *5 TVP*

Game Rules: *A limited version of the SA: Shielded, this upgrade is only effective against ion disruptor cannon attacks.*

Makeshift Armor

Since the beginning of time, soldiers have looked to the items around them to help stop or deflect an incoming round. Scrap metal, sand bags, railroad ties, etc. can all make do as armor in a pinch. Of course, this extra weight comes at a price, but doesn't everything that's good for you?

- **Makeshift Armor**
  Special Attributes: *NA*
  Model Restrictions: *None.*
  Upgrade Cost: *15 TVP*

Game Rules: *This upgrade allows a model to use any number of items to increase their AV by (+1) but decreases their MV (-2).*

This upgrade cannot be used in conjunction with any other armor upgrade.

Barrel Bomb

A barrel bomb is an improvised explosive device made from a barrel filled with high explosives and shrapnel and dropped from an aircraft. While a barrel bomb can be attached to the undercarriage of an aircraft, using a rudimentary release switch wired to the cockpit, it can also be rolled out of a cargo door on a transport while in flight, dropping to the ground below.

- **Barrel Bomb**
  Range: *NA*
  RAV: *2/4*

Model Restrictions: *Available to aircraft models only.*
Upgrade Cost: *10 TVP*

Game Rules: *This upgrade allows an aircraft to mount a "bomb" without the need of a pylon. While providing a massive blast, barrel bombs are extremely inaccurate and will automatically drift (no strike-point roll required).*

While a single-use item, multiple barrel bombs may be purchased and mounted to the same model.

Loadmaster

The loadmaster of a transport is responsible for getting every square inch of cargo space filled while maintaining the safety of the craft. Sometimes a little ingenuity is required to squeeze out that little extra bit of room, from pulling out the seats to making troops sit on each other's lap.

- **Loadmaster**
  Special Attributes: *Transport +1*
  Model Restrictions: *Available to aircraft, CAV (quad), and vehicle models only.*
  Upgrade Cost: *10 TVP*

Game Rules: *This upgrade allows any model with the SA: Transport to increase their capacity by (+1).*

Jump Pack

Jump packs are used by infantry to increase their mobility, especially across more rugged terrain areas.

- **Jump Pack**
  Special Attributes: *Bulky*
  Model Restrictions: *Available to infantry models only.*
  Upgrade Cost: *10 TVP*

Game Rules: *This upgrade allows an infantry model to equip a jump pack, adding a +2 to their base MV, that can be used to make "short hops" to bypass the terrain below (Move Class: Air).*

A model is not allowed to have more than one movement-based upgrade.

Linked

A power-armored infantry model can be wired to accept a direct neural interface with their weapons, allowing for quicker reflexes and improved targeting.

- **Linked**
  Special Attributes: *NA*
  Model Restrictions: *Available to power armor infantry models only.*
  Upgrade Cost: *15 TVP*

Game Rules: *This upgrade allows a powered-armor infantry model to receive a (+1) to any direct-fired ranged assaults.*

Motorized

Non-powered infantry can be equipped with personal transport vehicles (typically hover/anti-grav skimmers or motorcycles), allowing them the extra speed to get from one point to another on the battlefield without the need to dismount from larger, specialized transport vehicles.

- **Motorized**
  Special Attributes: *NA*
  Model Restrictions: *Available to infantry models only.*
  Upgrade Cost: *10 TVP*

Game Rules: *This upgrade allows a non-powered-armor infantry model to equip a personal transport, adding a +3 to their base MV and changing the model's move class to: wheeled, hover, or anti-grav (player's choice).*

A model is not allowed to have more than one movement-based upgrade.

Medic

A medic provides immediate triage on the battlefield to an wounded solider, stabilizing them for movement to a dedicated medical facility behind the lines.

- **Medic**
  Special Attributes: *NA*
  Model Restrictions: *Available to infantry models only.*
  Upgrade Cost: *15 TVP*

Game Rules: *This upgrade allows an infantry model to add a medic that can be used to "triage" (Repair Action) any infantry model in the same squad they are currently in B2B contact with and recover one point of damage.*

Non-Commissioned Officer (NCO)

The "backbone" of every armed force, a non-commissioned officer (typically sergeants and corporals) is responsible for the day-to-day training of the soldiers below them and executing any mission they may be tasked to perform within every star-nation's military. The NCO makes sure everyone understands what is expected of them and verify they follow the orders as given.

- **Non-Commissioned Officer (NCO)**
  Special Attributes: *C3*
  Model Restrictions: *None.*
  Upgrade Cost: *5 TVP*

Game Rules: *This upgrade can only be purchased for one model in each squad, designating it as a NCO and adding +1 to the force group's starting C3 pool.*

UPGRADES

Officer

The officer is the overall commander of an armed force, responsible for its deployment and general strategy when in combat. An officer will generally give an order to the NCOs rather than to the force as a whole, and maintain a situational awareness of the battle as it unfolds.

- **Officer**
  Special Attributes: *C3*
  Model Restrictions: *None.*
  Upgrade Cost:
Lieutenant (+2 C3)	*10 TVP*
Captain (+3 C3)	*15 TVP*
Major (+4 C3)	*20 TVP*
Colonel (+5 C3)	*25 TVP*

Game Rules: *This upgrade allows one model within a force group to be designated as an officer, providing for a C3 bonus (based upon their overall rank) to the force group's overall pool. The Upgrade: Officer cannot be used on a model with a damage track less than x2 the C3 bonus amount within the force group. If there is no model available to meet this requirement, the officer may be placed in a model with the highest DT available.*

Example: *The Officer Upgrade: Major (C3 +4) must be placed in a model with at least an 8 DT rating level if available.*

Orbital Drop Strike Team (ODST)

While the actual ODST term applies to the Terran version of these specialized troops, each major star-nation deploys their own variant of this particular battle unit.

An ODST team is typically assigned by the military as a special operations force capable of long-range reconnaissance and unconventional warfare. Their training includes insertion in a battle zone by being "dropped" from orbit around a planet (using specialized "drop pods") and making pinpoint landings of the surface, often behind enemy lines and by complete surprise.

- **Orbital Drop Strike Team (ODST)**
  Special Attributes: *NA*
  Model Restrictions: *Available to CAV and infantry models only.*
  Upgrade Cost: *5 TVP (All models in a squad must be upgraded)*

Game Rules: *This upgrade must be purchased for EVERY model within the same squad. While an ODST squad does not deploy at the beginning of the game a player may decide, at the beginning of any subsequent turn, to deploy their ODST squad(s) by adding an assigned card to the draw deck during the shuffle. Once this assigned card is drawn, the ODST squad may immediately deploy as a free action, anywhere on the game board*

as long as it is no closer than 12" to any enemy model. and proceed with its activation.

If no legal deployment location is available, deployment is delayed to the following turn, repeating the process. Once a squad has deployed it no longer requires an assigned card and will activate like any other squad for the remainder of the game.

External Active Phase Array Pod

An active phase array pod can be mounted to the external surface of a machine, providing some of the functionality found in a more dedicated array system.

- **External Active Phase Array Pod**
  Special Attributes: *NA*
  Model Restrictions: *Available to aircraft, CAV, and vehicle models only.*
  Upgrade Cost: *15 TVP*

Game Rules: *An external APA pod is provides for the SA: Active Phase Array, but is limited in range and capabilities due to power and software requirements.*

As a result, the Upgrade: External Active Phase Array provides a (+1) to any friendly model's primary combat roll if the targeted enemy model is currently located within its area of effect (range: 18").

Reactive Armor

Reactive Armor is designed to reduce the damage from weapons that penetrate heavier armor (such as shaped charges and MAC penetrators) through an electromagnetic reaction triggered by the initial contact of an incoming round. Energy weapons typically will not activate this reaction, reducing the effectiveness of this armor type to these types of weapon systems.

- **Reactive Armor**
  Special Attributes: *NA*
  Model Restrictions: *Available to aircraft, CAV, and vehicle models only.*
  Upgrade Cost: *15 TVP*

Game Rules: *A model with the Upgrade: Reactive Armor receives a (+2) AV bonus when hit by any weapon system with the SA: Ammo/Limited Ammo. The model will also receive a (-1) to its AV when hit by any other weapon system type.*

This upgrade cannot be used in conjunction with any other armor upgrade.

Experimental Nano-Tech

Since the introduction of nano-repair technology by the AEC in 2210, researchers and engineers across the galaxy have tried to advance the technology in an attempt to make it use faster and more effective.

- **Experimental Nano-Tech**
  Special Attributes: *Rugged*
  Model Restrictions: *Available to aircraft, CAV, and vehicle models only.*
  Upgrade Cost: *20 TVP*

Game Rules: *This upgrade adds the SA: Rugged to a model; any critical failure repair roll will disable the system and prevent any additional repair attempts for the remainder of the game.*

Storm Training

Learning how to get off or on a transport as quickly as possible is a skill taught to every soldier from their first day in basic-training. Woe to the recruit who is last off the "cattle car" and the subject of scorn by the drill instructor.

- **Storm Training**
  Special Attributes: *Storm*
  Model Restrictions: *Available to infantry models only.*
  Upgrade Cost: *3 TVP*

Game Rules: *This upgrade adds the SA: Storm to an infantry model.*
A model is not allowed to have more than one movement-based upgrade.

Turbo-Charged

A favorite modification of gear-heads everywhere, the top-end speed of a machine can be increased through a variety of after-market modifications to add to it's top horsepower.

- **Turbo-Charged**
  Special Attributes: *NA*
  Model Restrictions: *Available to aircraft, CAV, and vehicle models only.*
  Upgrade Cost: *10 TVP*

Game Rules: *This upgrade is used to increase a model's base MV by (+1).*
A model is not allowed to have more than one movement-based upgrade.

Veteran Pilot

Veteran pilots have survived countless battles, learning the ins and outs of war that only experience can bring (with a little dose of luck), providing the enemy the chance to "die for their country".

- **Veteran Pilot**
  Special Attributes: *NA*
  Model Restrictions: *Available to aircraft, CAV, and vehicle models only.*
  Upgrade Cost: *15 TVP*

Game Rules: *A Veteran Pilot will add a (+1) to any non-secondary combat die roll made by the model they have been assigned to.*

Battlefield Upgrades (Alternate Ammo)

Every arm of a modern military force is on the look-out for even the smallest advantage they can get over the enemy. Alternate ammo selections allow for a quick "change-up" without the need for an all-new weapon system design.

Using an alternate ammo upgrade can be used to supplement the basic load-out of some weapon systems. Any alternate ammo upgrade must be purchased for EACH weapon system of a specific type equipped by a model.

A player choosing to use alternate ammo during an attack MUST declare their intent to do so before making the combat roll or the "basic" ammo will be used by default.

Alternate Ammo: Field Artillery System

Smoke Shell (SS)

Smoke shells generate a circular smoke screen around the impact point in an attempt to disrupt the targeting of enemy combatants.

- **Smoke Shells (SS)**
  Light FAS
  Special Attributes: *AoE 2, Smoke*
  Upgrade Cost: *2 TVP*

  Heavy FAS
  Special Attributes: *AoE 4, Smoke*
  Upgrade Cost: *4 TVP*

  Rocket Artillery FAS
  Special Attributes: *AoE 3, Smoke*
  Upgrade Cost: *3 TVP*

Game Rules: *Smoke shells are used to fire a smoke-generating munition that generates a circular smoke screen around the final strike-point to disrupt LoS.*
Smoke from this type of ammo will remain in effect until the beginning of the firing model's next activation.

FASCAM

FASCAM is an artillery shell designed to burst in the air over an impact zone and scatter the ground with anti-personnel and antitank sub-munitions (mines).

A laser-guided (LG) upgrade version is also available, requiring a target-lock with the SA: TAG.

- **FASCAM**
  Heavy FAS
  Special Attributes: *AoE 3*

RAV: 5/5
Upgrade Cost: *10 TVP (LG 15 TVP)*

Rocket Artillery FAS
Special Attributes: *AoE 2*
Target Point Roll: *7+*
RAV: *4/4*
Upgrade Cost: *10 TVP (LG 15 TVP)*

Game Rules: *After determining the final strike-point of the "attack", place a minefield template equal to the AoE of the round (see Battlefield Assets, pp. 137) to represent the area that has been "mined" by the FASCAM round.*

FASCAM "mines" will go active immediately, "attacking" any model that moves into or through the indicated template location.

A laser-guided FASCAM round will receive a semi-guided bonus (+1) to the strike-point roll.

SADARM
SADARM is an artillery shell that is fired toward the designated target area, bursting in the air approximately 1,000 meters above the ground and releasing an armor-piercing sub-munition that deploys a parachute to slowly spin at a slight angle as it searches for a target below.

- ● **SADARM**
  Light FAS
    Special Attributes: *AoE 6, Blaster 1, Strike*
    Target Point Roll: *7+*
    RAV: *4/4*
    Upgrade Cost: *10 TVP*

  Heavy FAS
    Special Attributes: *AoE 6, Blaster 2, Strike*
    Target Point Roll: *7+*
    RAV: *6/6*
    Upgrade Cost: *15 TVP*

Game Rules: *The successful TAG of any single enemy CAV or combat vehicle within the SADARM's effective range (AoE), centered on the final strike-point location, will immediately be subject to a direct-fire ranged assault.*

If no target becomes available, the sub-munition will fall to the ground and self-destruct at the beginning of the firing model's next activation.

AXLE
The AXLE is a breeder-pumped x-ray laser munition using ions to produce a high energy beam that can punch through the heavy armor of a CAV or other hardened target.

- ● **AXLE**
  Heavy FAS

Special Attributes: *AoE 3, Ravage, Shock (6+)*
Target Point Roll: *7+*
RAV: *8/8*
Upgrade Cost: *20 TVP*

Game Rules: *An AXLE munition has several single-shot laser-bolt guns "wrapped" around a breeder core designed to explode directly above a final strike-point location. The explosion provides the necessary fuel to produce several high-energy beams that shoot out into various directions in an attempt to hit any targets in the area of effect.*

Nano-Disassemblers
Similar in operation to the nano-tech used by modern fighting equipment for emergency field repairs during a battle, nano-disassemblers seek to instead tear down the integrity of a targeted area, using the components they scavenge to increase their numbers and the area they cover until they reach a terminal point in their life-span and become inactive.

The main drawback to this type of weapon is the lack of control once it is unleashed, as nano-disassemblers are unable to recognize friend from foe and will attack both indiscriminately.

- ● **Nano-Disassemblers**
  Heavy FAS
    Special Attributes: *AoE 3*
    Target Point Roll: *NA*
    CCV: *7/7*
    Upgrade Cost: *20 TVP*

  Rocket Artillery FAS
    Special Attributes: *AoE 2*
    Target Point Roll: *NA*
    CCV: *5/5*
    Upgrade Cost: *15 TVP*

Game Rules: *Once the final strike-point for the attack is determined, a nano-disassembler cloud template is placed on the board at the impact point, "attacking" any model caught within the AoE with a close-combat assault. Any model that remains or moves through this cloud during their activation will immediately be subject to an attack.*

If, at the end of a turn, there are no models and/or structures caught within the nano "cloud", it will randomly drift (p. 56) in search of a new target.

Nano-disassembler "clouds" will remain active for the duration of the game or until destroyed. Nano-disassembler "clouds" will be automatically destroyed when targeted by a model using anti-nano dispersion systems, flamethrowers, or ion disruptor cannons for the attack.

Alternate Ammo: Guided Missiles

HARM

High-speed anti-radiation missiles are designed to detect and lock-on to a "radio" emission source. Radar, jamming units, and even some high-powered radio transmitters can be targeted.

- **HARM**
  Special Attributes: *Locked-On*
  Target-Point Roll: *NA*
  RAV: *NA*
  Upgrade Cost: *15 TVP*

Game Rules: *Only a model with the SA: Active Phase Array or SA: ECM and a guided missile weapon system may equip HARM munitions.*

Alternate Ammo: Pylon (Aircraft Only)

Bomb Rack

Bomb racks allow aircraft to carry multiple bombs that can be dropped at the same time to saturate a target-area in short order.

- **Bomb Rack**
  Special Attributes: *Ravage, Shock (6+)*
  Target-Point Roll: *7+*
  RAV: *4/4*
  Upgrade Cost: *10 TVP*

Game Rules: *This is a single-use upgrade that can be purchased multiple times (x1 per equipped pylon) by an aircraft model to perform a carpet-bomb attack.*

An aircraft model, at the beginning of it's activation, may declare it will be making a carpet-bomb attack. This type of attack produces a 2" wide corridor, centered on the aircraft, in a straight line equal to the current MV of the model. Any turns or other types of movement will end this "corridor".

Any model caught in the final corridor of the carpet-bomb run is subject to an attack.

Alternate Ammo: Rockets

Cluster Munitions

Similar to the FASCAM rounds used by artillery, rocket launchers can be used to deliver anti-tank and personnel sub-munitions (mines) to a specific target area in an attempt to deny its use to the enemy.

- **Cluster Munitions**
  Special Attributes: *AoE*
  Target-Point Roll: *7+*

RAV: *½ RAV*
Upgrade Cost: *Light 5 TVP (Heavy 10 TVP)*

Game Rules: *After determining the final strike-point of the "attack", place a minefield template equal to the AoE of the attack (see Battlefield Assets, pp. 137) to represent the area that has been "mined" by the cluster munition rockets.*

Cluster "mines" will go active immediately, "attacking" any model that moves into or through the indicated template location.

Semi-Guided

By adding a guidance and control section to the front end of an unguided rocket, small corrections can be made in flight by the weapon if a TAG is available to increase the chance of a successful hit.

- **Semi-Guided**
  Special Attributes: *NA*
  Target-Point Roll: *NA*
  RAV: *-1/-1*
  Upgrade Cost: *5 TVP*

Game Rules: *A model with one or more rocket launchers may upgrade their ammo to include semi-guided rockets, allowing the model to receive a (+1) when making the strike-point roll provided the target area is currently subject to the SA: TAG.*

The addition of the guidance and control section reduces the payload of each rocket, resulting in a (-1) to the weapon system's RAV.

CAV
Extra-Large Chassis
Butcher
The Steel Dragons
Mercenary Company

Appendix E: Force Group Specialization

Battlefield Support Assets

Battlefield Support Assets are used by a commander to increase the effectiveness of their force group and attempt to force the enemy to fight on their terms. Battlefield Support Assets are purchased with TVPs from a force group's Specialization Bonus Pool and/or as part of the overall Threat Value Pool available for force group selection. A Battlefield Support Asset is typically a single-use item unless noted otherwise. Multiple selections of the same Battlefield Support Asset are permitted.

Unless otherwise noted, a Battlefield Support Asset deployed during play requires a model with the SA: *Combat Engineer* and a special action during that model's activation. A Battlefield Support Asset requiring a die roll that fails still results in the Battlefield Support Asset being expended.

Minefields

Minefields are generally a defensive weapon, designed to harass and slow down an advancing enemy as well as denying certain areas to them, but they can cause serious damage to a model if not taken seriously.

Minefields purchased as a Battlefield Support Asset may be placed during the deployment phase (minefields may not be placed in the opposing force's deployment zone) of a game (no SA: *Combat Engineer* required). Minefields deployed during play may not be placed within 6" of an enemy model (with the exception of a FASCAM minefield). A minefield covers a 6" diameter circle and should be represented by a minefield template. Once a minefield is deployed, it is immediately active and if any eligible model comes in contact with the minefield template, a combat roll is made.

Modern "smart" minefields are designed to monitor any gaps in their coverage and to redeploy in order to maintain maximum effectiveness. At some point enough mines will have been detonated, limiting the number of times it can perform an "attack" on an enemy model. After placing a minefield, set a d6 next to the minefield template with the "1" side facing up and each time a minefield is breached (combat roll) increase the die by (+1), removing the minefield when the die reaches "6".

"Smart" minefields are capable of recognizing the IFF code on a friendly model and will not attack should they pass through the minefield during the game.

De-mining

Placing a minefield is quick and simple; removing a minefield (known as de-mining) is slow and dangerous work, requiring specialized training. A model with the SA: *Combat Engineer* may attempt to remove a minefield by performing a special action.

The model must move into base-to-base contact with the minefield, making a 10+ Roll and adding (+) its rating level to the die roll before the minefield makes a combat roll.

On a successful +10 Roll, the minefield is removed from play and no further action is needed. If the roll is unsuccessful, the player controlling the minefield can now proceed with the combat roll and apply damage (if any).

Anti-Air (AA) Minefield

Often referred to as "Volcano Mines", an anti-air minefield is designed to take out low-flying aircraft (Nap of Earth) that cross over the area being covered. These mines fire a liquid jet of molten metal in a blast-focused stream that can cause catastrophic damage to an air-based model.

- **Anti-Air (AA) Minefield**
  Range: *B2B*
  Special Attributes: *NA*
  Target-Point Roll: *7+*
  RAV: *-/4*
  Specialization Cost: *100 TVP*

Anti-Personnel (AP)/Anti-Tank (AT) Minefield

Most minefields are made up of both types of mines to prevent combat engineers from having an easy time of removing the larger anti-tank mines and vehicles by just driving through and clearing anti-personnel mines.

- **Anti-Personnel (AP)/Anti-Tank (AT) Minefield**
  Range: *B2B*
  Special Attributes: *NA*
  Target-Point Roll: *7+*
  RAV: *4/4*
  Specialization Cost: *100 TVP*

Bunker

A bunker is a hardened structure equipped with one or more firing slots to allow infantry to fire out at an enemy target from inside. A model inside a bunker cannot conduct or be the target of a close-combat attack from a model outside.

All bunkers must be placed on the game board before play begins and has room for one infantry model. Larger bunkers may be purchased (+25 TVP for each additional 2" square-section) permitting space for more models to be inside.

A model may begin the game inside a bunker if it is located within their deployment zone. An empty bunker may be occupied by either side.

- **Bunker**
  Range: *NA*
  Special Attributes: *NA*
  Target-Point Roll: *NA*
  RAV: *NA*
  Specialization Cost: *25 TVP*

SPECIALIZATION

Bunker: Weapon Emplacement

A bunker can be equipped with a single weapon system, mounted to fire into a single firing arc from one side of the structure, through a firing port or from a turret on top, allowing it to fire in any direction.

The weapon emplacements for each side (if any) are grouped in a single squad, adding a single card to the draw deck of the appropriate suite/color.

Weapon emplacements have one action point each to use during their activation.

- **Bunker: Weapon Emplacement**
  Range: *NA*
  Special Attributes: *NA*
  Target-Point Roll: *NA*
  RAV: *NA*
  Specialization Cost:
No Turret*	50 TVP
With Turret*	75 TVP
  *+ Weapon Systems TVP

SIGINT

SIGINT or Signals Intelligence represents the collection and analysis of tactical data for use by a force group to gain the initiative over the enemy and is represented by the addition of SIGINT bonus cards.

For each SIGINT bonus card purchased, a force group may add an additional card of the appropriate suit to the draw deck for their side for the entire battle.

- **SIGINT**
  Range: *NA*
  Special Attributes: *NA*
  Target-Point Roll: *NA*
  RAV: *NA*
  Specialization Cost: *250TVP*

Infantry Fighting Position

An infantry fighting position is a series of foxholes and/or sandbag placements that allow infantry models to take cover and remain fighting. Each position will be approximately 3" in diameter and can be used by two infantry models. An infantry model in a fighting position negates any open-cover penalties and receives a heavy-cover bonus to any attack.

All infantry fighting positions must be placed on the game board before play begins.

- **Infantry Fighting Position**
  Range: *NA*
  Special Attributes: *NA*
  Target-Point Roll: *NA*
  RAV: *NA*
  Specialization Cost: *25TVP*

Level I Deployable NanoTech Barrier

A model with the SA: *Combat Engineer* may use a special action to deploy a 3"long barrier wall (elevation level 1) that is 1" wide in any direction from its current location, one end remaining in B2B contact with the model.

The nano used for the barrier is sprayed on the ground; converting materials from the surface into a hardened wall to provide a temporary shield from incoming fire. The barrier will remain for the rest of the battle, but will eventually disperse, turning into an ash-like material and crumbling to the ground.

A CAV model adjacent (within 1") to the barrier receives light cover while combat vehicle and infantry models receive blocking cover.

- **Level I Deployable NanoTech Barrier**
  Range: *B2B*
  Special Attributes: *NA*
  Target-Point Roll: *NA*
  RAV: *NA*
  Specialization Cost: *25TVP*

Level II Deployable NanoTech Barrier

A model with the SA: *Combat Engineer* may use a special action to deploy a 3"long barrier wall (elevation level 2) that is 1" wide in any direction from its current location, one end remaining in B2B contact with the model.

The nano used for the barrier is sprayed on the ground; converting materials from the surface into a hardened wall to provide a temporary shield from incoming fire. The barrier will remain for the rest of the battle, but will eventually disperse, turning into an ash-like material and crumbling to the ground.

A CAV model adjacent (within 1") to the barrier receives heavy cover while combat vehicle and infantry models receive blocking cover.

- **Level II Deployable NanoTech Barrier**
  Range: *B2B*
  Special Attributes: *NA*
  Target-Point Roll: *NA*
  RAV: *NA*
  Specialization Cost: *50TVP*

Level I Repair Module

A model with the SA: *Combat Engineer* and a Level I Repair Module may automatically repair one point of damage (using a special action) to a single non-infantry model that it is in B2B contact with.

Lingering damage cannot be repaired with a Level I repair module.

- **Level I Repair Module**
  Range: *B2B*
  Special Attributes: *NA*

Target-Point Roll: *NA*

RAV: *NA*

Specialization Cost: *50TVP*

Level II Repair Module

A model with the SA: *Combat Engineer* and a Level II Repair Module may automatically repair two points of damage (using a special action) to a single non-infantry model that it is in B2B contact with.

A Level II Repair Module can be used to repair a single point of lingering damage, provided that is the only damage point being repaired.

- **Level II Repair Module**
  Range: *B2B*
  Special Attributes: *NA*
  Target-Point Roll: *NA*
  RAV: *NA*
  Specialization Cost: *100TVP*

Recon Drone

Recon drones are employed by a force group commander to give them an "eye in the sky" and help track the movements of an enemy force.

For each recon drone purchased, a player can choose to skip the current card showing on the draw deck. The card will be flipped over and returned to the bottom of the deck and a new card will be drawn.

Once a recon drone is deployed, it is removed from play and only one recon drone may be used during a turn (per side).

- **Recon Drone**
  Range: *NA*
  Special Attributes: *NA*
  Target-Point Roll: *NA*
  RAV: *NA*
  Specialization Cost: *100TVP*

Re-Supply Drop

A re-supply drop can be used by a force group commander during the end phase of a turn to replenish the ammo bins (internal and external ammo bins included) of every model in the force group that has run "dry" up to that point during the battle.

- **Re-Supply Drop**
  Range: *NA*
  Special Attributes: *NA*
  Target-Point Roll: *NA*
  RAV: *NA*
  Specialization Cost: *100TVP*

Revetment

Revetments are retaining walls dug into the ground with a sloping "floor", and supported by stone, wood, or sandbags on three sides for a CAV or combat vehicle model to use for cover, but still allow it to engage the enemy.

A CAV revetment is three levels deep and is built with a step the model can use to rise up and take a shot, temporarily granting a CAV model the SA: *Pop-Up*.

A combat vehicle revetment is one level deep and allows a vehicle model with a turret to use hull down.

Any revetments must be placed on the game board before play begins and designated as a CAV or combat vehicle-type revetment.

- **Revetment**
  Range: *NA*
  Special Attributes: *NA*
  Target-Point Roll: *NA*
  RAV: *NA*
  Specialization Cost: *50TVP*

Satchel Charge

A satchel charge is a demo device (generally a bag filled with a Thermex explosive) with a pull igniter that can be used as an anti-CAV or tank weapon by infantry when they are in close proximity to an enemy machine, generally by placing it in a leg joint or drive system to disable the target.

Satchel Charges Asset will equip an entire infantry squad and can be used by any model from that squad when they are the primary attacker in a close-combat assault. Satchel Charges are a single-use item, but may be purchased multiple times for the same squad.

An infantry model that uses the satchel charge during a close-combat assault will receive a (+3) when making their opposed combat roll.

- **Satchel Charge**
  Range: *B2B*
  Special Attributes: *NA*
  Target-Point Roll: *NA*
  CCV: *+3/+3 vs CAV and combat vehicles only*
  Specialization Cost: *50TVP*

Trench

Trenches are "slits" dug into the ground and supported by stone, wood, or sandbag retaining walls along their length to provide infantry a place to seek cover from incoming fire, but still allow it to engage an enemy model.

Trenches are 3" inches in length and 1" wide with an elevation of one depth. Multiple trenches can be purchased and "connected" to form an even longer construct. Each section provides room for two infantry models to use and blocks LoS to the model (unless the enemy model is also in the trench) from

S P E C I A L I Z A T I O N

any direction.

Trenches are constructed with a step that allows the infantry to rise up and use the SA: *Pop-Up*.

All trenches must be placed on the game board before play begins.

- ●**Trench**
  Range: *NA*
  Special Attributes: *NA*
  Target-Point Roll: *NA*
  RAV: *NA*
  Specialization Cost: *25 TVP*

Battlefield Support Strike Packages

Unlike Battlefield Support Assets, where a specific item is purchased with TVP, Battlefield Support Strikes are divided into Strike Packages. When designing a force group, players may assign a portion of their Threat Value Points to one or more Strike Packages. During play, a model with the SA: *FIST* may use a special action during their activation to call for a Battlefield Support Strike from any of the Strike Packages with enough remaining points to pay for the attack.

Once the attack has been declared, place a strike-point counter anywhere within the range of the attack (measured from the model with the SA: *FIST*) and proceed with the attack as detailed in the following descriptions.

Strike Package: Artillery

Artillery Strike

An Artillery Strike will automatically drift (no strike-point roll), subtracting 1" for each rating level of the coordinating model's SA: *FIST*. The drift distance cannot be reduced below zero.

- ●**Artillery Strike**
  Range: *36"*
  Special Attributes: *AoE 2*
  Target Point Roll: *7+*
  RAV: *4/4*
  Specialization Cost: *50 TVP*

Artillery Barrage

An Artillery Barrage will automatically drift (no strike-point roll), subtracting 1" for each rating level of the coordinating model's SA: *FIST*. The drift distance cannot be reduced below zero.

- ●**Artillery Barrage**
  Range: *36"*
  Special Attributes: *AoE 4*
  Target Point Roll: *7+*
  RAV: *4/4*
  Specialization Cost: *100 TVP*

Artillery Bombardment

An Artillery Bombardment will automatically drift (no strike-point roll), subtracting 1" for each rating level of the coordinating model's SA: *FIST*. The drift distance cannot be reduced below zero.

- ●**Artillery Bombardment**
  Range: *36"*
  Special Attributes: *AoE 6*
  Target Point Roll: *7+*
  RAV: *4/4*
  Specialization Cost: *200 TVP*

Artillery Smoke Screen

An Artillery Smoke Screen will automatically drift (no strike-point roll), subtracting 1" for each rating level of the coordinating model's SA: *FIST*. The drift distance cannot be reduced below zero.

Once the final strike-point has been determined, a smoke screen, using the strike-point as its center, will be set using the drift roll to mark the direction/angle to set the screen.

An Artillery Smoke Screen is 2" wide and 12" long and will block any LoS and SA: *TAG* that pass through the affected area. The smoke screen will remain on the board until the next activation of the model that requested the fire mission for it.

- ●**Artillery Smoke Screen**
  Range: *36"*
  Special Attributes: *AoE 2x12*
  Target Point Roll: *NA*
  RAV: *NA*
  Specialization Cost: *50 TVP*

Artillery FASCAM

FASCAM is an artillery shell designed to burst over a strike-point at an optimum altitude and cover the area with anti-personnel and antitank sub-munitions (mines).

An Artillery FASCAM will automatically drift (no strike-point roll), subtracting 1" for each rating level of the coordinating model's SA: *FIST*.

A minefield template should be used to represent the area that has been "mined" by the FASCAM round once the final strike-point has been determined. A FASCAM will go active immediately, "attacking" any model (no IFF responders) that moves into or through the indicated template location.

- ●**Artillery FASCAM**
  Range: *36"*
  Special Attributes: *AoE 2*
  Target Point Roll: *7+*
  RAV: *4/4*
  Specialization Cost: *75 TVP*

SPECIALIZATION

Strike Package: Air

Gunship Assault (Death From Above)

Circling gunships will be called in to deliver a concentrated stream of fire to a designated area in a series of strafing runs, attacking any model within the zone.

A gunship assault will automatically drift (no strike-point roll), subtracting 1" for each rating level of the coordinating model's SA: *FIST*. The drift distance cannot be reduced below zero.

Once the final strike-point has been determined, the gunship assault may proceed, using the strike-point as its center and will use the drift roll to mark the direction/angle to set the attack.

A gunship assault will create a "corridor" that is 2" wide and 12" long, making a ranged-attack on any model caught within this area.

- **Gunship Assault (Death From Above)**
  - Range: *36"*
  - Special Attributes: *AoE 2x12*
  - Target Point Roll: *7+*
  - RAV: *4/4*
  - Specialization Cost: *100 TVP*

Cruise Missile

A model with the SA: *FIST* may request the firing of a cruise missile, placing the cruise missile model on the controlling player's deployment zone table edge. A cruise missile has two action points (see data card) to use for movement only and will activate in the following turn(s) along with the model that initiated the strike.

If the cruise missile model comes into base-to-base contact with any model it will immediately conduct a ranged attack as a free action and removed from play.

Cruise missiles may be targeted by other models and can be destroyed. Cruise missiles remain in play until they find a target or are shot down.

- **Cruise Missile**
  - Range: *NA*
  - Special Attributes: *NA*
  - Target Point Roll: *7+*
  - RAV: *6/6*
  - Specialization Cost: *100 TVP*

Advanced Cruise Missile (Super Thermex)

A model with the SA: *FIST* may request the firing of an advanced cruise missile, placing the cruise missile model on the controlling player's deployment zone table edge. An advanced cruise missile has two action points (see data card) to use for movement only and will activate in the following turn(s) along with the model that initiated the strike.

An advanced cruise missile is loaded with Super Thermex, a nanotech explosive compound that allows for massive detonations on par with small nuclear devices, without the radiation and fall-out inherent to those types of weapons.

Move the advanced cruise missile model to the desired detonation point and, using a free action, make a ranged attack combat roll against any model with the SA: *Hard* caught in the AoE of the blast. Any models with the SA: *Soft* are automatically destroyed and removed from play.

Advanced cruise missiles may be targeted by other models and can be destroyed. Advanced cruise missiles remain in play until they find a target or are shot down.

- **Advanced Cruise Missile (Super Thermex)**
  - Range: *NA*
  - Special Attributes: *AoE 4*
  - Target Point Roll: *7+*
  - RAV: *10/10*
  - Specialization Cost: *500 TVP*

Massive Ordnance Air Blast Bomb (MOAB)

A Massive Ordnance Air Blast Bomb will automatically drift (no strike-point roll), subtracting 1" for each rating level of the coordinating model's SA: *FIST*. The drift distance cannot be reduced below zero.

SPECIALIZATION

Designed to damage and destroy fortifications, the impact of this bomb creates a massive fireball and a wave of over-pressure that will automatically destroy any non-Hardened structure caught within the AoE. Any other structure or model caught within the AoE is subject to a ranged-attack combat roll.

- **Massive Ordnance Air Blast Bomb (MOAB)**
  Range: *36"*
  Special Attributes: *AoE 3, Blaster 1, Ravage, Shock (10+)*
  Target Point Roll: *7+*
  RAV: *8/8*
  Specialization Cost: *300 TVP*

Strike Package: Space

Orbital Missile Strike

A model with the SA: *FIST* may request the firing of an Orbital Missile Strike (direct-fire attack) by an orbiting spaceship or satellite. Orbital Missile Strikes are highly accurate (no drift) and designed to decimate the target area.

- **Orbital Missile Strike**
  Range: *36"*
  Special Attributes: *AoE2, Blaster 1, Strike*
  Target Point Roll: *7+*
  RAV: *6/6*
  Specialization Cost: *200 TVP*

Orbital Precision Strike (Hammer Strike)

A model with the SA: *FIST* may request the firing of an "Hammer Strike" by an orbiting spaceship or satellite.

A Hammer Strike is a SABOT-delivered set of tungsten carbide cermet rods designed for an accurate (no drift) strike against a single target. The targeted model will receive three ranged-assault combat rolls from the attack.

- **Orbital Precision Strike (Hammer Strike)**
  Range: *36"*
  Special Attributes: *Blaster 2, Strike*
  Target Point Roll: *7+ (x3)*
  RAV: *10/10*
  Specialization Cost: *300 TVP*

Orbital Bombardment (Steel Rain)

A model with the SA: *FIST* may request the firing of "Steel Rain" (direct-fire attack) by an orbiting spaceship or satellite. Similar to a Hammer Strike, an Orbital Bombardment is launched as a series of "pods", each containing several bundles of small (as compared to the single rod fired by a Hammer Strike) tungsten carbide cermet rods. Once positioned in orbit in a roughly rectangular pattern, the pods are activated simultaneously to fire their cargo at hyper-velocity speeds towards the ground below, raining destruction upon anything caught within the strike area.

- **Orbital Missile Strike**
  Range: *36"*
  Special Attributes: *AoE3, Blaster 1, Strike*
  Target Point Roll: *7+*
  RAV: *8/8*
  Specialization Cost: *250 TVP*